Dream a Little

Dream a Little

Land and Social Justice in Modern America

Dorothee E. Kocks

UNIVERSITY OF CALIFORNIA PRESS

Berkeley   Los Angeles   London

University of California Press
Berkeley and Los Angeles, California

University of California Press, Ltd.
London, England

Library of Congress Cataloging-in-Publication Data

Kocks, Dorothee E., 1957–.

Dream a little : land and social justice in modern America /
Dorothee E. Kocks.
    p.   cm.
Includes bibliographical references and index.
ISBN 0-520-20286-4 (alk. paper). — ISBN 0-520-22280-6 (pbk. :
alk. paper)
    1. American fiction — 20th century — History and criticism.
2. Landscape in literature.   3. Literature and society — West
(U.S.) — History — 20th century.   4. Women and literature —
West (U.S.) — History — 20th century.   5. Social justice — West
(U.S.) — History — 20th century.   6. Johnson, Josephine Winslow,
1910 — Political and social views.   7. Sandoz, Mari, 1896–1966 —
Political and social views.   8. Baker, Ella, 1903–1986 — Political
and social views.   9. American fiction — Women authors —
History and criticism.   10. Landscape — West (U.S.) —
History — 20th century.   11. West (U.S.) — Historiography.
12. West (U.S.) — In literature.   I. Title.
PS374.L28 K63   2000
813'.520932 — dc21   99-056435
                                                                    CIP

Manufactured in the United States of America

09 08 07 06 05 04 03 02 01 00
10 9 8 7 6 5 4 3 2 1

The paper used in this publication is both acid-free and totally
chlorine-free (TCF). The paper used in this publication meets
the minimum requirements of ANSI/NISO Z39.48-1992 (R 1997)
(Permanence of Paper). ♾

For Mark

CONTENTS

ACKNOWLEDGMENTS

This book was long in gestating. Consequently, I have many people to thank. Peggy Pascoe read and reread the manuscript with great kindness. Under her tutelage, I have been treated with profound decency at the same time as I have been excellently challenged. Also, Elizabeth Jordan Moore has been my stalwart friend throughout this process. Her writing counsel is as nourishing as it is wise.

Several writing groups have sustained me through the years. Among the many people to thank are Jane Gerhard, Krista Comer, Ileana Porras, Laura Santigian, Jim Cullen, Michelle Totland, Diana Sterne, Steve Trimble, Margot Kadesch, Greg Totland, Howard Bartlett and Bob Nelson.

I am indebted to the University of Utah and Dean of Humanities Patricia Hanna for leave time to write this book. Many colleagues provided helpful commentary along the way, as did several former students, including Steven Park, Liza Nicholas and Thomas Harvey.

I am grateful also to John L. Thomas, Susan Smulyan, James T. Patterson, Mari Jo Buhle and George Hicks at Brown University for their stimulating teaching. For the title of this book, I am indebted to the artist Patrick Coffaro, whose artwork by the same name is reproduced on the cover.

To my gracious and generous parents, Marianne and Fred Kocks, I extend my heartfelt gratitude. And to Mark Etheridge, I whisper my devotion always.

Introduction

"Imagine," urges the song by John Lennon — a world with nothing to kill or die for, where there is no greed or hunger, where all the people can share all the world. "You may say I'm a dreamer," the song continues. Listening to the music in the car, you might find yourself singing along. You might admit, out loud, to imagining peace, justice, freedom, fairness, all the most extravagant hopes of humankind. But confessing to these hopes is something that happens more often in lyrics, or prayer, or protest chants than in sustained discussion. Begin to try to realize those dreams, and the details immediately will trip you up. Not only is it hard to define what we mean by such ideals, a competing goal starts to interfere: the noble purpose of being realistic, not naive, astute even. If you join in the extravagant hopes for humanity in one context, there is still the moment when you come down to earth. When you get real.

How to give in to idealism at all in a century of world wars, multiple genocides, vast and growing inequalities, and monopolized democracies? How to dream a little? One answer has been to take literally the advice to come down to earth. Dreamers often use the earth and all it stands for as a visualizing aid. Blueprints for an ideal society seem to reveal themselves in the wilderness or the desert, in the image of a small town nestled in fields and valleys, in lessons learned while quietly contemplating a river. It is a very old habit, from various cultural traditions, to find ways to solve the most confounding social problems by turning to the mountains or forests, or by taking lessons from people who seem to live close to nature. The tradition of using landscapes to reveal and elaborate our dreams for social justice is the topic of this book. I call this tradition the geographic embrace.

I mean to take advantage of the historical conditioning that leads us to find ideals in landscapes. To get help for the difficult task of dreaming, I focus on certain landscapes that contain layers upon layers of ideals: the West, the family farm, the local community. These are symbolic places. Their place is not so much on the earth as in books, movies and political speeches. To tease some meaning for today out of these thickly handled symbols, I turn to three women who embraced these geographies before me. Two, Mari Sandoz and Josephine Johnson, were writers; and one, Ella Baker, was a political activist. With their examples before me, I use ideas about land to imagine a better world.

More often, the tendency in books about myths about place is to debunk them, to engage in mythbusting, to show the little man behind the curtain in Oz. Indeed, the fact is that nature is extremely fickle. The lesson of a landscape such as the West's red butte wilderness can be that nature teaches cooperation. In the dry desperation of this climate, people can learn that mutual aid is the dictate of nature, which is intricately interdependent. Conversely, the same landscape can teach the survival of the fittest. From this latter point of view, society should celebrate the daring, antisocial exploits of free individuals.

Nature provides slippery moral grounds. The content of nature's lesson depends in large part on the content of the viewer. But still, we need myths. Regardless of what the West *actually* teaches, we need a stage on which to contrast cooperation and individualism, or to invent new words or images that teach us how to appropriately combine both. We need to go through the mistake, if you will, of being idealistic in order for there to be any change. This book answers to the call to dream a little rather than the call to wake up.

My reasons for expecting disagreement on the value of myth-making come from much more than the ordinary inhibitions of daily life. I am a trained academic. I have spent years in the hallways of reason, where logic is continually refined and sharpened and every idea is tested and retested against competing claims. It is an atmosphere in which faiths can corrode. I believe that scholarly inquiry, though, actually can contribute a great deal to the process of social dreaming. This book seeks to convey some of the more extravagant, theoretically complex thoughts about landscape myths and their truth or consequences to dreamers inside and outside academia.

The approach that I take to questions of social justice draws from a variety of intellectual traditions. My main debt is to theories of language and its role in corralling our sense of the possible. If you want to dream a little, the first dilemma you will face is that language limits your imagination. To see the subtle control of language over thought, imagine for a moment a sharp, clear photograph of a scene — let's say a picture of that same red butte wilderness that is so typical of the West. The photograph has edges — what lies beyond the frame? The fact that the sliver of life *inside* the frame appears realistic coexists with another fact: if you change the borders around the picture, a different reality can emerge. For example, show a bit more of the sky, and the frame might show a fighter jet on a practice bombing run, flying over the open space. In the same way that photographs speak to us by virtue of what they *don't* show us as much as what they do, words help to create, rather than simply reflect, reality. For example, consider that "science," by common definition, is not art. Consider that "nature" is generally understood in opposition to society. These distinctions actually serve to *create* a situation in which scientists and artists find it difficult to share their findings and in which nature is set aside in parks rather than seen as existing within the human soul. As one theorist said, "Grammar is politics by other means."[1] My emphasis on language means that in this book you will read much about *how* we talk about land and little landscape description or nature writing. If I can show the frame around the picture, maybe we will be able to envision new possibilities.

The intellectual traditions that call attention to the shaping qualities of language belong to the larger family of ideas that questions the scholarly claim to objectivity. To be objective commonly means to be dispassionate, to be driven by the facts, to avoid the taint of subjectivity. As part 1 of this book explains, the pursuit of objectivity hobbles discussions of myth in particular. Myths of the good society require passionate engagement, I argue, even in expert or academic debate.

Rather than seek objectivity, this book will do more than

admit to bias. I aim to cater to subjectivity, not just acknowledge my own. We need myths, we need to imagine what a better world might look like, and to do so, we need ways to *discover* our opinions. To be subjective means to reveal one's own, constantly emerging, ideas about the world. Part 2 offers an example of what such expert but simultaneously subjective discourse might sound like. I include stories about my life and the process through which I acquired the knowledge that made it possible for me to write this book. Rather than a bird's-eye view, my discussion of land and social justice includes me and some of my personal history.

In addition to dreaming a little in an intellectual context, this book offers some specific contributions on the topic of land and social justice. The opening argues forcefully that a major social justice initiative in the history of the United States has been largely forgotten: the "frontier." The land giveaway program may be slathered with remembrances, many fond, many horrified. Still, a key aspect of it disappears in most discussions, including academic ones. The frontier was a big-government program. It was, I argue, a predecessor of twentieth-century welfare, and it was more generous in its intent than the safety nets of our time. Rather than beginning with the New Deal, large-scale government welfare initiatives have a long history in the United States, and that history begins with expenditures of land.

I argue in chapter 1 that before there was a welfare state, there was a frontier state. Why is the frontier *state* forgotten; that is, why is the federal government's intervention in the economy of poverty so typically postdated to the early twentieth century? The answer has something to do with land's linguistic aura. Land could be spoken of as free, even while it was being bought in the Louisiana Purchase, being paid for with vast expenditures of military might to conquer it from defending natives, being surveyed and mapped and distributed by government-funded bureaucracies, and so on.

The forgetting of the frontier state is part of the larger phenomenon of the geographic embrace. In the geographic embrace Americans forget and remember land in historically conditioned ways. Our customary language habits, or discourses, invite us to erase the politics and history in landscapes that appear as nature's gift. At the same time, we slip easily into the habit of calling on land or nature when it comes time to invent a new politics or alter the course of history. Chapter 2 takes a broad look at the origins of the habit to turn to land — to remember it — when asking questions about political morality. Those origins relate to the separation of scientific from religious authority in the nineteenth century, a division of reason from faith that left the choosing of political values marooned somewhere in the middle. To heal this gap, people appealed to geography to confirm their values independently. The final section of chapter 2, and the conclusion of the argument of part 1, suggests that leaning in to the geographic embrace could be a better strategy than trying to rise above it, than trying to be objective about it.

The geographic embrace is a common gesture in the twentieth century. It is a habit of seeing land as a setting for moral insight, a setting that transcends history and politics. But habits of seeing — like the geographic embrace or the convention that science is not art — are not the same as addictions. There is a lot of play in culture.

In part 2, I journey into three symbolic landscapes: the West, the family farm and the small community or "local" ideal. In each of them there is the broader sense that landscapes bring us closer to important truths. I look at these icons of the West, the family farm and the local ideal through individual eyes. Mari Sandoz, Josephine Johnson and civil rights activist Ella J. Baker guide my quest for inspirations that fit, rather than omit, what I have learned from the study of history.

Through Mari Sandoz, I discover that culture is like landscape. You are always already in one. Trying to escape culture for some omniscient high ground is as unlikely as escaping earth, and as unpleasant. Following her lead, I find that changing the world in the direction of greater social justice might begin with a cultural politics: a sense that our imaginations, at some deep level, can be transformed even as we are embedded in them. The complex interaction between what is and what can be had a precedent in her life: the interaction with what is and what was the Great Plains landscape.

Josephine Johnson loved nature. Yet she feared being a "weak woman birder"; escaping to nature horrified her. She wrested herself out of the corsets of a language that divides nature love from human love. Appropriately, she named her solution via a re-visioned family farm, a setting that by long tradition symbolically joined nature and social justice goals. First, however, she had to reject the old beliefs. She criticized especially the undemocratic family and also the parsimonious, practical outlook that disapproves of the indulgence of beauty. Later, she had to dispute the emerging, midcentury definitions of liberalism. A politics of abundance for self, nature and society is what emerges from Johnson's family farm.

Looking toward an almost imaginable future of transnationalism, I explore in the final chapter what "acting locally, thinking globally" might someday mean. The answer begins by relinquishing the sense of geography that our elementary school teachers cultivated in us with map tests. Borders between nations or between towns are actually much less permanent than that convenient geo-graphy (earth writing) might suggest. In what other way might we imagine the "local," if not as a fixed small community on a map? I find my answer through the larger philosophical orientation of Ella J. Baker. Drawing on a transatlantic, African-American orientation toward geography, I learn to read *place* more as a verb than a noun. In her civil rights activism, Baker cultured community. The local invented itself through her leadership. In this myth of a small town, Baker's local communities are like nomadic ones. Her perception of place requires fluidity. The local is an attitude of awareness to "where the people are."

My search for meaningful myths leads me to lean in to the ideas of these women, crafting not so much a sense of place as a sense of direction. I name these directions "a politics of memory," "a politics of abundance" and "a politics of identifying." Although the chapters in part 2 move through the century from the last homestead to transnationalism, and though they include western, midwestern and southern places, I do not mean to offer a survey. Instead, I offer the view from here; where I am.

Given the title of this book, you would likely want to know what I mean by "social justice." As a starting point, I ask you to join me in recognizing that many people remain utterly destitute even though our species has created the machinery to feed, clothe and shelter everyone on the planet. What the opposite of that injustice might be, or how to define fairness or justice, is much more difficult. This book describes attempts to reach such a definition using geography's guidance. But I don't mean to be evasive. I can offer you my general definition. In a world of social justice, there would be equality between the sexes and races; democracies would serve all their subjects as well as they do the rich; there would be an end to poverty, to nefarious discrimination, and even to war as we know it. Part of the point, however, is to experience how the meaning of social justice is not fixed and to participate in its reformulation. This book is about trying to name (and claim) ideals. But it is also about how those ideals cannot be easily extracted from their situations.

Another point of definition: you will notice that I use the words *geography, land, landscape* and *nature* nearly interchangeably. For another study, a more precise usage of terms would be necessary. My purpose, though, is to evoke a family of meanings using words that resemble each other as cousins do — a shared nose here, similarly dark eyebrows there.[2] What I am looking for are colloquial meanings. Colloquial meanings too are what I mean to provide: "as distinguished," says the *Oxford English Dictionary,* "from formal or elevated language."

In the final section of this book, the epilogue, I return to the suggestion of subjectivity, including why the main examples in the book are from women. The explanation is that their ideas resonated with me more than any others did. Those inclinations have to do with my own history, my personal experience of the world. Why do you need to know about me in a book about history and place and social justice? Because interacting with culture, just as interacting with landscape, requires the very personal experience of the senses as well as intellectual truth, as Sandoz taught me; because, as Johnson said, the self's cry for life is the motor of change; because where I am, as Baker would acknowledge, is the beginning of where this book can go. Despite its academic roots, my work on this book has been a political and personal journey. I invite you to contemplate a legacy of ideas passed down to modern Americans. I invite you to cultivate judgment, with the help of others who have gone before you, about which myths you yourself might want to uphold.

PART ONE

The Geographic Embrace

CHAPTER ONE

A Tale of Forgetting

Before there was a welfare state, there was a frontier state. Instead of money, the frontier state spent land. The similarities between welfare and frontier programs are striking. Both involved huge public investments. They aimed at nothing less than the solution to poverty. Both were rife with fraud. But talk show hosts, political commentators and historians never talk about a frontier "state" in the same way that they talk about a welfare "state." The absence of the frontier from typical accounts of the history of government handouts is part of a larger phenomenon. I refer to this phenomenon as the geographic embrace.

Land, nature and geographic symbols like the "West" — all these are part of a genealogy of ideas that plays a trick on us. Like a set of blinders, the tradition I aim to describe focuses attention in one direction at the expense of others. In this way of thinking, the frontier was free; it was given by nature, not paid for by the government's commitment of resources.

The geographic embrace has twin effects. On the one hand, land tends to erase, or encourage us to forget, its economic and political aspects. I will elaborate on the example of the frontier state to show how this forgetfulness works. On the other hand, words on land not only divert attention from certain directions but also turn attention toward others. Americans habitually look to landscapes like the West or to nature to find an answer to the question, what would a good society look like? In this way of thinking, landscapes give us clues to how nature intended the human world to be.

Images of land overlap a great deal with ideas about how to fashion a better, fairer world because of a way of seeing and not-seeing that developed over a long period. I believe that becoming aware of this historical pattern will help us to think better about the ideals we want to uphold. I do not mean to suggest, though, that we need to wake up and smell the proverbial coffee. The trick played on us by land is just one of many such historical patterns that we inherit subtly in how we use language. The end of part 1 takes up the question of how to deal with the geographic embrace. The best strategy, strangely enough, will be to lean in to it. But first we need to become familiar with the cultural and historical context that words on land bring with them.

On an especially bad day in February 1934, a middle-aged woman in Kansas wrote a letter. "Dear President and Mrs. Roosevelt," began Lizzie Crane — an ordinary woman, of ordinary education, writing in a gentle cursive penmanship directly to the leaders of her country. She wrote more than one hundred pages, nearly a book. Sitting in the cool reserve of the national archives, I turned page after heartfelt page, following the terrible comedy of hard luck that was the thirties.[1] Her husband and she had owned a farm, she wrote, but then he developed asthma, which made hay gathering nearly impossible, and then lightning struck down a family horse, and soon after her husband's condition worsened, and he died in steady stages that exhausted their savings and even lost them, finally, a rented farm. And then things got seriously bad. In the early years of the Great Depression, she and her children had to rely primarily on her eldest (but still young) son's income, as he vagabonded from job to job whether in Florida or near home. She remarried, and her second husband beat her. Finally she chose even greater destitution over the tyrannies of this home life. "It has taken much thought and nerve for me to make up my mind to write you my story," she confessed to her well-placed betters. Indeed.

"There surely must be a way out of this where we are all able and willing to work," she wrote, and she knew what that way was too: a homestead. She had read in the newspaper about a revival of the old program with the newly created Division of Subsistence Homesteads, and she had her spot picked out. Never mind that the "homestead" she asked for would include a boardinghouse as well as five to ten acres, not just bare, unscraped earth. She did not consider her request unusual because the gist of the formula was still there. The gift of land washed clean any hint that she was asking for "something for nothing." She was not needing, that is, what is today commonly called welfare.

Asking for land is not asking for welfare. This assumption is broadly and deeply shared in American history. Asking for welfare involves shame and defeat. But land feels different. Ordinary people like Lizzie Crane, as well as their well-placed betters, have combined to make land-based welfare the only truly venerated government assistance program in the history of the United States. In Europe the inherited strata of wealth determined people's lives, but in the United States—politicians announced in tones that came perilously close to boasting of radical intent—the conditions would be different. Here a bedrock of equality cut into 160-acre sections would mollify the differences of birth.

Homestead programs sound so much cleaner than "welfare." You can be sure that Nebraska farmers today would not welcome very kindly the comparison of their ancestors to recipients of Aid to Families with Dependent Children (AFDC). I sympathize with those farmers, and I also regret that the welfare moms must take their aid with such a large helping of shame. The fact is that our society has intervened in the private economies of families for a long, long time. The government program to give homesteads to heads of households was the earliest version of welfare, and it began in earnest as early as the 1830s when the federal government started to formally recognize "squatters" on government land as legitimate owners. Frontier handouts continued into the 1920s, making them the longest-running government assistance program in American history.

The word *welfare* calls forth all kinds of negative associations, and the descendants of frontier recipients would understandably shrink from the comparison. But the land-based giveaway had many of the same problems so frequently associated with government programs. Consider the example of Henry Miller of the semiarid Central Valley of California (there, where so many of our fruits and vegetables now grow). To collect his million-plus free acres from the government, he allegedly drove a team of horses with a boat tied aback through a loophole in the Swamplands Act. All the law said was that a boat had to cross the land to qualify it as swamp and therefore free to those who would drain it.[2] Welfare cheating in the frontier state puts today's able-bodied dole junkies to shame.

Well, you might say, the homestead programs weren't "really" welfare because at the time people didn't think of these programs as such. They too hated big-government intervention, and what's more they judged the poor more viciously than anyone does today. In the nineteenth century the poor were blamed for their predicament, and sympathy for them was at best condescending. There's some real truth to these objections. But then there is that statue in New York harbor. Bring me your hungry and poor, it says. There's nothing wrong with them, it implies.

People who came in search of free land didn't have a "culture of poverty." They had lousy luck in the bingo game of birth. At the same time that poverty was condemned, the political discourse of the time contained a deep sense that unfair privileges (in Europe) required a vast experiment (in America) to offer hope to those born without silver spoons in their mouths.

The point of the comparison between welfare programs and the frontier is that we must be forced out of our assumptions to see it. Surely there are significant differences between currency and real estate–based aid programs. However, we are blinded from seeing the similarities that do exist because words on land have a habit of erasing the political maneuvering that fills the background. If you believe that nature gave us the frontier, then large-scale government assistance to the poor began in the 1930s. But look again. As in the creation of welfare, politicians of different outlooks fought hard about whether to bring the frontier state into being. The Whigs insisted that the land swelling the government coffers ought to be kept like savings in the bank. The land should be used to generate revenue — at the highest return possible — rather than be distributed cheaply. White southern leaders also objected to the idea, seeing a program that subsidized small farmers as a threat to slave economies. Some conservatives of that time might have "spent" some land to prime the economy, but the idea of handing it out to Tom, Dick, Harry (and later Jane) was anathema to many. Consider the words of Timothy Dwight, president of Yale University and Congregational minister in the early republic. He took as dim a view of the future recipients of frontier largesse as any contemptuous critic of welfare today. In 1821 Dwight wrote that the people surging to get land in Maine "will, almost of course, consist of roving, disorderly, vicious men." Men who already owned land or property, he believed, had risen to their station by virtue of their worth. People without property, equally, needed to submit themselves to the traditional hierarchy where they belonged and not rise up. "In the regular, established society in which they were born," Dwight commented longingly, "they were awed and restrained."[3] Especially in the midst of the Civil War, when the 1862 Homestead Act was passed, the opposition loudly urged that such assets should not be "squandered" when a war was on.[4]

Politicians disagreed and maneuvered to create a government-sponsored land program against poverty. The frontier did not just appear out of nowhere to these nineteenth-century thinkers. It came out of battles played out in legislatures and newspapers. Among the harder questions was how to provide land for future seekers of a fresh start. People today find it easy to assume that the free land somehow ran out of its own accord.

Those who lived through the political struggle to make the land available in the first place were not under this illusion. From Workingmen's party advocate Charles Henry Evans in the 1830s to gadfly economist Henry George in the 1890s, they tried to invent a mechanism for creating a land bank to finance the program over the long haul. The methods included restrictions on inheritance. They included laws to return land on the death of its owner back to the commonwealth.[5] Land could be a resource for equality but only if the law made it a renewable resource, said antimonopolist voices like Horace Greeley and the National Land Reform Association. These people were not yet burdened with the West of the twentieth-century imagination, where the end of the frontier seems as inevitable as its beginning.

The similarities between modern welfare and nineteenth-century frontier programs are especially striking when you look at the intentions of the legislators. I will turn later to how the outcomes of the two programs compare and also to the very good question of whether the homestead program was really more like workfare, or an employment program. First, though, I want to insist that the architects of the homestead programs and their allies undertook a massive government assistance program deliberately. Far from fleeing government intervention, nineteenth-century politicians openly assigned themselves the role of social engineers — when dealing with land policy, that is. A government that will last, insisted Kansas senator Samuel C. Pomeroy on the floor of the Senate during the debate over the 1862 Homestead Act, should provide for the "houseless and homeless" and give a hungry man first "the comforts of life." Otherwise, the United States, like Europe, will become the refuge of a splendid aristocracy while laborers find their aspirations extinguished. Indeed, give free land to the homeless of our country, "yes, and of every country," said the exuberant Pomeroy, rather than continue European history where "untaught millions, without aspirations, without hope" are squashed by the nobility, "perishing of want of a few acres of God's earth in which to raise their daily bread."[6] Sympathy for the downtrodden and something almost akin to class politics were among Pomeroy's reasons for supporting the bill. In addition, he argued that the proposal coincided with the legitimate purposes of government, which were to promote freedom, prosperity and happiness; and it would create new consumers, able to pay the import tax on goods they could afford as home owners, thereby increasing the nation's treasury. Money counted — Pomeroy spelled out why he thought the act was a good investment and not a squandering of the public purse.

The 1862 Homestead Act passed in Congress. To suggest that Pomeroy's idealistic speech was the primary reason the bill overcame objections would be a vast exaggeration. The Kansas senator himself could have been part of the backroom negotiations that turned the handouts quickly into what is today commonly called corporate welfare — that is, government aid to railroad magnates and other corporate interests. Nevertheless, it is important to notice these nineteenth-century people who could admit, out loud, that the U.S. government's role was to banish homelessness and economic insecurity.

You can hear the assumption that the federal government ought to help the poor repeated again in an 1879 congressional commission convened to evaluate the success of homestead legislation. Although their agenda was to reckon with fraud, they assumed they were to set the ship of state back on this course: to use government land to save millions of people from the condition of being "homeless."[7] It is clear from their prose that they proposed to intervene in a fate that might otherwise have befallen "the majority" of the four million people they estimated had filed claims on the act they were charged to review.

Reading the documents the homestead legislators left behind, it becomes clear that they intended to parcel out livelihood, especially to those who had no secure income. They meant to use land to address problems such as the rise of urban poverty. The commissioners of 1879 understood this and sought to act on it. Homelessness meant much more to them than the absence of shelter. A home, by their sights, was a working farm. Their calculations about the right acreage make this clear. An appropriate translation is that the frontier state's "entitlements" promised no less than a natural right to subsistence.[8] The scale of their social engineering ambitions drew on more than a century of rhetoric on the natural right to the fruits of (especially agricultural) labor. This natural rights tradition proposed that you did not have to *earn* the right to life, liberty and happiness; you were born with it, and any government that did not guarantee it deserved a revolutionary thrashing. Private landownership was at the very top of the list as a means of fulfilling this natural contract. And it was a helluva promise. After all, getting your own land in Europe would have been like John Doe today winning the Lotto. Two Lottos, the same day. (In fact, land could easily be turned into cash, and many homesteaders did so as soon as they could.) With feudal traditions fresh in their minds, the American promoters of free (or in the beginning, cheap) lands for the poor hardly were being modest in their aims.

The legislators intended to provide land to the homeless, and land promised food and shelter. Proponents of homesteads meant, in other words, to help families gain the minimum comforts of life. As if the promised economic advantages were not enough, they actually meant land to provide many other benefits. The many strands of support for land giveaways included the idea that farms would guarantee not just life-sustaining jobs for a whole family but also the right to *good,* worthwhile work. Farming was a growth opportunity for the soul. "By the exercise [agriculture] gives both to the body and to the mind, it secures health and vigour to both," John Taylor of Caroline summarized succinctly in 1803.[9] There's more: the farm would be like a private country for each family. The original conception of landownership in American law guaranteed "absolute dominion," so that each landowner was like a despot whose power included stopping neighbors from infringing on the "quiet enjoyment" of his or her private kingdom.[10] Economic security, worthwhile employment and an independent mini-kingdom were the types of associations that the proponents of homesteads brought to the land giveaways. In addition, people in this camp argued that the programs would benefit the nation as a whole. Anyone with such a "home," they believed, would be so certain to want to protect it that they would not join a revolutionary mob, they would not chop off the heads of the rich with sharp guillotine blades, they would vote their own minds because they had no boss to fire them for it — they would, in other words, become citizens. This had been very much a concern for the representatives of a still-new nation who had to deal with quiet doubts of their own about the experiment in democracy. And the concern lingered. Through independent property ownership, the commissioners of 1879 wrote, the farmer was to imbibe a "feeling of responsibility to society and [a] sense of dignity." The word *homeless* evoked in the nineteenth century vastly different associations than would come easily to the commission's suburban descendants. Home was title to earth; it was title to employment; it was title to respect in citizenship. And they meant to give homes away.

Such was the mainstream bombast of the nineteenth century. The rhetorical commitments of the New Deal–cradled welfare state, in other words, were not without any American precedent. When Franklin Delano Roosevelt declared that "freedom from want" was among the essential elements of a good society, he was building on a long tradition.[11] The beginning of modern "safety nets" in response to the Great Depression continued an old, familiar role of government: to stem the condition of homelessness and make possible the basic "comforts of life" for all. The difference is that earlier legislators distributed gifts of land.

Perhaps the comparison between the welfare and frontier states should not see the frontier only as *equally* interventionist but as *more* generous. The homestead proponents of the nineteenth century envisioned starting kits parceled out at the front door, not safety nets hung regretfully out back. There was no minimum level of destitution to which you must first fall. To speak freely in Congress about a natural right to the comforts of life was easier in the political climate of a nation that still prided itself as revolutionary. Then the great goal was to prove the United States better than Europe. When the welfare state came into existence, politicans were at pains to distinguish the United States from the Communist Soviet Union. The European comparison could push political dreaming toward the left; the Soviet challenge helped drive politics further right.

The mainstream bombast of the nineteenth century disappears in today's common assumption that government invented a new role for itself with the start of modern welfare programs in the 1930s. The evidence for the similarity between welfare and frontier programs, however, goes beyond the vast social engineering intentions of the legislators. The frontier state consisted of more than just speeches. There is also the scale of financial commitment involved. What if we were to describe a frontier state that spans circa 1841 (the General Preemption Act that first legalized some squatters' rights to land) to 1916 (the Stock-Raising Homestead Act)?[12] Considerably more tangible than the political rhetoric that justified it, the frontier state commanded a war chest dedicated to the acquisition of territories, a vast commitment of assets that alternatively might have been used (as the Whigs had earlier urged) to generate revenue, and incidentals such as the cost of exploring and mapping territory, adjudicating disputed lands and staffing the land office bureaucracy. This does not count the secondary commitments like the public financing of a transportation infrastructure or the colleges built to educate the farmers, both funded together with the Homestead Act of 1862. Then there was the cost of the reservation system to house the stubbornly unvanishing Indians. How much might all this have added up to? Conventional yardsticks bend and crack when asked to perform this task. Standard measures to compare the relative size of the public versus the private sector across different time periods rely on governmental spending on goods and services.[13] Of course, the contrast then looks stark. The frontier state did not spend much cash; it spent land. To fulfill its commitments, it did not raise taxes; it drew new borders. In a recent effort to begin a small portion of such a calculation, James Oberly estimated the forgone revenue from just the pre–Civil War land warrants at $62 million. By comparison, the total federal budget in 1855 was $59 million.[14]

One might argue that the frontier is generally not counted as welfare because it did not work as welfare. It failed. The tawdry outcomes of the frontier programs have been the subject of study by historians of the West for a long time. It is worth facing up to these findings in some detail. For decades students of the American West have been engaging in a heartily good brawl about whether the frontier had been even moderately successful in its generous aims; whether land had, in historical fact, helped to build a more just society. The findings of the demythologizers, in roughly chronological order, might be encapsulated as, first, the "good idea corrupted" school. Honorably led by public lands historian Paul Gates in the 1930s, this version sees greedy, well-positioned speculators snapping up the deserving poor's marginal chances, assisted therein by venal legislators who passed a chaos of conflicting laws.[15] In the books on this shelf, we read about Henry Miller and his clever boat trick, we read how frequently birdhouses substituted for the domiciles required to secure a land claim formally, and most especially, we focus on the railroads and mining companies that collected most of the spoils.

More fundamental than the "good idea corrupted" school, the second set of frontier debunkers pronounced good riddance on the whole ideological kit and caboodle in the 1950s. These historians saw a veneer of ideology over consistently greedy and often naive behavior on the part of the farmers as well. It was not just the railroads and money-burning monopolists that had doomed the idea. The presumably earnest and incorruptible farmers were also land speculators, much more interested in joining the mad scramble for market advantage than in settling quietly down to the simple life — which in fact had never been simple but exhausting and perilously insecure anyway. The whole agrarian mystique, argued this school of thinkers such as Henry Nash Smith, had doomed the nation to avoid facing its urban problems; to drape monopolistic practices with an imaginative veil of pioneer glory; to demand naively that ecologically arid land behave like eastern pasture, and more. In snapshot form, the gathering of charlatans and hopefuls in 1891 near Midland, Texas, seemed to say it all. There, drought-stricken westerners cheered as leftover explosives from the Civil War thundered upward into a still-bare blue sky. They had been told the dynamite could change the weather.[16] To these historians, the agrarian myth had only been rainmaking on a larger scale.

The failures of the frontier to fulfill any of its grander, social justice aims came most starkly into focus with the rise of civil rights activists and historians in the 1960s. Rather than just window dressing for land-grabbing farmers and corporations, this new generation of scholars placed American "manifest destiny" squarely inside the context of the worldwide age of imperialism. The settlers were part of a conquering force, and imperial interests underwrote the farmers' occupation of the territories. The justifications for the movement westward were frankly racist. There is a great deal of evidence to support this interpretation. To take only one of the more succinct examples, Senator Thomas Benton in 1846 flatly declared the continent a gift from God for the white race.[17] Such religious justifications joined with opportunism to obliterate other peoples' sovereignty. During the last thirty years, this civil rights–inspired revisionism has developed into a subtle set of stories about how conquest actually works. Historians such as Patricia Nelson Limerick, Peggy Pascoe, and Richard White have captured the complex, kaleidoscopic variety of encounters that eventually added up to a history of domination. The stories of these historians featured confused missionaries; frankly lost explorers led by black scouts; crisscrossing and changing alliances among Iroquois, French, Algonquians and Anglo-Americans in historically changing formations; and farmers of every color and gender, only some of whom were favored by the land giveaways.[18]

The insights of the civil rights era forced the racial bias of the frontier out into the open. Even the most liberal intentions of the frontier land giveaway took on an ironic aspect. The relevant snapshot in this collection is the Dawes Act of 1887. It forced Indian groups to divide tribal or clan-owned land into individual homesteads. As nothing before had so plainly done, the act revealed the homestead formula as ethnocentric. What was wrong with Indian forms of communal landownership? How was the family farm more "just" as a system? Despite their seeming good intentions, the reformers only made the racist landgrab worse. By insisting on individually owned land, the architects of the Dawes Act reduced Indian sovereignty to a tiny vestige of their treaty rights. The white land speculators benefited the most, once more.[19] These smaller parcels proved easier to gobble up. Conquest was the bottom line.

The value of the comparison of the frontier to twentieth-century welfare programs might, however, be strengthened by the failures so evident in the execution of the frontier ideals. In our time, it is common to cite every example of bumbling government intervention as further evidence for cutting Washington down to size. Why are the failures of the frontier not included in such diatribes? Why is the frontier state not cited as proof of the failure of government? There is a blind spot that prevents seeing the likeness. Large-scale public assistance programs began in the thirties, is the popular assumption. Western history seems to be a separate and unrelated chapter because it comes from land.

The blind spot that erases land-based welfare from other accounts of federal government intervention affects scholars as much as popular editorializers. This includes even scholars who otherwise aim to combat the popular stereotype that big government began in the 1930s. While enumerating other programs, they tend to omit land from their reckonings. Sociologist Theda Skocpol, for example, works hard to deflate the illusion of a "night watchman" state — an image of government as a part-time, moonlighting, nearly insignificant force. From the "night watchman" point of view, today's overwhelming size of big government contrasts with a bygone time of freewheeling market competition. In those good old days, goes the story, local and state governments at most parceled out a few favors to orphans and widows while private charities and evolutionary competition took care of the rest.[20] To dismantle the presumed timing of welfare provision, Skocpol underscores the extent of Civil War pensions and mothers' and children's benefits. Land, though, appears nearly parenthetically in her treatment.[21] A similarly demythologizing historian, Alan Dawley, pushes the origins of the social responsibility of the New Deal back a half decade to Herbert Hoover. While he occasionally acknowledges an earlier "revolutionary liberalism," it disappears under generalizations about the long continuity of "laissez-faire liberalism."[22] Like a page missing from a diary, references to the Interior Department or the General Land Office are missing from histories of the formative years of the leviathan of big government.[23]

Evidence of a consistent blind spot in counting land as a government-funded handout goes way back. Lizzie Crane in the 1930s was only continuing a long tradition of seeing land as very different from other kinds of aid. Consider, for example, this justification of the homestead giveaways from a frequent recipient of such government largesse, a man named Ebenezer C. Hardy. "I am strictly an uneducated man," wrote Hardy to the congressional commission of 1879. But he proceeded to explain why he believed the homestead-type acts were the "best of any laws that are now or ever have been in force." He acquired his first parcel in Oregon in 1852 through what was called the donation law; then he mined gold and lead ore before acquiring new land (160 acres for himself, 160 for his wife), this time in Elko County, Nevada. To anyone who might think this was a large meal at the public trough, Hardy responded by emphasizing how hard he worked. Easterners didn't understand, he gently conjectured in his justifying letter to the commission, the responsibilities that are "thrown on frontiersmen in general." In addition to working the land, the frontiersman (according to Ebenezer) helped to build the common schools, roads and bridges and also rose to defend his property claims against Indians. All this in a day's work. (His solution to the labor crunch: annihilate the Indians and, with them, the irritating Bureau of Indian Affairs bureaucrats.) He closed the letter by apologizing again for its failures, saying that every day his zealous schedule kept him from answering the commission's survey until finally he did it poorly in the evenings — "when," he wrote, "I ought to have been at rest."[24]

The most reasonable objection to linking the frontier with what is today called welfare is that it was fundamentally an employment program, not an assistance one. I will readily grant that there is something to this insistence. Like workfare, homestead programs included the expectation that the recipients would work hard for their aid. And yet notice also that the history of workfare or even employment legislation does not generally cite the frontier as a precedent. The government's role in creating the frontier disappears. Again, land's seemingly *natural* properties obliterate the political and economic background of choices made and choices left behind.

In addition to the exchange of labor for aid, frontier programs resemble workfare in the attitude that both the recipients and the benefactors bring to the aid they receive. Unlike contemporary welfare mothers (or "welfare queens," as Ronald Reagan called them), the heroes of pioneer dramas may step forward proudly to accept their handouts. They celebrate their low-down circumstances without a hint of shame in their voices. They are led to believe they offer their labor in exchange for nature's real estate. But the frontier recipients avoid acknowledging the larger government apparatus that made the exchange possible. The homesteaders avoid counting a great deal when it looks like their labor is an even trade for land. They ignore the state that buys up land, hires surveyors to corner it, subsidizes railroads to build the country up, pays bureaucrats in the Land Office to distribute it and funds investigators to hunt up and deal with fraud. It was a huge government program, not a simple Lockean trade of sweat in soil translating to rightful ownership.

Although the central role of labor in the idea of the frontier does offer some reason to compare the frontier to workfare rather than welfare, there is a serious problem. The historical reality was that the recipients of government land did not all settle down and work the soil. By some estimates, the overwhelming majority in fact converted their warrants and titles as quickly as possible into cash, collecting thereby sometimes the equivalent of a half year's pay.[25] The way the system worked, Congress distributed what was called land "scrip." These scrips could be redeemed for land. As White argued, "Land scrip was the nineteenth-century equivalent of food stamps," only more valuable, because scrip, unlike food stamps, could be sold or traded.[26]

The labor implied in land handouts diminishes the shame associated with government aid, and yet it is still government aid. Land could become cash, it could become a tradable investment security; land scrip was a handout that could be used in many ways, only one of which was to get a "job" as a farmer. In the end, the comparison to an employment program only once more erases the level of government commitment involved.

Land should not escape the political accounting of who got what. Fairness demands looking where we are disinclined to see. Benefits that accrue to one group at the expense of another ought not disappear just because those benefits arrive hidden by land. The blind spot that erases the frontier from government programs that address homelessness is part of a larger habit of not seeing. This tendency is as strong today as ever.

The most obvious, current examples of the blind spot about land are the vast government assistance programs that underwrite middle- and upper-class homes. Between 1920 and 1970, the percentage of Americans who rented their dwellings dropped from 41.9 to under 20.[27] In these years and continuing today, government aid significantly underwrote the expansion of home ownership. The biggest of these support programs is the tax deduction for mortgage interest. Even flat-tax and other reform-minded thinkers, who would like to undo this mortgage aid, talk about this program as an untouchable subsidy. Costing the treasury billions of dollars every year, the tax deduction for mortgage interest is arguably the biggest public housing program on record. But addressing it is anathema. "This is the sacredest of sacred cows," argued Stephen Moore, an analyst for the libertarian Cato Institute. "The dirty little secret of the mortgage deduction is it is the biggest rich man's subsidy."[28]

The heir to the frontier *state* is the government assistance program provided to Americans via a network of home-ownership-related benefits. Since the 1930s the federal government has insured mortgages so that banks can risk putting up 95 percent of the price of a home. The loaning institutions can invest confidently knowing that if there is a foreclosure, the government purse will pay. Historian Stephanie Coontz has argued that middle- and upper-class Americans take for granted large-scale programs of government assistance while damning lower-income claims for help.[29] Those programs that they take for granted tend to be washed clean by association with land handouts.

The frontier state of old and its current manifestation of sacred-cow benefits is only one example of how land erases political choices being made today. Another extremely significant example is the deep assumption that voting districts should be drawn on the basis of location. It seems "natural" that a voting district be defined geographically. History does offer other examples. In most states between 1820 and 1840, for example, the conservatives sought to have at least one house of the state legislature represent the propertied interests[30] — creating a legislature that represents a class rather than a region. To the framers of the Constitution, residential voting districts were only one of several controversial choices. The new democracy wanted to avoid "virtual representation," the British system that permitted a legislator to represent the interests of an entire empire regardless of location (and so therefore permitted an Englishman to represent Virginia). One idea was to avoid group representation altogether and permit each individual one vote. But how to count these individuals? As political geographer Fred Shelley and his coauthors explain in a summary text on American political geography, "Since there was already a strong attachment of people to places, in part because of land ownership, territory became the major criterion to early framers of the constitution, for it could be clearly defined using surveying methods and the defined spaced could be depicted on maps."[31] In other words, it looked easy. Just draw a circle around a certain geographic area and say that the people who live here get one representative. But, of course, it didn't turn out to be that easy. Because people don't stay put. They move. In the American case, they move a great deal. Before you knew it, some urban districts had millions of people but the same meager number of representatives as a nearly empty county.

Land blinds us to the decisions we make. It is not "natural" to count votes inside geographic units. It is a political choice. And using geography to define voting districts might actually be a poor choice. "The case can be made," speculate Shelley and his coauthors, "that Americans are living under a system of political organized spaces that still represents the relatively immobile and parochial population of two centuries ago." Land-based units imply that people who live in the same place by definition have a significant shared interest. But often geography has less meaning today than other group identities, including race. Not long ago, Lani Guinier, a daring lawyer and nominee for U.S. assistant attorney general, made just that case. Race deserved more of a hearing as a basis for representation, she argued. People do not vote as individuals, they participate in "communities of interest." Politics is a group phenomenon. Geographic constituencies, Guinier argued, "are a form of group representation in which common territory is a proxy for common interests."[32] So, perhaps, Guinier suggested radically, we should choose our communities of interest instead of letting geography *seem* to do it for us. Her article that included these speculations later doomed her nomination — so dangerous is it to suggest alternatives to the natural-seeming order. Land seems apolitical, but it is not.

Changing the way we vote away from geographic constituencies, however, is another of the most sacred of sacred cows — another example of how difficult it is to see the effects of land-based politics. In the second half of the twentieth century, the courts have tried, mightily, to recognize that people move and that geographic units do not. Change is up to the courts because state legislators are loath to alter the districts that voted them in. Starting with the Supreme Court's *Baker v. Carr* decision in 1962, the "reapportionment revolution" redrew lines on U.S. maps to try to match population numbers with legislative representatives.[33] Of course, if they get carried away with this principle of equal representation for equal population areas, the five intermountain western states could end up sharing two representatives.[34] The status quo, however, rests firmly on the general assumption that geography is destiny.

Finally, the clinching evidence for the blindness toward the politics involved in geography is the blank look you get if you suggest that we open a new frontier today. In a provocative essay, urban studies scholar Frank J. Popper calculated the amount of earth that was sparsely populated or held in federal ownership in 1980 and found it comparable to the acreage of the nineteenth-century frontier. Combined with a suggestion that Great Plains settlement be abandoned for a vast "buffalo commons," the gag earned him some talk show slots, but the idea quickly sank under the weight of the common sense of our time.[35] As we turn toward the twenty-first century, it is "nonsense" to talk literally about a new frontier in land.

"We ran out of land" is the common explanation for why there are no homesteads today. But what we ran out of is a conviction for how to use federal property. Now the public land divides, not into homesteads, but into grazing allotments, recreation areas, wilderness protection and so on. We could change our minds and write a new homestead act. The land is still there. What has changed is our ideas for how to secure freedom from want. We didn't "run out of land." But the popular assumption that there is no land left has the effect of suggesting that the disdvantaged have no "natural right" to the claims they now make, only a politically evolved one. Occasionally an odd voice will once again try to assert the old claim. The Division of Subsistence Homesteads program, to which the desperate Lizzie Crane referred, was an early example of a twentieth-century effort to update the homestead idea. Its founders meant the project only as an illustrative experiment, however, and they quickly found themselves the objects of ridicule for highly publicized mistakes.[36] Foundations were off; construction errors multiplied. In 1973, near the end of the civil rights movement, Samuel C. Jackson, an inspired former Department of Housing and

Urban Development (HUD) official, urged the creation of a new urban homestead act. He proposed that city properties be granted outright to low-income residents willing to invest their time and labor in improving them.[37] Nearly twenty years later, at a news conference to which almost nobody came, Jesse Jackson would make the same appeal for the bonanza of properties now owned by the federal government because of the savings and loan bailout.[38] Meanwhile, some community activists had followed in the footsteps of nineteenth-century squatters or "preemptors" and simply taken up residence in foreclosed properties in Denver and elsewhere. These are the proverbial exceptions that prove the rule.

When asked to comment on the public land laws, Edward Eldridge, a farmer in Whatcom, Washington, made this prediction in 1879:

> Have you ever thought whether my grandchildren and their
> grandchildren will be able to get 160 acres each for nothing
> also? . . . They won't be bluffed off with the answer that if
> they wanted land for nothing they should have been born
> a hundred years ago. They will answer that the soil of
> America was not made for the exclusive use of those who
> lived a hundred years ago, but the general use of all who
> inhabit it through all ages.[39]

Unfortunately, Eldridge has proved to be quite wrong; we are bluffed.

Why are we blinded to how land was once used and how it is still used to naturalize deeply contestable political decisions? Why are we bluffed? There are many explanations for why hard moral choices about the role of government disappear under land's magic spell. It should never be forgotten that land's legerdemain has benefited certain privileged interest groups. The history of white supremacy is a case in point. As the "New Western" historians suggested, a racist ideology of "free" land buttressed the conquest of the West. Note that at the end of the Civil War, the federal coffers swelled with 850,000 acres of Confederate land. But in this case the land was not seen as nature's gift to the destitute; instead it had previous owners to whom it was returned. The land by and large went back to the white Southerners. The freed slaves argued that the land by rights ought to be recognized as theirs because they were the ones who had worked it. As Jacqueline Jones recounts in her history of the South, the slaves demanded that the government give them the land because their labor created its value and also because of their other sacrifices — "Our wives our children our husbands has been sold over and over again to purchase the lands we now locates upon."[40] The homesteaders of the West had no such prior claims and yet received the largesse of government lands. White supremacist logic employed land myths in its interest.

The history of established elites twisting land formulas to dovetail with their own interests continued into the twentieth century. The various programs underwriting modern home ownership have been infamously slanted on the basis of race. Through the "redlining" of loan programs, only whites could qualify for most mortgages in the forties and fifties, regardless of financial stability. Suburbs got more government support than the multicultural cities because the laws were written to favor new construction over urban renovation. In this way suburbs got vast infusions of funds while inner cities deteriorated and racialized ghettos hardened into their current shape. Whites benefited with easier mortgages and construction loans for new homes, and then, because the new suburbs required commuting, the government financed the massive highway construction of the fifties, sixties and seventies. Despite all this financial support, the mainstream bombast of the twentieth century failed to embrace these programs as "public housing." But the suburbs represent a clear public housing initiative: the government is responsible in large part for their flourishing. Instead the stigma of "public" funding stuck only to the vast inner-city housing projects like Cabrini Green in Chicago and not at all to subsidized suburban growth. Inner-city public housing and the suburban home-ownership boom are actually legislative twins. Often the very same legislative acts funded them.[41] They are "colored" very much as the geographies of the South and West were, only now we have a "south" and "west" equivalent in each city.[42]

While the hard economic and political interests of established elites tell part of the story of why land benefits erase the political background that produces them, the causes go deeper. The geographic embrace has a long history of momentum. The "forgetting" of land happens because it is difficult to twist language out of its ruts. It is hard to speak about land without falling under the spell of its naturalizing influence.

Cultural assumptions create the reality we see, of a frontier as separate from welfare. Richard White neatly makes the point of the central importance of cultural assumptions by citing range managers who define 83 percent of the West as range. "Think about that," he urges. "What if someone said parking lot attendants consider 83 percent of the eleven contiguous western states as parking lots. . . . You probably can park a car on 83 percent of the West. But such statements confuse a potential use of the land with the intrinsic character of the land itself."[43]

Free land is no more a natural category than is a parking lot.

In the nineteenth century, the land that became "free" could have become investment property for the federal government, a separate Indian nation-state, the Mormon nation of Deseret and so on. Similarly, any new legislative act could transform current Bureau of Land Management lands into planned utopian communities, car parks, suburban home lots or, again, livestock grazing areas. "Free" land — land set aside for claims by homesteaders — is a cultural invention.

Seduced by the many varieties of agrarian and pastoral thought, however, a very human — that is, cultural — habit is to assume that land is naturally there and not filtered through cultural invention. Long traditions of ideas lead us into the habit of thinking that land has qualities that transcend history; that soil has its own agenda to which human beings submit. My purpose is not so much to logically refute such agrarian faiths, of which there are many and some surely edifying. Instead I want to note the traditional grooves that permit land to be seen as transcendentally different, as outside history, and consider some of the consequences of this habit of thought. Postmodern theorists tell the story in abstract language: "We must be insistently aware of how space can be made to hide consequences from us, . . . how human geographies become filled with politics and ideology."[44] So urges Edward Soja, one of a band of critical intellectuals determined to show how maps make rather than mirror reality.[45]

Forgetting the frontier state is part of a larger story, which is that land is difficult to "see." This is because land seems more natural than money. Gifts of land come from God or Nature; they are a birthright. Food stamps, unemployment insurance, education — all the other modern entitlements — cannot escape their too-human origins. Land does, for very human reasons.

CHAPTER TWO

A Tale of Remembering

Why does land cast such a spell that a large-scale government assistance program vanishes from our collective consciousness? Why do public handouts become invisible when they involve squares of earth? Undoubtedly there are lots of reasons. Among them is this: an excess of regard. We turn to nature for moral guidance. Appealing to the higher authority of nature requires the illusion that the landscape before you is free of politics.

In chapter 1, I suggested that cultural blinders often keep people from seeing the role of land in American history. I pointed to a deep-seated inclination to avoid counting land in the plus-or-minus ledger of who gets what. Land handouts seem to come from nature, not government, I said. It's "non-sense," I argued, to speak in contemporary discourses about creating a new frontier of welfare. All this is part of habitually disregarding the politics in landscapes.

But, in an odd way, a devoted attention to land actually permits this forgetting in the first place. The same cultural habit lies at the root of both the erasing and the memorializing: the geographic embrace. Where do people go to find their politics? How do we name our beliefs, our ideologies — our ideas for the good, just society? Often, we do so by referring to the West, to nature — to landscape and geography more generally. By "the geographic embrace," I mean that Americans tend to hold on to land, even cling to it, as a last certainty in an uncertain world. Nature will tell us what to do. We turn to land for help in naming our politics for very specific, historical reasons. It will take me a while to explain this.

In the first years of the 1900s, a young man grouched his way through his farming chores, cursing the dry Texas plains that left him no time to explore the rest of life's delicious possibilities. He hated living where he was. One night, inspired by the despair of his youth, he dared to contact a national magazine. I want to be a writer, he said in his lonely letter, but I don't have the means. What happened next should only take place in the movies — but even screenwriters don't dare plots as unlikely as this. A wealthy stranger read the young man's words, and, after exchanging a few letters and cartons of books, the stranger sent him money for a good college education.

The young man became historian Walter Prescott Webb, and the strangest part of the story, yet also the most predictable, is that the disillusioned boy returned later to Texas. He moved back literally, becoming one of the state's favored sons, but he also moved back allegorically. He turned back to Texas to find hope. As a scholar, he agonized again about the contrast between human potential and the drudgery of so many lives. Society was so obviously unfair. His Texas, for example, suffered, as did the entire U.S. West, because of the capricious, illogical privileges that the East had accumulated over two centuries. How to fix things?

Webb's answer was that the best society fit itself to nature's designs. And in the Texas of old, there had once been a civilization perfectly synchronized with its environment. This is what he argued as a historian. In the Texas he had missed by just one or two generations, he found "a social complex which is a thing apart." It was the right social complex, the model of the good society, that he discovered in the western past.[1] Here is what it looked like to him: men could play like boys, ride hard and talk little and share in the great wealth of free grass for cattle. No wonder, given their environment, that they were individually strong and communally fair. No wonder that no one lorded over anyone else, as their place and their technology (horses) were so suited to each other and to human life. A nature-based democracy was what Webb saw in his Texas of yore.

Learning the contours of a better human world by studying nature is a common habit in literature. People of very different political perspectives equally fall into the geographic embrace. Mary Austin wrote a book in 1927 that was not published until much later, in part because the ideology of the book was so radically feminist. But as in her other, more mainstream work, Austin wrote about the wisdom of nature in *Cactus Thorn*. The plot takes a white political reformer out of New York, where he has lost sight of his sense of truth, and relinquishes him to the wilds of a southwestern desert. There he falls in love with an Anglo woman, Dulcie, who spends time with Indians and knows the desert inside out. Following her lead, he finds his vision restored by communion with nature. True democracy, he discovers, follows an inner sense of justice that is like instinct. Exploitation of one class by another would not be imaginable in an active democracy. People have no right to seek their own way at the expense of other people. Unfortunately (and here is the radical part), he does not quite get it. He applies the democratic lessons of the landscape only to public life, not to family values. Women can be used and discarded. Women do not fully count as partners, as citizens, as fellow teachers and learners of nature's lessons. Backed by the authority of the desert, Dulcie kills him for betraying his own medicine — his own realization of the desert's lessons.

Writers such as Webb and Austin rely on the authority of nature out of a kind of cultural intuition. Rather than truly learn about nature, I mean to suggest, they are driven to nature by their historical, cultural circumstances. They are pushed into the geographic embrace. Webb and Austin wrote the way they did partly out of a choice foisted on them. They and many other modernists easily slip into asking nature to confirm their beliefs. Sometimes they go directly to landscape description; other times they turn to the folk, to authentic local communities, to Indians, because they see these groups as closer to nature.

The habit of turning to the hills, to the plains, to the mountaintops and riverbanks for answers to life's most troublesome questions is an ancient one. "Injustice is the opposite to nature," said the Greek philosopher Democritus, circa 400 B.C.E.[2] Some look to American Indian philosophies rather than Greek ones for the source of this tradition. Some say the habit is universal. More interesting to me is why the habit continues. There are specific reasons related to the modern standoff between religion and science that permit geography to maintain this special connection to truth. Modern theories of knowledge are otherwise very corrosive of certainties of any type. Landscapes have not survived these challenges unscathed, but they have, generation after generation, reemerged nevertheless as settings for the exploration of the good society.

Several long-term intellectual trends set up the conditions for this particular dance with landscape, the naming of ideals. These are familiar old stories. Thomas Jefferson and agrarians such as John Taylor left a legacy connecting the origins of democracy — that most ideal hope for human society — to the farming and agricultural life. Close contact with the earth would create good citizens, they said. Enlightenment philosophers Jean-Jacques Rousseau and Thomas Hobbes took for granted that nature provided blueprints for human social organization — all they needed to do was decipher those determining influences. They came up with famously different answers, but they shared the assumption that nature could lead us. In literature, the "noble savage" was a familiar figure — a person tutored by nature who shows up his or her more "civilized" counterparts by being more just, honorable and true. James Fenimore Cooper's Leatherstocking was only one of these many characters who demonstrated that nature teaches ideals of human society. The romantic poets and then the American transcendentalists furthered the tradition, looking to nature to find out how to be authentically human.

But despite all these historical sources for the geographic embrace, there are also historical reasons for predicting that the nature myths might recede rather than become more prominent at the end of the nineteenth century. Modern philosophy and politics have been notoriously hard on certainties of any kind.

God was dead, according to Friedrich Nietzsche. From many quarters, this pronouncement had less to do with religion itself than with doubts about whether any "center" would hold. "All that is solid melts into air," Karl Marx intoned. There were many different ways to become skeptical of inherited certainties, whether one read science, philosophy or novels. Meanwhile, on the streets, the migrations of the nineteenth century brought people in closer contact with other religions and other convictions — with information that could threaten the local minister's or elder's or village authority's hold on truth. No one had the ultimate say.

Given the broad challenges in modern life to singular, universal sources of truth, it is actually strange that nature remained a trustworthy social counselor. One of the best historians of European ideas of "nature," Raymond Williams, was also puzzled at the immunity of nature to this challenge: "Even [those] who were prepared to dispense with the first singular principle — to dispense with the idea of God — usually retained and even emphasized that other and very comparable principle: the singular and abstracted ... Nature."[3] In a place so willing to abide contradictions as the U.S. House of Representatives, an exasperated W. W. Payne begged his colleagues in 1846 to give up recruiting nature for their favorite partisan hobbyhorse.[4] But it did not stop; in fact, rather than abandon nature as counselor, various historical factors converged to make landscape myths more necessary in moral arguments.[5]

The geographic embrace survived modern corrosions because of a power vacuum in the cultural imagination. In early America, ministers counseled the colonial and then early revolutionary elites; the clerics headed the universities. But a kind of earthquake had been shaking loose the timbers of this worldview for some time. That earthquake was the competing claims to truth by science as opposed to religion.

As scientific authority competed with religious authority, an unstable truce was finally established in which truth was divided into two spheres. In one sphere, there was scientific fact based on analysis and reason; in the other, there was religious truth based on conviction and feeling. Intellectual historian James Kloppenberg describes the resolution succinctly:

> [The dispute] culminated in the proclamation of a truce on terms offered by scientists, who confessed that they could not account for religious feelings, and accepted by religious thinkers, who admitted that theology could no longer dictate its beliefs to science. When both religion and science recognized each other's sovereignty in their enlarged spheres and no longer represented immediate threats to one another, an unsteady intellectual peace seemed possible.[6]

But here's the problem: how, then, to weigh one social ideal — individual freedom, for example — against another — such as personal sacrifice for the common good? Who do you call then? The scientist? The minister? This is what I mean by a gap in the cultural imagination. The "intellectual peace" of which Kloppenberg spoke marooned political morality in a rhetorical never-neverland.[7] The two spheres separated reason from faith, but some human activities require both simultaneously.

The truce between science and religion left out the problem of political morality. The common good is more subjective a thing than science can determine; and one of the main American contributions to politics is the conviction that no one particular religion should dominate the decision-making process. Who, then, has the authority to settle disputes about what constitutes the common good?

At the turn of the century many Progressives believed that science could solve political questions. They set up independent bureaucracies to avoid any taint of partisanship and subjectivity. Instead, scientific methods would be applied to establish, for example, a "fair" railroad rate for transporting wheat. But definitions of a "fair" rate stubbornly differed if you asked farmers or railroad executives. How could science determine whether entrepreneurial freedom is the greatest good and should be protected regardless of the scale of misery it might produce? These are questions of values. By definition, asserting one value over another cannot be done "objectively."[8] The Progressives' use of polls and other scientific-seeming mechanisms disguised the fact that the truce between religion and science uncomfortably squeezed the passionate expression of social values.

Nature emerged ever more strongly as the source of political values just at the historical moment when this trade-off between scientific and religious authority became dominant or hegemonic. Among the effects of this trade-off was a change in the style of newspaper reporting. The vivid, impassioned prose of the early century gave way to an apparently more neutral language. Historians likewise sought to set aside myth in the name of the noble dream of scientific objectivity.[9] In the larger context of this celebration of neutrality and objectivity, the "West" emerged as a popular symbol. In the "West," on the "frontier," nature offered seasoned advice on the classic questions of the science of society: how to define and achieve democracy, the obligation of the strong to the weak and so on. Nature taught society in equations distinguished by leaps of logic. Owen Wister popularized the Social Darwinist views in the 1902 cowboy classic, *The Virginian,* as his unimpeachably natural man instructs an overcivilized easterner on the distinction between "quality" (evolutionarily fit humanity) and "equality" (the masses). The Virginian plays, cries, and succeeds in nature, proving his evolutionary worth over the Shortys of the world, the character in the novel who must die because he is stupid. The popular Western to this day easily dispenses political homilies as if read from the backdrop of mesas and sage.

Nature could make passionate declarations of the ultimate public good *sound* objective. It worked like a charm, in part because nature observation was the touchstone of scientific inquiry. Frederick Jackson Turner's famous frontier thesis in 1893 epitomizes this trend.[10] Turner described the "frontier" as essentially a laboratory where the same social experiment was repeated again and again. The wilderness spit out Americans who were "inventive," "practical," "individualistic," if a bit "antisocial."[11] People needed ways to debate political values. And so they appealed to evolution, to the West, to nature's "obvious" lessons.

Part of the reason that nature remained a viable higher authority in this cultural climate was because it was so pliable. Political ideals drawn from landscape could draw on the authority vested in scientific observation such as Charles Darwin's. But they could also draw on the equivalent of gut reactions. In nature, principles can be proven as if by laboratory experiment, but they can also be experientially true — tested by experience. To illuminate this pattern, a comparison is useful. One of the distinguishing characteristics of modernity, argued French theorist Michel Foucault, is that people search the body for truth about the self. "'Do you really mean it?' 'Are you being honest with yourself?' These are questions people have come to answer through trying to chart what the body desires."[12] Just as individuals turn to their "gut feelings" for truths about themselves, people like Webb and Austin searched landscapes for their social lessons.[13] It is as if nature contains society's gut feelings. We try to chart nature's desires as if they are the physical body of society. These are rhetorical devices. They work because of the cultural imagination beneath them.

People debating greater and lesser social values gravitated toward vocabularies of landscape for these various historical reasons: the geographic embrace worked because it built on a long tradition; it worked because claims about nature's lessons could sound objective and scientific; it worked because those claims could also sound as incontrovertible as gut feelings. I could assemble many more reasons. Literary critic Jane Tompkins, for instance, argues that the new popularity of the West was the result in part of gendered battles for authority. Earlier in the nineteenth century, literature and social expectations set white women on a pedestal — they were purer than men, who were condemned by their masculine nature to the soul-dirtying realms of business and sexual desire. White women were a society's treasure — from them came the light of moral instruction. But some women began to use these myths to climb into the political sphere. Since they had a special insight into morality, their duty was to clean the public house. As Abraham Lincoln famously remarked, the little woman who started the Civil War was Harriet Beecher Stowe. Her novel of outrage over the evils of slavery played on the belief in women's moral superiority over men. According to Tompkins, as white women more and more entered politics based on this claim to moral superiority, the Western emerged. A shift in the cultural imagination took place. Cowboys like the Virginian went outdoors, symbolically away from women, to learn to manage society in an evolutionary way. Thus, Tompkins suggests, men tutored in the wild replaced women in the home as the arbiters of the "good."[14]

How to convince someone else that the common good resides in a free market or in a regulatory state? When the historical arguments run down and when the battle of statistics reaches a draw, there is finally not much left other than: I believe it to be so. In the face of this convergence of reason with conviction, it is very tempting to enlist some other authority to your side. Because religion only further revealed the subjective character of your conviction, nature became even more important as the independent judge.

The key to nature's role was its purity. No human taint hovered over the mesas of the "West" when Owen Wister or Mary Austin or Walter Prescott Webb sent their characters out into the desert to learn from the landscape. Indians were guides, in these writers' imaginations, but Indians did not alter nature's unbiased, independent truths. Nature was external to, or outside of, the human context. Erasing the politics and history in a landscape like the West, in other words, was necessary to maintain the illusion that there exists some higher authority to which one could appeal.

Forgetting, or erasing, the social context that shaped a landscape like the "West" made it possible to retain or remember nature as umpire in political disputes. Land — if it had no history, if it was "free" in many senses of the word — made political dreaming possible. Like an alphabet that could be assembled into many combinations of meanings, landscapes offered an escape from a rhetorical rock and a hard place. The philosophic task of defining social justice was difficult to pursue in a realm called "science" that aimed more and more for the noble dream of objectivity, and it was equally difficult to pursue in the confines of personal religious conviction and the private sphere.

To be clear, the geographic embrace is a pattern lodged in the conventions of language use. These discourses exert a subtle influence on the cultural imagination, a shared sense of what is normal or what disappears as white noise. These discourses are not straitjackets: plenty of people take their convictions from the church to the legislature without heeding any subtle suggestion that they are violating some border. Furthermore, the strength of the conventional divide between the spheres of science and religion waxes and wanes. Still, a legacy remains in the gestures of literature, the mappings of symbolic geographies and the definitions of government aid. It requires some conscious effort to see this legacy.

And so now we have arrived at an interesting point. This is a book about how Americans enlist ideals about land for the sake of social justice. Social justice ideals are difficult to define. I have just suggested that the truce between religion and science marooned political idealism in general. It is hard to speak about political values. Do you claim to draw on scientific truth? Do you use science to set railroad rates? If you claim to draw on religious truth, how far can you get in a political sphere dedicated to freedom of religion? How do you have a discourse about political morality inside this set of choices? The compromise between these sources of authority created a gap in language. Nature filled the gap.

The geographic embrace was a response to the standoff between religion and science. Once we understand it with our minds, once we understand that it is an induced response to the spheres of influence wielded by religion and science, do we then "know better"? Are we cured of the illusion? Do we want to be?

Myths of a good society emerge in Americans' representations of the land. Can we escape the choices foisted on us by earlier generations? Can we think more freely about political possibility without leaning on the crutch of nature? Can we "dream a little"? What would that mean, and how would we speak it?

The West is "the native home of hope," wrote Pulitzer Prize–winning author Wallace Stegner.[15] He spent much of his lifetime elaborating his vision of the West, including the following straightforward definition of what exactly the West could teach us to hope for: "[When the West] fully learns that cooperation, not individualism, is the pattern that most characterizes and preserves it, then it will have achieved itself and outlived its origins. Then it has a chance to create a society to match its scenery."[16] Like many others before him, Stegner falls into the geographic embrace. He preaches cooperation and confirms the rightness of his politics by appealing to the lessons of landscape.

Examples of the geographic embrace abound in literature, politics and art today. Like hawkers at a street fair, commentators and opinion makers will urge their solutions to modern problems on you with scenery and isolated facts from nature's great book of knowledge. Are they all wrong? Stegner's example is a good one to keep in mind. He was a complex and subtle thinker. Exposing such culturally trained instincts like the geographic embrace seems to imply the next step: let us shed our illusions; it is time to bust the myth. Allow me to exaggerate to make the point. Hear the sneer: how foolish, for a person like Stegner, to imagine that tree and dirt and rock would have the commandment to cooperate written on them. He is simply projecting his own ideas onto landscape.[17]

What is the best way to react to the geographic embrace? This turns out to be a complicated question. There are good reasons to go running in the other direction. I noted above that the geographic embrace draws us into the habit of forgetting the frontier state, the modern subsidy of home-ownership tax breaks and the like. In fact, one can argue — with good reason — that the "geographic embrace" as a whole tends toward conservative ideals and toward the defense of existing inequalities. Myths of the West seem to have a consistent spin. Literary critic Martin Green put the matter plainly. The cowboy myth that emerged at the end of the nineteenth century, he argued, "was a fairly conscious adaptation of popular legends to ruling-class purposes."[18] Western myths uphold a status quo in which Wister's Virginian worships rather than criticizes his upper-class betters. By the time of the mass production of Westerns, many critics seem to agree, conservative writers had co-opted the potential to use nature as "an engine of attack on the authority of tradition."[19]

Reasons for turning away from the geographic embrace multiply especially when nature's lessons for society combine with biology's presumed lessons about race and gender. At the turn of the last century in particular, nonwhite intellectuals and many white women scientists proved not nearly as quick to invoke nature as the last certainty in an uncertain world. After all, Harvard men like Dr. Edward Clarke still drew on nature's dictates to argue that women were physiologically unsuited to intellectual work. It would stunt their reproductive capacities, insisted Clarke in 1873.[20] Avoiding invocations of nature is a common strategy for many oppressed groups. One of the major themes of minority literature is to resist being typecast as nature's children and therefore oversexualized or comparable to animals. Geographic destiny and biological destiny seem part of the same Euro-American imperializing tradition that is called "nature-talk" by historian Giovanna Di Chiro.[21] Such "nature-talk" has been an ideological hammer used against people of color and women. Not for everyone has utopia ached to be revealed in landscapes perceived as nature's home.

The reasons to be suspicious of the geographic embrace are legion for those who dream of social justice, of equality, of some fairness. And yet I will be leaning in to the embrace in this book, rather than fleeing it. My explanation for doing so makes up the rest of this chapter. In a nutshell, the answer is that the geographic embrace offers one way to dream a little, and ways to combine political dreaming and analytic thinking are hard to come by. I seek a dialectic between realism and the implied idealism of this book's title. Leaning in to the geographic embrace means recognizing that the lessons presumably drawn from landscape are actually drawn from human perceptions. But, while recognizing the "trick" of projecting ideals onto landscape, it is still possible to engage those notions further.

The geographic embrace is a myth, and like many myths, it can mislead us. But myths are also necessary. A conventional divide in our language segregates myth from good history. Habitually, novels and popular fiction about the West are expected to be infused with adamant convictions and subjective visions for a good society. But good history is meant to stick to the analytical interpretation of facts. By this way of thinking, myth and history divide as do religion and science — messily, uneasily, with considerable overlaps, but still the distinction remains.

If we want a history like this one about the geographic embrace to speak to the deeply subjective task of naming political morality, the old divide between myth and history must give way. By this way of seeing, myth is not history's opposite. Instead, it is a vision of human possibility. As literary critics Hayden White and Northrup Frye suggest, "Whatever else a myth may be — a verbal equivalent of a ritual, a poetic account of origins, a projection of possible last things — it is also . . . an example of thought working at the extremities of human possibility, a projection of human fulfillment and of the obstacles that stand in the way of that fulfillment."[22]

A history that caters to myth or to "thought working at the extremities of human possibility" would require a different, more idealistic tone. By comparison, historical scholarship often contrasts what people set out to do with what actually happens. The dissonance between what people attempt and what they achieve offers us stories full of irony, but as White once asked, "Where does such irony leave us? Irony does a lot of things, but it doesn't stir people's souls."[23] Ironic detachment is a common stance in academia. The cry for a different way to react to intellectual insights like the geographic embrace is part of a larger movement concerned with reviving the role of the "public intellectual."[24]

Bending toward myth is a different strategy also than reminding readers that myths are not true. It is demoralizing, and boring, to keep saying, again and again, that human views of geography are "only" social constructions; are opinions masquerading as truth. We do need opinions, after all. Desperately. Acting morally in the world requires knowledge — but what kind?

To look deeper into what it might mean to merge myth and history, the following pages examine the history of the western United States as a case study. The inclination to correct false and often imperialistic myths by appealing to objective history has been an honorable and profoundly necessary step in the study of the U.S. West. But "correcting" myths has created problems of its own. The scholars who undertook this revision are often labeled the New Western historians. Their ideas have been extremely controversial. Their dilemmas can help me to explain why leaning in to the embrace of myth has pragmatic, historical and philosophic advantages. We must find new ways of reacting to historical phenomena like the geographic embrace rather than dismiss it as myth. Perhaps we can become better, more skilled dance partners in the embrace. May we yield to it and may we lead too, palms pressing against the back of the future.

In books and movies, in history and in drama, the region called the "West" has been made to symbolize the nation's promise. For this reason, historians of the West feel bedeviled by wishful thinking, or, in one of its most familiar usages, by "myth," the habit of seeing in the past what one wants to see instead of what was. Segregating myth from history is a difficult task under any circumstances, but popular devotion to Westerns magnifies this debate when it comes to writing good histories of the West. By uncovering the choices available to current historians of the West, we can perceive the alternatives presented to us by the geographic embrace more generally.

In the late 1980s journalists scaled the walls of the ivory tower and reported that a "New Western History" was in ascendance.[25] In the pages of *USA Today* and other popular media, the "new" history was quickly squared off against an old, mythic West, despite pleas for greater subtlety by some of the startled academics.[26] The debate quickly blossomed, as did roses of rage on cheeks of infuriated defenders of the Old West. In the pages of the *New Republic,* Texan novelist Larry McMurtry slammed the revisionists as the "Failure School." McMurtry insisted that we need our myths, our quixotic windmills, instead of always wanting to shine "the sober light of common day" on the West of the imagination.[27] Other pundits focused their outrage on an exhibit at the Smithsonian Institution that reinterpreted Western art as ideological propaganda in the service of a conquering imperial civilization rather than a democratizing frontier. From Hollywood, popular culture spread the revisionist news with movies like *Dances with Wolves* and a television mini-series looking at George Armstrong Custer from both Native American and Euro-American points of view.[28] Meanwhile, Patricia Nelson Limerick, one of the leading revisionist historians, welcomed the breakdown of barriers between academic and public debate and took her story of the West on the road as lecturer. By and large she found an audience whose common sense corresponded with her findings. One appreciative Sacramento listener allowed that he had enjoyed her speech but quipped, "Since I'm not a western historian, everything you said was obvious to me."[29]

Amid this rethinking of the western past, the various parties found themselves forced into a philosophical standoff. The new historians who had overturned the most egregiously ethnocentric accounts of the western past claimed a victory of History over Myth. With the popular media replaying the debate with all the subtlety of a noon-hour shoot-out, historian Donald Worster in 1989 pronounced:

> For this region that was once so lost in dreams and ideal-
> izations, we historians have been creating a new history,
> clear-eyed, demythologized, and critical. We have been
> rewriting the story from page one and watching it be
> accepted. That has been a slow, hardwon victory, and
> I think it is time we celebrated the achievement.[30]

Professional historians more typically recognize the inevitable gray area between fact and fiction, between analytic observations and the burdens of subjectivity. But particularly in the realm of western history, there is a temptation to leave these epistemolog-ical questions behind in graduate school in order to shout louder than the celebrants of western expansion.[31]

On the other side of the line in the sand, celebrants of the Old West articulated a philosophical defense of myth. One of the best equipped to do so was McMurtry, who had first made his mark in the opposite camp, despising what he called histories that glorified "ruthless race warriors" like the Texas Rangers.[32] His early novels are exposés of the West, crafting a stark realism out of the stunning scenery and heroic tales. By the time of the New Western history, however, McMurtry had changed horses. With his Pulitzer Prize–winning Western novel of 1985, *Lonesome Dove,* McMurty began a long streak of best-sellers that re-create the old myths. When the range war between historians broke into the news stories, McMurtry entered the fight with all the enthusiasm of a convert.

McMurtry's challenge to the New Western history is interesting. It helps to reveal a key reason why leaning in to myth is justified, first of all, on pragmatic political grounds. McMurtry makes the following case: the Old Western history was better because it provided a very necessary salve to modern readers caught in suburban, mechanical lives. The crux of McMurtry's arugment is that the revisionists are wrong for throwing off the Quixotean task, and he reminds us to consider what happens when "the crazy old Don surrenders his fancies and lets the tough little realist have his way."[33]

The point to draw from McMurtry's attack on the New Western historians lies beneath the surface of his general defense of myth. Look closer at why he likes the Old Western history, and you'll see him promoting one particular version of the western myth. "Freedom and opportunity" are the political hopes he sees in the West. For Wallace Stegner, cooperation was the hope. For others, equality and democracy are the main promises of the West. Any elementary school child might identify any of these as belonging to the "traditional" western myths. McMurtry's defense of the "West of the Imagination" proves ultimately not to be a general commitment to myth in all its variety but to a specific political dream. In the article attacking the revisionists, he has a particular freedom in mind: that enjoyed by his fathers and eight brothers. Those men had seen the West in its "fresh beauty," in its "wild" state, but, more important, they had lived at a time when they could have genuine callings in a tough environment. The idea of the Wild West gave that earlier generation of men the guts to go on against formidable odds, and for McMurtry the memory of that time assuages the dismal realities of modernity. Myth is food for the psyche, he argues. "Explorers and pioneers of all stamps needed imagination, much as athletes need carbohydrates. Fantasy provided part of the fiber that helped them survive the severities that the land put them to."[34] After the age of explorers and pioneers was over, the yearning for the fantasy only increased. "For if that West is lost, then it's all just jobs."[35]

The justification for leaning in to the geographic embrace arises, in fact, out of what McMurtry is able to ignore. At the same time as he tags the New Western historians as the "Failure School," he paints them with the brush of nihilism, by which he means the absence of any ideals. He claims the glory of conviction solely for his side. In the process he is able to assign to himself the role of defender of ideals in general, rather than (and this is the politically consequential point) one particular "fancy" or dream of the good, true and beautiful. As McMurtry's article makes clear, the myth-history divide casts the civil rights–trained historians as nonidealistic, a historical development of some considerable irony and ominous political consequence.

What McMurtry is able to ignore are the quixotic windmills that the New Western historians do tilt toward. Racial and gender equality, a softening of class lines — these are some of the ideals that suffuse the project of re-visioning western history. The unwitting consequence of claiming a clear-eyed, demythologized history, as the revisionists did in the battle to upend imperialistic assumptions, is that the mist in their own eyes became invisible. But clearly, these sixties-inspired historians do dream a little.

One good reason, then, to admit to mythologizing and to cater to the geographic embrace is for political strategy. The New Western history suffered for seeming to be about failure to the exclusion of future hopes. The nihilistic charge sticks — in spite of the transparent idealism on the part of the New Western historians — in part *because* of their claim that their business is to demythologize.

In addition to strategic advantages, intellectual honesty demands a more explicit recognition of the role of myth. Such intellectual honesty is legitimately very hard to deliver. To explore the difficulty of speaking directly about one's myths, let us look closer at the work of Worster. While Worster made the statement celebrating a "demythologized" western past in the context of a media-covered conference, a closer reading of his landmark book, *Rivers of Empire,* reveals a much more complex picture.[36] The driving argument of the book is that the history of gaining control over nature — specifically by damming rivers — produced a culture of efficiency at the expense of humanity. The technological experts with the knowledge to control vast rivers found themselves joined to the interests of large-scale capitalists, especially in agribusiness. The power of the experts and the money men combined to create an oligarchy, cloaked in the sweet rhetoric of democracy. In the name of the family farmer, the oligarchs harnessed water to the maximum output of goods and services. What Worster wishes to do is invoke a more idealistic or spiritual kind of economic accounting than a rationality that would, in effect, prefer every river to be straight and not waste itself in meandering curves. He quotes Max Horkheimer, a Marxist of the Frankfurt school, who decried the Enlightenment for the "disenchantment of the world; the dissolution of myths and the substitution of knowledge for fancy."[37] Worster's most fundamental critique of the managerial relationship to nature is that it fails to consider social ends, especially those that underwrite spiritual rather than economic advancements. The instrumentalist attitude toward nature only looks to making means more efficient. It always seeks more; but it never asks more *for what.*[38]

Worster's complex relationship to the role of myth begins with the contradiction between his celebration of demythologizing in one context and his lament elsewhere for myth, fancy, imagination. Additional paradoxes demonstrate that he feels caught by both positions. On the one hand, at the beginning of *Rivers of Empire* he aims to contrast the ecological and social transformation of the U.S. West to wild-eyed idealism. Wake up, he seems to want to say. He writes sarcastically of "the mythic imaginings of Thoreau . . . dreaming beautifully of the wild, the free, the democratic, the individual."[39] But then, at the end of the same book, he dreams equally beautifully of the wild, the free, the democratic. He imagines that the U.S. West might be approached "deliberately as an environment latent with possibilities for freedom and democracy rather than for wealth and empire."[40]

Worster's solution to the dilemma of reckoning with his ideals or myths is to project his views onto the landscape. Worster, in other words, falls into the arms of the geographic embrace. In a classic example of the rhetorical tradition I have described, Worster combines his final, hesitant exposure of his own ideals with what the desert West would say to us:

> Relieved from some of its burdens of growing crops,
> earning foreign exchange, and supporting immense cities,
> [the desert West] might encourage a new sequence of
> history, an incipient America of simplicity, discipline, and
> spiritual exploration, an America in which people are wont

to sit long hours doing nothing, earning nothing, going
nowhere, on the bank of some river running through a
spare, lean land.[41]

Worster's own commitment to demythologizing the West leads
him to emphasize knowledge and realism rather than myth and
fancy in most of the book. Bound by the terms of the discipline
of professional history, his own exploration of social ends is
pushed to the final pages. When he does dream a little, he does
so by re-visioning a river landscape. In its lessons, he allows his
values to be revealed. Worster repeats the unconscious sub-
terfuge that inscribes into the landscape the lesson of ultimate
truths. So he invites his readers to visit a riverbank and asks
them to sit quietly, doing nothing, earning nothing, to discover
what really matters. He believes that nature would teach the listener that life is unitary and interdependent and requires cooperation and small-scale technology and government. Adapting
to nature is the rhetorical maneuver he uses to urge this fine
myth, this "thought working at the extremities of human possibility": that people would care for each other and the earth more
than for materialistic rewards; that wealth would be shared
more equally and suffering would be replaced by time for fancy.

Leaning in to the geographic embrace means allowing readers to see the visions of human possibility that inspire you.
Honesty requires a little less contempt of the fact that other people "mythologize." The mistake is in thinking that texts can
either be mythic or "clear-eyed"; either fanciful or critical; either
romantic or ironic. Instead, the works of the new historians, of
their contemporary ideological opponents, of their like-minded
and their distant forebears all demonstrate the murky combina-

tion of idealism and realism in historical writing. Two plots combine: there is the long-running effort to which Worster refers in which factualists correct myth. At the same time, however, there is a coincident plot of myth itself correcting myth; of one utopian hope fighting another for the heart and mind of the reader. This second plot is the one I mean to bring to the foreground in this book.

If everyone, though, willingly reveals his or her ideals, if the embrace of myth becomes a routine honesty in history, will we not just be left with people shouting their own preferred convictions over the fence at each other? Here we come to the philosophical justification for leaning in to the geographic embrace. The problem, to repeat, is how to react to a discursive tendency, a habit of language, that bends us toward articulating ideals indirectly, projecting them onto landscape. My suggestion to respond in kind, matching myth for myth, and to relinquish the safety of detachment and irony draws on a school of thought about history's larger role.

Engaging, rather than demythologizing, the ideals that suffuse geographic writings builds on a philosophical tradition that demands dialogue more than truth from the past. At its best, the study of history is a "conversation with the dead about the things we value," intellectual historian David Harlan once suggested.[42] Reading Stegner's or Thoreau's mythical fancies, by this school of thought, is an opportunity to discover and elaborate one's own ideas in the context of a larger, ongoing dialogue. Harlan suggests that this way of reacting to the text of the past shares a resemblance to rabbinical scholarship. The Torah is a place for bright students to find new meaning. This tradition distinguishes itself particularly from fundamentalist Protestantism, in which readers search the Bible for incontrovertible truth. Leaning in to the geographic embrace means not cutting off the conversation about ideals by dismissing them as myths but instead reacting to another's myths by using them to discover your own.[43]

Conversing with the dead about the things we value is one way of explaining the philosophical justification for leaning in to myth. Built on a long and very complicated set of ideas about the limits of objectivity, the core insight for our purposes here is the dialectic nature of human understanding. The process of arriving at historical truths, from this point of view, is a series of zigzags with no clear final destination. A dialectic implies a back-and-forth interchange of ideas. The hope is not so much that one genuine, repeatable truth will eventually emerge out of all the interchange. Instead, it is the conversational process itself that is the desired result. In the case of a history that yields to the mythologizing impulse, the conversation process would refine and elaborate the ideas that may begin as gut feelings. The philosophical hope is that, while there may not be much gained from shouting convictions across the fence at each other, some good may come of a longer, thoughtful exchange.

The philosophical justification for leaning in to the geographic embrace, however, includes much more than the "dialectic" nature of truth telling in human discourse. There is in fact a historical imperative to break the presumption of a gap between myth and history. Here postmodern feminist ideas add an element of "play" to the serious business of how to write good history — how to write "good" truth, in the many senses of the word. In the history of science, Donna Haraway argues for a proactive joining of opposites. Analytically, her work joins nature and society, those traditional opponents. She shows how social conventions have slanted perceptions of nature, including even those precise descriptions of nature arising out of scientific research. From a springboard of observation about the "invention" and "reinvention" of nature in social contexts of colonialism and other oppressions, Haraway leaps into a larger call to create and celebrate cyborgs, bastards, and previously unimaginable unions of opposites. Like nature and society, myth and history are such a union of opposites. The hope is that, by jarring the old conventions, new ones will come into play. And old usages will lose some of their naturalizing or normalizing power. By joining opposites, we might create a "cyborg" politics — using our inventiveness to create new creatures out of old habits. The key is to disrupt "truth." Any one truth ignores others. "Cyborg politics is the struggle for language and the struggle against perfect communication, against the one code that translates all meaning perfectly. . . . That is why cyborg politics insist on noise and advocate pollution, rejoicing in the illegitimate fusions of animal and machine."[44] Unlike the "dialectic" justification, this more radical philosophy rejects the view that history could be demythologized, that "one code can translate all meaning perfectly." One code of meaning is an inaccurate understanding of humanity. One code is also complicit, often in the subtle coercions of grammar, in reproducing traditional oppressions. It is therefore urgent to fuse opposites, like myth and history, to create new options.

I will grant, quickly, that the philosophical justifications for leaning in to the geographic embrace are debatable, radical and esoteric. Just getting an elemental understanding of what Haraway and her postmodern fellows are saying is extremely difficult. As language is itself the instrument of change, the words she uses defy ordinary conversation. Postmodernists speak in seemingly incomprehensible sentences in part to act on their convictions about language. Still, a basic, fairly straightforward philosophical point can be made: the reason to join opposites like myth and history is to reclaim choice and agency in human history.[45] Students of society, history and philosophy have many reasons to doubt the simple notion of free will. There are too many cultural influences, both hammer-handedly obvious and delicately subtle, and too many psychological impediments, especially in the notion of the unconsious, to permit an easy reliance on free will. Instead, choice — including the choosing of visions of human possibility — requires a recognition of the limiting contexts of culture, history and, more generally, language. It is out of this complicated sense of the world of coercions that the proactive call to unite opposites comes. It is a contrarian's strategy: by defying conventional opposites, we might have better "conversations with the dead about the things we value."

The highly debatable philosophical grounds for yielding to the geographic embrace lead me to make one further point: I do not mean to suggest that all historical writing should follow this course toward a combination of myth and history. First, in the trenches, it is abundantly obvious that there is such a thing as inaccurate history. Western lands were not "free," rain did not follow the plow, and women and people of color were not absent. As Harlan argues, the contention that there are no universal truths does not preclude the existence of particular truths. There are still, in other words, plenty of occasions to demythologize, or, more precisely, to expose prejudgments. Philosopher

Richard J. Bernstein suggests in *The New Constellation* that thinkers as diverse as Richard Rorty, Thomas Kuhn and Michel Foucault converge in assigning this role to history: "to expose prejudgments, prejudices, and illusions."[46] Countering the tyranny of ideology might be seen as one kind of history. The invention of new ideologies requires a different kind of history that is more self-consciously mythic. One exposes prejudgments; the other seeks to cultivate good judgment.[47]

If you will grant, on an experimental basis, that one legitimate way to react to the geographic embrace is not to demythologize it, that still leaves the question of what exactly it would mean to "lean in" to the geographic embrace. I have said that it would require allowing readers to see the author's visions of human possibility. That suggestion could imply an encouragement to let it all hang out. But the trick is to combine "monstrously" (as Haraway says) the task of dreaming with the task of analytic reasoning. We must resist the cultural training that asserts that heart and mind are distinct and separable; that emotion and reason can be cleanly divided; that faith and learning belong in different spheres. My method requires a resistance to the cool detachment of the demythologizers, but equally it rejects resorting to gut feelings without any accompaniment of reason.

To lean in to the geographic embrace means to converse in a particular way with the dead about the things we value. The type of dialogue I envision at the extremities of human possibility combines a conversation among friends with a scholars' roundtable. Particularly among women, in my experience, conversations explore feelings — their roots, their consequences, the confusion over what to do next. In a supportive climate, new reconciliations or even new hard lines are made possible. The scholars' roundtable adds to this conversation the presence of people who have come before us. Widening the circle beyond the limits of the current company, no matter how excellent that company may be, necessarily opens more options.

That is my myth of history, my vision of what could be possible from understanding the past. The second half of this book offers some examples. It contains my conversations with three women whose ideas and ideals profoundly resonated with me. These conversations aim to be both subjective and analytic, colloquial and scholarly. My aim in this book is to "study" the links between landscape ideas and social justice visions. In part 2, to "study" will mean to engage, to have a dialogue with, to play with the myths. The pages that follow explore my own and my historical subjects' struggles to make good political use of landscape.

PART TWO

The Dance of Ideals

CHAPTER THREE

The West of Words

Mari Sandoz and a
Politics of Memory

Mari Sandoz was a writer. She did not live off the land. She visited it, dramatically.

Mari, who was Marie before she became a writer, grew up close to the soil. Her parents were homesteaders. She learned about hardship there, her own and others', and from the land she drew lessons about how to seed, to really seed, a new world. What I want to know from her is why words on the land were better than land itself. The story I am going to tell, with Sandoz as a guide, explains why my words about her words about land might have anything to do with creating a better world. A more fair one.

We will begin with her mother, a young woman traveling alone from Switzerland to Arkansas, U.S.A., in the early 1890s. The migrants to the North American Great Plains came from so many different places for so many different reasons. For Mary Fehr, the daughter of a butcher in Schaffhausen, the journey began unconsciously in the shape of a possibility. It was ghostly, this possibility, made of the wisps of impressions from newspaper advertisements and published letters. Land in America! they promised; a new start. We might well ask why a doctor's daughter believed that rural America would liberate her. Why not Paris or education? Land, a promise attached to acreage, drew her. Seductive whispers — the long tradition of pastoral literature, a whole layering of cultural history — beckoned her to abandon Europe for western America. These whispers might have fallen on deaf ears if there hadn't been money with which to travel. Mary Fehr owned savings in the bank. But she also had gumption. Then she had a drunken father who sent away the sweet, black-haired musician who had asked for her.

Off she went, carrying the address of an uncle in America and the satisfaction of having told her father exactly what she thought of him. But, as for so many others, the golden dream always seemed to stay in the distance even as she raced toward it. The climate in Arkansas aggravated her asthma; then she nearly died in one of the typhoid epidemics. She chased her hopes again to St. Louis, where she found good work in the household of a doctor and his wife. But again health problems and also ambition pushed her on. This time she would claim the brass ring itself: a homestead. She sent money to her brother Jacob in Switzerland to come help her. But how to find a square of land to work and own? The occupation that arose to fill this need is no longer with us. Now the public domain is in the hands of rangers and foresters, aided by fishing guides, river-running outfits, and Ticketron or Internet campsite reservation services. What Mary Fehr, Mari Sandoz's mother, sought was a public land "locator," a person who knew where to find the corners of acres surveyed by the government. She found Jules Sandoz of Mirage Flats, Nebraska, and wrote her brother to meet her at

Sandoz's station stop. Not only could Jules Sandoz, who also was originally from Switzerland, physically point to free land, but he also offered to house Mary Fehr and her brother for six months while they established themselves. Sandoz was an enthusiastic booster of his adopted western Nebraska region. He primed the pump of immigration by writing boastful letters about the area to European newspapers. He had ulterior motives: he hoped to encourage white women to emigrate, and so he was not at all unhappy when Mary's brother Jacob failed to make the rendezvous that day.

Mary Fehr wore a brown traveling dress. Jules Sandoz had squeezed a shoe over his stinking foot, injured in an early homesteading accident. With no brother in sight and the knowledge that Jacob had turned out to be pretty shiftless anyway, with her trunk misplaced and not enough money to make it back for another start in St. Louis, Mary accepted a ride that evening out to Sandoz's place on the Niobrara River. Within a few hours he had proposed, and she made one more of the desperate decisions that the flight away from her father seemed constantly to demand of her.[1]

As it turns out, the man that Mary Fehr hastily married also was in the process of giving his own father a piece of his mind. Jules Sandoz threw away his bourgeois prospects in Switzerland for life in America because his father had refused his choice of a working-class bride, the sweet and never-to-be-forgotten Rosalie. And Mary Fehr's and Jules Sandoz's daughter, the author Mari Sandoz, continued the family tradition of objecting to their fathers. She began her literary career with the publication of a book that pictured her pioneer father in decidedly unromanticized terms.

Escaping the rule of fathers — the tradition of patriarchy — is not the primary subject of this chapter, however. There will be many reasons to flee from fathers, but the harder struggle is to know toward what you might turn.

Mary Fehr, Mari Sandoz, and I too, it appears, have this in common: we dare with land. I think there are historical reasons for this. And I think I can make history with this — by which I mean not like a politician or war leader "makes" history but the way a memorist does. I want to take something from the background of social consciousness and move it to the foreground: to memorialize it, capture it, so you will see what I am talking about.

To get a glimpse of the larger story, let me tell you a bit more about Mari Sandoz's habits with land. She wrote *Old Jules,* which is widely acclaimed as an American classic. Being thirty-nine when it finally was published, she was old enough to have accumulated many rejection slips. One of the reasons earlier editors ignored her work was that she had some hard truths to tell. Here is a short list. Her father, the subject of *Old Jules,* brutally beat his wife and children; feuded irreconcilably with neighbors; made ludicrous the idea of democracy for which his region so often was made to stand. And Indians not only lost lands that they believed were rightfully theirs but so did, by and large, the homesteaders. The winners were the wealthy and well connected.

As Kurt Vonnegut said over and over again in *Slaughterhouse Five:* So it goes.

Mari Sandoz focused her attention on her father. Read the book, though, or any of hers, and you will be struck by how many words about landscape fill the pages. The epigraph of *Old Jules* begins, "One can go into a wild country and make it tame, but, like a coat and cap and mitten that he can never take off, he must always carry the look of the land as it was." Then the first page starts with three paragraphs describing a rhythmic alteration of human and nonhuman forces in the surrounding environment. The towns of shacks and tents "were shaking off the dullness of winter." In the hills beyond, grass was starting. "Fringes of yellow-green crept down the south slopes or ran brilliant emerald over the long, blackened strips left by the prairie fires." Only after the cast of wolves and rustlers, grass and galloping hooves — only after a great deal of scene setting, in other words — do we get this sentence: "And out of the East came a lone man in an open wagon, driving hard."

Why do we have to know first about the "monotonous yellow sandhills unobtrusively soak[ing] up the soggy patches of April snow"? Or the deep canyons of the Niobrara, a river located at the crossroads of the railroad's black path, of covered wagons pushing westward, of the looks of a hundred thousand head of cattle and on and on?

Let me convince you that her habits of land use are worth wondering about. In this and the rest of Sandoz's considerable opus, she means to do much more than establish a context with the details of shrubbery, soil or animal and human geography. I think her intentions evolved over time, and to keep your attention, I will start with her last, best thoughts on the subject. But then we will slow down and I'll tell you how she, and I, got there.

At the age of sixty-two and already once a survivor of cancer, Mari Sandoz yearned for a helicopter. "I should like to go hovering over the Great Plains, spying out long lost historical sites," she said. "With a roll of maps, a camera, a pad of paper and a little shovel for a bit of digging I could have a wonderful time."[2] Her longing had some staging and vanity to it, expressed as it was in a letter to the *Saturday Evening Post* to describe herself to readers. But here is the bigger picture: in land, Mari Sandoz experienced memory. I mean to say that experiencing memory is different from "having" a memory or recalling some particular thing. And I am talking about public, not private, memories, what some thinkers call "social memory."[3]

When Sandoz experienced memory in a particular landscape, she interacted with the vague, amorphous presence of what we call "culture." Culture is more than the sum of its parts, more than individual attitudes that add up to trends or patterns. It is a presence, a force, exerting its influence at the subtlest levels.

When I say Sandoz interacted with culture, I mean to suggest a two-way street: she felt its shaping influence, and at the same time she shaped it. Conjugating with this beastily insubstantial, influential presence required an attitude of receptivity and aggression all at once. Of sensation and sense, of Zen-like aware-ness and logical dissection. Of wordlessness and wordiness.

And here is the key thing: this way of being, of interacting with culture, had a precedent, a model, an example in her life, namely, interacting with landscape. It was the background that shaped the foreground, the wild country that is the coat, cap and mittens we can never take off. She was interested in landscape's subtle influence, the way it contains the past geologically and archaeologically in its layers, its mysterious and almost unname-able power. She would take maps, a shovel and the most techno-logically marvelous conveyance of her time to the Great Plains. She was not after communion with nature in the way Thoreau had been. She was finding a realm where nature and culture merged.

She turned to landscapes for idealistic reasons; for the dream of a better world. In the decade following *Old Jules,* she conceived her ambition to write a grand, seven-part history of the Great Plains region. Just as Sandoz's body of work began to shape itself more and more around her sense of the importance of place and, in particular, the Great Plains of the past, she said this: "The underprivileged child, if he becomes a writer, is interested in social justice and in the destruction of discrimination between economic levels, between nationalist levels, between color levels, and so on."[4] She was such an underprivileged child, and the destruction of discrimination was her goal. Sandoz scrawled toward that goal with the same intensity that her father had in those letters cast out to immigrants. While he used literal blocks of land, she used literary ones.

Why write about the sweep of time across the Great Plains if you were interested in righting social wrongs? Because readers caught up in stories about people and their environment might get a sense of the oneness of things; of the interconnectedness of even the past and future and present. If environmentalists later conjured up a sense of the living unity of the planet with the newly applied word *Gaia,* then Sandoz was after a similar concept that would include human cultures. The parallel is that for Sandoz, culture (like nature) looked more like a "being" than a "thing." Anthropologists and historians took snapshots of cultures, freezing them like landscape painters did nature. She sensed motion. Life, of a sort.

If these sound like New Age sentiments, maybe they should.

Sandoz went in for things like palm readings and numerology, as her biographer, Helen Stauffer, shyly hints now and then.[5] There are so many traps to fall into — errors of mysticism, of overgeneralizing across cultures, of too-stubborn rationalism. I will be talking about these further on, some of which she anticipated, some she did not. But I believe her enough to stop trying to telegraph what she meant and instead unfold in place and time her geographic embrace.

What was it like to grow up on a homestead? One truth (but not the only one) is that homestead life was brutish. Mari Sandoz was born the year after her mother's unexpected marriage in a spring that turned quickly to hot, sticky summer. Her infant cries of discomfort woke her father in the night, and he beat her until she lay blue and trembling.[6] In the course of those early years, she would see her mother whipped with barbed wire and would stand one day with her father's rifle pointed for a long moment at her chest. He stood, completely ready to fire at her. To others, he would preach philosophically on the innate inferiority of women, departing from his own Populist party's preference for women's suffrage.

From the very first, she had cause to doubt the West of opportunity that her youthful mother had believed in. As if to drive the point home, one morning she was sent to wake the well-known stranger who had stopped at their house. She opened the door and stared at his false hair, at the fact of his famous golden locks being a wig. So much for Buffalo Bill.[7]

The better life envisioned by all those Europeans looking westward also dimmed in the face of the physical labor involved. Hard work was no idle pulpit chatter in her life. The eldest of six children, she was fully responsible early on for tending her siblings, one seeming to grow from her hip where she carried him the whole day. Then, one summer in her young teens, she established residency for her parents on a new claim. She survived there on game and berries with only a younger brother's help.[8] Later, when a snowstorm threatened their cattle, she rode a long day rescuing them and returned with her eyes scalded by the light and wind. She went blind in one eye as a result.

All this hard, physical labor inevitably cut short her time for learning. Even after other local children were sent off to school, Sandoz was kept home. Her tempestuous father had alienated the county officials. Finally, at age nine, she made what she called the greatest discovery of her life as small black marks on the page became an alphabet.[9] The silent companionship of written words remained a luxury for which she had to fight hard throughout her childhood. Family friends slipped Thomas Hardy and Joseph Conrad into her attic hideaway against the wishes of her father, who preferred the socialist periodical the *Appeal to Reason* and forbade fiction because it was, he said, for housemaids and servants. After she had broken away and begun to write, her first success — honorable mention in a short story contest — brought this emphatic response from her father: "You know I consider writers and artists the maggots of society."[10]

She left the land of her youth as soon as she could, traveling not far in miles but considerably in experience. Lincoln, Nebraska, boasted not only electric lights and elevators but a university, libraries, archives. And paying work for women. She left behind an extremely brief marriage to a man she rarely mentioned thereafter. She left country for city for the same reasons thousands of the underprivileged had done and would do.

Still, "good riddance" was hard to proclaim. At some point, she hit on the idea of talking back by writing about her father. She says in her introduction to *Old Jules* that on his deathbed Jules asked her to tell the story of his life. Sandoz's sister, Caroline Pifer, once gently wondered if she might have fabricated this justification.[11] Because of the artistic result, we who come later can discount any justification as ultimately unnecessary. Living in inexpensive, small, dark rooms without a glimpse into her future, Sandoz did not have any such comfortable certainty about whether to proceed.

Out of range of his voice and his fists, one might expect the daughter who became his biographer to condemn the man and the West for which he stood. She might have unfurled her own wrath and produced what some critics today would call a tale of victimization.[12] In fact, in the many early drafts of *Old Jules,* the tone apparently drifted toward blaming.[13] Even in the final work the cruelties were not glossed over but told in a spare forward language, distressingly frank for the times. Before an editor on the Atlantic Press's prize committee yanked it from oblivion, another publisher suggested the story be fictionalized, unable perhaps to bear the exaggerations of evil that occur in real life.[14]

The struggle was to find a way to tell the story, the history, of the homestead dream truthfully. But the truth was so utterly complicated. Historical "verisimilitude," as she put it, was hard to approach in any circumstance but especially when her subject touched her so personally. She realized early on that she would need psychological independence from her own ingrained habits and tried tricks like changing her appearance. She grew the hair that her mother always had chopped short for practicality. She dyed it at home, her experiments sometimes producing literally purple results.[15] Her name became Mari instead of the childhood Marie. She denied herself intimate pleasures such as music, which she found aroused her emotions too powerfully.[16] She needed control.

In addition to her private prejudices, she was up against the New York publishers' expectations and the assumptions of generations of readers about the "West." All her life Sandoz insisted that stories of universal significance could be found here where eastern publishers expected primarily exotica and adventure. The weight of earlier tellings — both the romantic versions and the newer social realism — failed to satisfy her desire to render her father. Other authors began in the 1920s and 1930s to describe the society in which she found herself as a "plundered province."[17] By 1937 Walter Prescott Webb was raging against the imperial control exerted by the eastern establishment in a livid book-length tract called *Divided We Stand,* and he was by no means alone. In some limited ways, the context approached what today is being called postcolonialism, with its dynamics of resistance to long-standing cultural dominance.

As Sandoz prepared to approach her truth about the West, she took courses now and then at the University of Nebraska where John Hicks, a disciple of Frederick Jackson Turner, taught western history. She was not likely to succumb to easy answers. She had been schooled to question the presumptions of authorities by her father's political pronouncements and once bragged that her family had given up religion seven hundred years before.[18] Still, these are pieties of their own, and she had before her the faces of her neighbors and friends at her favorite café in Lincoln; all the living relatives of the people she studied by reading every newspaper account of the region in the local archives; any number of voices that might dispute, claim offense or be slighted. Her mother, still living in the sandhills beyond the first Niobrara homestead, refused to endorse the project.[19] Then there was the ex-husband who was reckoned with by a consistent and lifelong silence on the subject. What could telling the truth about a community of which she had been a native possibly mean? What might the truth look like?

The solution she crafted to the dilemma of truth telling was to take the perspective of the land. From the witnessing presence of the landscape, she unfolded her story.[20] The method she began to choose here would later lead to a conception of the relationship between land, truthful memory and social justice. Pushing the reader constantly back to the land to view the action from a weathered distance, she offered a variety of simultaneous conclusions.

Here is an example. The passage comes at the end of the book, as the author describes her thirty-year-old self traveling by train from Lincoln to Jules's deathbed in Alliance, Nebraska:

At daylight Marie looked out upon the first low sandhills, huge sprawled bodies under dun-colored blankets. So they must have looked from the east in 1884, a little grayer from the winter wash of snow, when Jules drove up the Niobrara. But then there were still deer, antelope, elk, wolves, Indians, and white men armed to turn back the westward invasion coming with the spring. Now ducks swam in melancholy file on the summer-shrunked ponds. Geese circled high to catch the swifter blasts of the north wind that moaned a little over the frost-reddened bunchgrass. The sunflowers, Jules's index to good soil, bowed their frost-blackened faces and rattled their fear of winter winds. And sometimes for ten, twenty miles through the choppy country along the south road there was no house, not even a horsebacker — only the endless monotony of stormy sea, caught and held forever in sand.

In this, her earliest use of the tool of land, she relied on a rhetorical device that other writers had made familiar: the landscape becomes a kind of wise, knowing presence. The final words of the book make this unmistakable: "the late fall wind [tore] at the low sandy knolls that were the knees of the hills, shifting, but not changing, the unalterable sameness of the somnolent land spreading away toward the East." In the constancy of Sandoz's landscape resides a witness capable of calm understanding.

With land as a setting for philosophical detachment, Sandoz plays out her multiple judgments of Jules. The recollected comments of a county clerk are the most generous toward this man and his legacy. (The clerk was "a woman, and for that reason despised as an officeholder by Jules," Sandoz cannot help inserting.) The clerk called Old Jules "a prophet who remains to make his word deed." The positive sentiment is plausible despite Jules's barbed-wire whippings and other cruelties because the story also includes many incidents of the rough man finding aid for desperate settlers, fighting to establish a community, staying on when others left. The clerk's words showcase his heroic side, a man who stubbornly fought in "the eternal conflict of the small man against the big."[21] He founded and refounded a town in the face of terror campaigns by cattle giants. His orchard, which he planted likewise on the very edge of perennially hostile, almost desert circumstances, survived him while his community did not. And so the heroic cast gives way elsewhere to a sense of classical tragedy, of characters caught in forces beyond their control — again, the eternal political conflict of the small against the big. This tragic judgment comes particularly into focus in the final pages. The train passed homes that were "empty-eyed, a door swinging open and shut"; passed an old signboard that read "Forty miles to Old Jules." Sandoz wrote that the man was like a tiny cloud that had grown "to flash and thunder and roar and bring rain to the needy earth, only in the end to disintegrate, to drift in a pale shred of nondescript cloud."[22] While tragedy reigned on some pages, bitter irony did on others. In Mary Fehr, the reader experiences a constant "harumph" — an ironic counterpoint to the old man's windy pronouncements about democracy.[23] She works on, rolling her eyes, while he schemes another start at a community. She remarks, characteristically, that he will not even earn enough money to pay the year's taxes with his efforts. And the buffoonery of an unkempt, limping pioneer waging war with cranky letters to bureaucrats and judges makes the comedy.

By drawing on the land as eyewitness, Sandoz was able to answer equally yes and no to the question, was there a hint of hope for justice in the homestead dream? Her father made a good representative figure, and she judged the past with his example. From the point of view of the landscape, the voices who evaluated him were like seasons, differing, equally "true" and consequential.[24] The centrality of the regional setting in the story of *Old Jules* permitted this shifting judgment from heroic to tragic humanity, from ironic to comedic reactions to the past. Chapters began, transitions were formed, always by standing on the tan-and-mauve hillsides or among the bunchgrass. It was a victory over the simpler alternatives of anger or appeasement that press ideologically on histories of conquest, whether of the American West or other empires. And it was a victory as well over the failure to pass judgment at all, a failure of nerve and commitment that presents itself compassionately as not wanting to apply the standards of the present to the poor innocents of the past. A sense of the landscape as witness helped Sandoz to combine myth and history for a greater verisimilitude.

However, the physical landscape began, even in this first book, to appear rather different from a quiet, judicious, removed and untouchable omniscience. The myth of geography she was beginning to create with this book took another tack. This physical landscape actually needed (dun-colored) blankets; it shook with fear of the winter wind. On one page she would declare it never changing, but on others antelope, elk, communities disappear, new ones form.

The radical potential of *Old Jules* hid in these hints of life, or lifelikeness, in landscape. She gestured toward this meaning in her introduction. Her intention, she wrote, was to create a "biography of a community." And then she added a definition of that community that, notably, was *not* the Swiss- and German-American pioneer community or some human-centered phrase. This would be the biography of "the upper Niobrara country in western Nebraska." Who ever heard of writing a biography of a geography?

So began Mari Sandoz's career in land use.

My own interest in land began as a local reporter in a small town in southern Maine. I fell for the promise of community. Three elected officials called "selectmen" ran the government: a churchman, a hardware store owner and a retired funeral home director. Under the cover of charm, we condescended to each other for identical reasons: they were forty years older and accustomed to the absence of women. We would sit silently for long minutes at a time, the three selectmen and I, as they passed the town phone and electric bills to each other for signatures at the weekly Monday night meetings. Beneath this rural calm lay plenty of newsworthy developments, including the drama of tiny towns courting the corporate favor of steady employment, the creep of subdivisions over the last farmland, welfare cuts and now and again a murder or a teenager's head lopped off in a particularly gruesome car accident. The difference between this rural place and the Chicago outskirts where I had grown up was that change seemed fathomable. In my position as reporter of planning board meetings, school board sessions, every kind of small government occasion, I watched realtors, homemakers, teachers, loggers, landscape designers — I watched ordinary people govern. Once a year the romance of this pooled into a single morning in mud season. The scouts served hot dogs and the women's Fire Department auxiliary handled the coffee and donuts while the voters of the town of North Berwick, Maine, filed into the elementary school gymnasium for Town Meeting. Those two words, Town Meeting, are like a personal name, I learned from my copy editors. The grammar turns the 150-odd neighbors who would show up into one body. In 1981 in North Berwick, recycling passed by two — just two — upheld hands. It was my political awakening. Before too many years passed, the relationship between geography and democracy became the topic I would pursue in graduate school.

I did not make much of a journalistic watchdog, charmed as

I was by the housework of local government. But in the privacy of my own mind, I struggled to write the truth of what I experienced. The draft of the novel that eventually emerged was too quiet and poetic for a first novelist to be able to sell, said the New York editors. I had sought to capture a sentiment that I can come the closest to summarizing as the willingness to participate. The selectman in it ought to have known from his personal life that even governance would confound him because human communication was so impossible, so elusive. But he proceeded anyway. And his visiting daughter (a young woman raised by her mother and adoptive father in Chicago) came to love him but also abandon him for that sentiment — the feeling of willingness, the illogical feeling of willingness.

Falling for a rural community turned out to mean, as it had for many people before me, an ache to believe in human agency; to believe that individual actions matter. I had grown up near Chicago visiting the Sears Tower on weekends; traveling up one hundred stories in an elevator with friends. I would stand before the dizzying sight of millions of lit windows and try to fathom that behind each one were people who imagined their lives to be as important as mine seemed to me. The first vote I cast in my life was in an aging, clanking voting machine in a Chicago ward. The location felt dirty and vaguely dangerous, the privileged university folks waiting in the same line as the mostly black residents of low-income housing. We were all of us unaccustomed to acknowledging our proximity. The power structures of the city overwhelmed my belief in human understanding.

In North Berwick I got a glimpse of why anyone would think that democracy could work. But as I fell for the promise of small communities, I faced an equally traditional problem: how was I to make a living, especially if I wanted time to write novels? I had come from somewhere toward the upper half of the wide, self-defining American middle class. My mother sewed our clothes. But we did have roast beef on Christmas, and fat steaks on special occasions. My parents took us on long vacations, which my father's scientific research job permitted. We could afford to travel back to Germany every few years to see my mother's and my father's families — the grandparents, my near-dozen aunts and uncles, the forty-some cousins. When it came time for college, my parents could pay — scholarships helped, but still, all four of us children went to college on a single bread-winner family's income, thanks to my parents' long foresight and good fortune.

I had come from an upper-middle-class childhood and married someone of similar means. Now we were on our own. With our educations and with the safety net of our families in case of emergencies, we had good prospects. We even soon bought our own home — a real fixer-upper in every sense of the word. I had taken photographs, as a journalist, of three houses being moved from the front lawn of a factory. When the contractors who had moved the houses ran out of money, I happened to stop by. We got one of the houses — still seamed between the first and second story from the move — at a bargain basement price. We borrowed some of the down payment from my parents' retirement.

Now Mark and I were nose to nose with the reality of making a living. We could make it, with both of us working full-time. I had a journalism job, Mark had a teaching position in a small private school — exactly what he wanted. But pay at private schools is considerably less than at public schools. Entry-level journalism salaries were even lower, at barely $7,000 a year.

This was the go-go eighties, but not in Maine. Our peers in New York City were celebrating making three figures at the age of twenty-three on Wall Street. We were hoping to make it to two figures each, sooner rather than later. I wanted to write novels, but I lacked some courage and I lacked the financial means. Still, I pulled my hesistancy inside me, quit my full-time job at the newspaper and began piecing together part-time work. I'd write in the morning, throw myself into money-saving projects like laboriously hand-sanding our deteriorating car, while fantasizing about making a killing growing herbal tea for market on our five acres. Eventually I came to my senses. I knew that very few writers become published writers. At my first writing workshop, I learned that very few published writers become best-sellers. Even established writers are mostly living hand to mouth. I liked security. I had grown up with it.

For a few years I waited tables some nights, worked weekend copy-editor shifts at another local paper on other nights. It was fine for now, I said. At age twenty-nine I looked myself in the mirror and realized with a sudden clarity that I did not want to be in the same position at fifty-five. There was an old woman at the newspaper, haggard and with shiny-seated pants, who gave me a glimpse into the future of part-time work at struggling rural newspapers. She took "obits" (obituaries) for four hours every morning and then was sent home, probably just in time to deny her the health benefits. Her skin was gray. She smelled bad. She had few, if any, options.

I had always been good at school. I would go back to university, earn a Ph.D. and teach college. Everybody "knows" that college teachers have plenty of time. I could be a college professor of American Studies, I decided — a field that combines literature and history and everything else into just the kind of grab bag I wanted — and I would write novels "on the side." It turns out I was very wrong about how relaxed a professorship would be, but for now I packed my bags with the seductive whispers of educational promise in my ears.

When I decided on an academic career, Mark dared with me partly because near Brown University in Rhode Island we could still find rural places to live. We found ourselves telling exotic stories of pig raising and chicken slaughtering at urban parties. We were both conscious of having selected the wardrobe, if you will, of a rural life. We were clinging to something though, and that clinging manifested in our walking, together or alone, in the woods. Where we lived on the western side of that tiny state, there were many acres of reforested countryside. Some of the pines were already again nearly one hundred years old and the size of ship masts. Colonial graves sank amid yuccas with their white spires of flowers. Rock walls, some built by slaves, remained so tightly stacked that you could not even hide a note in the cracks. Walking around Barden Reservoir on the weekends reminded me of the walking I did in Maine, the same path, day after day, year after year. Those wanderings had produced in me a different kind of knowledge than I had experienced before. In every season I knew the path, and the smell of the pine boughs leaning over the creek and the sound of the water playing the rocks. The only comparison I can make is the kind of knowledge from the many, many, many books I read in graduate school, which layered in me like a geology. The sediment of experience in landscape and, as it turns out, landscape reading began to work on me from the background.

These details of my own life are relevant to this story about

Mari Sandoz precisely because they are "personal." Her histories were too. What I mean to do is draw attention to how we learn things. How individuals learn things and how societies too can be said to learn. Understanding of the kind that Sandoz explored requires some muddling of the conventional separation between individual and social inspiration; between the experience of walking in woods and the act of reading about walking in woods; between a (personal) story about the slow process of learning some new understanding and the extracted, abstracted punch line of what is learned.

When I encountered Sandoz's work in a course that first year, I glimpsed a kindness in her books toward the learner in me. There was something ecological about her method, though I couldn't at first understand that. Mostly there was, in the background of my everyday life, the familiar divide between common sense (lessons drawn from experience, including from walking in the woods) and professional expertise (learned from words in books, especially the dryer books with abstracts and thesis statements and no sensual padding for comfort). My new classmates and I were becoming certified intellectuals, and we were, all of us, uncomfortable in vague ways related to the divides we were crossing. Each of us had come out of what is called the "real" world. One was the son of a New York City firefighter, self-conscious about having soft hands that never had worked machines. He was the first in his family to graduate from college, let alone earn a Ph.D. Then there was the pale, very young man who unbelievably had already come from a law office stint fighting Mafia links to unions. At the home of the lone African-American woman in my entering class, there was a life-sized portrait of her mother whose hard labor had helped to make her learned life possible. We all were uncomfortably aware that the divide between the academic and the real world could make us seem "better." The status of intellectuals is higher than that of manual laborers. Then again, we also had learned to distrust intellectualism, as most Americans do. "Only weenies get master's degrees," the cowboy boyfriend of a graduate student informed her, I later learned. In both the praise and the sneer, the separation between real life and intellectual endeavors was profound.

The physical setting of the university offered a corresponding code to this divide between the world of physical experience and the intellect. Flowering trees showered the streets with a ticker tape of petals in the spring. Benches purposefully invited readers out to the lawn, or onto the grass itself that was worn thin with the play of young women and men. But the lecture halls were dark, stuffy, sleep inducing. This physical context communicated things to me long before I could write this. I am reminded of an old Greek word for the subtle midwifery of ideas: *maieutic*. An 1868 use of the word listed in the *Oxford English Dictionary* (*OED*) defines the maieutic process as "drawing out intelligence before communicating knowledge."

Our bodies were supposed to be subservient to our sharp minds. One day a professor wore a taut pinstripe suit to class and startled us all by waving a gun. It was a toy, of course. The point he meant to make had something to do with the rise of organized crime in the history of the urban United States, but it's the startle I remember, the physical movement of eighty-odd people at once. Lecture etiquette (which can, of course, be broken) generally requires the teacher too to seem abstract, bodiless, a brain transported by tissue. I felt awkward when, several times a week in the swimming pool, I encountered the urban history professor. We would pass each other, barely seeing but yes, looking, noticing each other, through the chlorine curtain. Academic writing reproduces the same proprieties. Successful novelists were much admired for their passion, and the interdisciplinary program in American Studies in which I was enrolled happily included fiction, television, even Bruce Springsteen as legitimate historical subjects. But to write that way? I had to be told by one of my first professors that the margin comment "journalistic prose" was sharply negative criticism. Our style was to be formal, serious and — especially — impersonal. Or, to put it plainly, our writing was supposed to be dull.

Body and mind, passionate and intellectual expression, being "grounded" or with your head in the clouds: in reading Mari Sandoz, I sensed an alternative. The toughest questions got substantive answers in her page-turners. The teacher who introduced me to *Old Jules* was a tall, silver-haired Mainer who would habitually lean way back in a chair with his long legs on his desk. His name was John L. Thomas, and he often invited his seminar students home. He even served sherry as Ivy League professors do in Hollywood movies, and he did so without any sense of staging or ironic self-consciousness. A small heater in the living room attempted to make up for his stereotypical New England frugality, and we graduate students struggled to keep our voices from nervous trembling. Sounding intelligent was quite important. We took turns. Several antique clocks ticked; their bells rang syncopated for not being precisely, digitally coordinated. Upstairs was James Madison's desk, or his uncle's — I don't exactly remember. The link was somehow presidential. The learning here was of a different sort than in lectures. Original ideas, analysis, creative thinking were separated by space from information gathering, from wool gathering.

My assignment was to read everything by and about Mari Sandoz. Immediately, she moved me. Literally. I had been choosing uncomfortable furniture to keep myself awake through a sentence like this one by the French theorist Michel Foucault:

> It seems to me that power must be understood in the first instance as the multiplicity of force relations immanent in the sphere in which they operate and which constitute their own organization; as the process which, through ceaseless struggles and confrontations, transforms, strengthens or reverses them; as the support which these force relations find in one another, thus forming a chain or a system, or on the contrary, the disjunctions and contradictions which isolate them from one another; and lastly, as the strategies in which they take effect, whose general design or institutional crystallization is embodied in the state apparatus, in the formulation of the law, in the various social hegemonies.[25]

When it came time to read Sandoz, I could leave the straight-backed chair. I could sprawl in the graduate student lounge and read without effort into the night and the next day. Her *Old Jules* was a history that was not just "journalistic," it was downright novelistic. She *meant* to move me: to get me to feel the sting of snow's brightness in the young Marie's eyes; to taste the first cherries from Mary and Jules Sandoz's orchard; to imagine the "monotonous yellow sandhills."

At the same time that I lounged, the impact of those compacted sentences like Foucault's definition of power was also working on me. Until now I have been candid about the problems with dull, punch-line, thesis-driven academic writing. But there is the bathwater to throw out, and then there is the baby, which is bone-hard intellectual labor. Anti-intellectualism is a common malady, an understandable one, but Sandoz would have none of it. Her reading included the most difficult thinkers of her day. In fact, a favorite book that she reread every year was Franz Kafka's *The Castle*.[26] It is not the kind of book to make a best-seller, or even be popular like Kafka's most famous story about a man who wakes up as a cockroach. I read *The Castle* with my own thoughts about Sandoz coloring the pages. In it Kafka chronicles the attempts of a confused but earnest Land-Surveyor to communicate with "the castle," a place accessed only through the clumsy if well-intentioned messages of middlemen and bureaucrats. The Land-Surveyor never succeeds in getting a message through to the castle, or even in understanding the confused instructions that seem to come from above. He never gives up though. He tires in trying but is doomed to continue.

Trying to understand *how change happens* is at the root of the hard intellectual labor of the Kafka book that Sandoz read perennially, of the social theory I was struggling to understand and also of Sandoz's use of land. The question unites the idealism of activists trying to create a better society with the thinkers who bookishly ponder how the world works. To instigate change, you need strategic targets. In the social theory that I was reading in graduate school under the various labels poststructuralism, deconstruction and postmodernism, words were the targets. I came to understand that words could inhibit or inspire change. In language we saw a web of relationships that generally fell into the category of unnoticed background. Made invisible by its very commonplaceness, the habits or conventions of language began to seem more critical in sustaining (or disrupting) existing social orders. I used these insights to begin to question conventions like separating sensory experience from dull lecturelike knowledge. Conventions like distinguishing stories from histories.

As I lounged with my Sandoz books and forcefully attended to my other learning, background and foreground began to converge. I saw something in the periphery of the biography of community that was *Old Jules*. Sandoz had her own social theory, and she used a lifetime to develop it. She had learned something back on the homestead, but the commonplaces and conventions of the era in which she was an adult were constantly pushing her to forget it. There would be hard work ahead — as hard a labor of instinct and intelligence as crafting a subsistence farm on dry prairie land.

After *Old Jules,* Mari Sandoz wrote novels, pretty awful ones. They were no worse, really, than other self-consciously proletarian fiction of the thirties. In departing from the biography of community, she may not yet have understood how much she got right in *Old Jules*. In working on it, she knew she wanted the language to re-create her sense of the place and time she aimed to describe. It was hugely difficult. With each draft, she struck poses of great confidence in letters to eastern editors. But the bank where she deposited her meager earnings failed; rejections accumulated; and one fiery afternoon she assembled friends and dumped seventy stories in a washtub, dramatically incinerating her written work.[27] She recovered, but it would still be nearly two years before her own hunches about how to tell this story would be confirmed by a telegram from the Atlantic Press worded very ambiguously to avoid news leaks. The follow-up phone call days later set her heart pounding. She had won their prestigious prize and her book would be published. "It is curious that nothing has ever had the same impact on me as your voice that day," she recollected much later in a letter to her caller, Volta Torrey of the *Atlantic*.[28]

Success brought some immediate rewards. There was the money — "Yes! Five thousand dollars!" Mari whooped to her mother in a quick note with the news of the honor. There was some reconciliation. When Mary Fehr Sandoz attended a play based on *Old Jules,* years of protective reserve and silence over what they had lived through together vanished as Mary Fehr forgot herself and blurted out, "Yah, that's right! That's how it was!"[29] Other kinds of recognition followed, including the companionship of other writers and well-known people. Reviews of her book were largely positive, and her work became part of a larger regionalist revolt that would challenge easterners' grip on the cultural life of the nation.[30]

For all the benefits of her sudden stardom, however, ease did not follow. Partly, the fits and starts of an artist's financial and literary destiny ensured that she would work very hard during her remaining thirty years of life. But she pressed it far beyond even that. Sandoz wrote frantically. Thirteen books followed *Old Jules,* sometimes two at a time, and articles and short stories joined the stack on her shelf. When breast cancer first struck, she sat herself impatiently in front of a fan to quicken the healing of her mastectomy scar. Her sense of urgency was continuous, not just at the crisis of illness. She lived modestly to finance her work, maintaining the extremely minimalist diet to which she had become habituated in the years prior to her success. ("I know my resistance to starvation rather well by now and can predict when collapse will come," she wrote a friend once, apologizing for the melodrama of this detail.)[31] Now and then, she did permit herself a small luxury, such as the sealskin jacket she bought in 1952.[32]

The reasons she rode so hard into a world of black marks on a page had to do with conscious conviction. It was in 1940 that she described herself as a writer "interested in social justice and in the destruction of discrimination between economic levels, between nationalist levels, between color levels, and so on."[33] Her biographer, Stauffer, found a 1946 letter in which Sandoz suggested, in effect, that all writers "have a stern obligation to avoid any word or implication that might encourage human injustice."[34]

Driven by conviction, she also believed a door was closing on the possibility of real democracy. The problems were legion. Sandoz had read *Mein Kampf* and studied the rise of fascism abroad and at home. The rampant desire for individual power and wealth at the expense of the community drove the action in her novels *Slogum House* (1937) and *Capital City* (1939). Her greedy villains were homegrown, western types such as Gulla of *Slogum House,* a woman who preyed on her neighbors during the depression. "Hard winters make fat coyotes," Gulla declares sadistically.[35] Gulla's greed was part of a larger historical force: the pull of materialism was one of Sandoz's favorite themes. In *Crazy Horse: The Strange Man of the Oglalas,* she describes the insatiability of the new way of life: "Truly the man who follows the buffalo eats well if he eats, while he who chases the whites is like one who chases the rabbit; even when he eats he is hungry."[36]

Sandoz wrote against the tide of selfish materialism. She aimed to expose the fascist will to power, even at home. In addition, Sandoz condemned passivity. She blamed those who failed to oppose injustice. The weak-willed rebels were "caught and held . . . as the sand of the hills was held in the long, wire roots of the blue joint and the clumpy bunchgrass." Her critiques focused on the United States, though she kept abreast of world politics. In the United States she saw "dollars as big as cartwheels" overtaking everything else.[37] "No voice was loud enough to be heard above the drumbeaters for the railroads, the cattlemen, the miners and the army contractors," she summarized in *Capital City.*[38]

There was a way of life, including a corresponding language, that was being ground under by modern American society. Real democracy, or any hope of it, was disappearing under those dollars as big as cartwheels. As she tried to name what was being forgotten, Sandoz sought out examples of democratic cultures. She turned especially to Indian histories. In them she saw case studies of strong democracy. Like other white progressives of the time, Sandoz presented Native American peoples as more civilized than Europeans. In her histories she reiterated the stereotype that Indians are closer to nature. She did not see a Rousseauian innocence in Indians but rather a greater cultural sophistication, which to Sandoz meant a more democratic system.[39] Her biography of the Sioux leader Crazy Horse, which was published in 1942, upheld an example of a community in continuous participatory democracy: no one obeyed a leader or representative unless in that particular instance they agreed with the recommended course of action.[40] In one scene the Indians laugh at the idea of white soldiers carrying out patently foolish orders. By comparison, "not even the great chief among them told anybody what to do."[41] Likewise, women did not stay with men except as they decided to do so.[42] Strong leaders were necessary but ought to earn their power, as Crazy Horse had done, by his deep sense of the needs of the group, and with the active consent of his followers. In Crazy Horse's case, feeling the community within himself extended even to his unconscious life. He regularly went into the wilderness alone to seek a vision that would guide the people. Sandoz was very interested in his being called a "strange man," a mystic; she described his vision quests in detail. Nature, the "dead-alive" ones and other messengers helped Crazy Horse to serve the people well. He led them until he too was defeated by the forces much larger than himself.[43]

One could be trained to act in such democratic ways. The Sioux, she wrote once for *Reader's Digest,* did not feel the sting of sacrifice when individuals subordinated themselves to the group because they felt the group within themselves.[44] Likewise, the earlier generation of pioneers felt the group within themselves, felt their interdependence. Instead of "free land," what had beckoned in the West even in that earlier time was not soil itself but the disposition to use it in a certain way — for family farmers, not the J. P. Morgans.

Furthering democracy required cultural training, a kind of deep conditioning, and this democratic training was helped by having lived close to nature. Sandoz suggested that in the past, when people were more immediately dependent on nature and each other, the overlapping ties that bound everyone and everything to each other were more apparent. "Homesteader children," Sandoz wrote, could see "almost from their first steps" the need for dependence on one's neighbors and the "interrelationship of earth and sky and animal and man."[45] These interrelationships were complex and hard to fathom. Readers caught up in stories about people and their environment might glimpse something in their peripheral vision as she had. It was an eco-logical view, though that word wasn't popularized at the time.

But people were not living in close proximity to the natural world anymore. The "interrelationship of earth and sky and ani-mal and man" was less visible in the rapidly urbanizing, subur-banizing and refrigerated society that flourished during the early middle years of the twentieth century, when Sandoz wrote most of her work. In fact, Sandoz herself did not live in close proximity to nature. She took an apartment in Denver where she did not even feel obliged to touch fruits or vegetables or meats. She always ate out — she needed the kitchen space for her file cabinets. Of notes. Of words. She never herself was drawn by any back-to-the-land rhetoric.

It was the memory of those interdependent societies that she was after. Understanding why memory should provide solu-tions to the "destruction of discrimination between economic levels, between nationalist levels, between color levels," goes to the heart of Sandoz's thinking. For her, the memory of a different time united the listener or the reader with that web of interrelationships, regardless of his or her current situation. In the memory of an earlier, participatory democracy, modern readers could find the impetus for change. That was her hope.

For memory to be an effective tool for bettering society, how-ever, the history had to re-create the experiences of the world of another time and place. The reader had to relive the past. To achieve the result she wanted, she demanded that her histories evoke, not just report, what happened. She drew in the land-scape, including its sounds and smells; she gave readers maps; she put her readers imaginatively into the past, even inventing dialogue for long-dead actors because her readers would forgive the imaginative stretch for the sake of the power of "verisimilitude."

Memory could only work as a political tool, if even the deeper truths could be re-created. The background of sights and sounds and sensual detail was part of the picture. But even more difficult was reproducing the background of language. Sandoz talked openly about her efforts to get the words right in the introduction to her 1953 book, *Cheyenne Autumn*. In it, she chronicled the desperate, failed flight of the Northern Cheyenne back to their home territory from a reservation. "To convey something of [the] deep, complex, and patterned interrelationships" that had been understood by the old Cheyennes, she had tried "to keep to the simplest vocabulary, to something of the rhythm, the idiom, and the figures of Cheyenne life, to phrases and sentences that have flow and continuity."[46] Phrases that have flow and continuity meant unusual verb tenses, rhythmic arrangements and colloquialisms.[47] "We will make a talk with the soldier chief" is one example.[48] Sandoz puts this sentence in the mouth of the Cheyenne named Medicine Arrow as he prepares to surrender a battle. "Make a talk" suggests that a conversation is an act of mutual creation, not two individuals counterposed against each other. "I will talk with the white captain" is not just grammatically different; the phrasing represents a different worldview.

Sandoz declared language a "live instrument" and took inspiration from the abstract modernist painters she admired. It was an uphill battle. She was ahead of her time. Sandoz did constant battle — not with some grand, clear ideological enemy (though she took pride in some of her books being banned), but with legions of copy editors.[49] Battles with editors provoked Mari

Sandoz into furious outbursts and into yet another scene with her eastern publishers. She moved from publishing house to publishing house in this continuing feud. She had good reasons to wage this fight. The effect Sandoz was after was profoundly out of kilter with the standards conventionally applied to manuscripts. Note, for example, how she words Crazy Horse's father's perception of the boy's emerging leadership qualities: "And beside the fire that night the father felt something else in the boy that was new — something that one could know without seeing, as the sap that rises in the tree is known long before the leafing."[50] Phrases like "before the leafing" drove Sandoz's editors to distraction, but Sandoz refused to budge.

Despite some acknowledged flaws in the craftsmanship, she managed sometimes to create the impact she wanted. And so literary critic Bernard DeVoto praised *Old Jules* as "an experience in citizenship."[51] She had re-created the experience, not just reported it. She was proudest of *Crazy Horse,* especially when a delegation of Lakotas and Flatheads appeared in her apartment with a copy of the book in a sack and surprised her with a ceremony including orations, sign language and formal handshakes. She recalled later: "It was the finest thing that could ever happen in my house and I felt terribly small and insignificant for a week."[52]

Words on the land were themselves a kind of power. With them, Sandoz could re-create a sense of citizenship. To put language at the forefront of political change emphasizes the extent to which one's imagination shapes the reality one sees. To inspire change means altering a society's imagination. Deciding what is possible and what is "unrealistic" begins in the background that is language. Words that seem only to reflect reality actually create it. The sense of interdependence, of "deep, complex and patterned interrelationships" assumed by the Northern Cheyenne, Sandoz argued, was matched in the style of speaking, in patterns of word choice, in the assumptions of language.

From societies that had lived in close interdependence with nature, Sandoz came to believe that memory was alive. The past and the present merged. She was most explicit about this view, which she said she herself only "dimly perceived," in the introduction to *Cheyenne Autumn*.

> The old Cheyennes, even more than their High Plains
> neighbors [the Lakota], had a rich and mystical perception
> of all life as a continuous, all-encompassing eventual flow,
> and of man's complete oneness of all this diffused and eter-
> nal stream. It was a stream of many and complex dimen-
> sions, one in which man, the tree, the rock, the cloud and
> all the other things were simultaneously in all the places
> they had ever been; and all things that had ever been in
> a place were always in the present there, in the being and
> occurring.[53]

In the same way that the rock, the tree and humanity are bound together, she saw the disparate peoples of the human race united by memory. Her readings of Carl Jung, Erich Fromm and William Faulkner reinforced this view.[54]

Mimicking language patterns, re-creating smells and sounds, imagining the dialogue of long-dead speakers — Sandoz used these methods to draw the past into the present. The past she re-created would not be simple; there were no pure heroes. Her father remained the archetype. The key was to sort among relationships, not separate good from evil individuals, races or nations. The model relationship to be mimicked in society, in the home, in the economy, was nature's interdependence.

Sandoz struggled to communicate this complex vision of the deeper interdependence uniting peoples, times and the nonhuman world. Her attention to nature would be so easy to misunderstand. All around her there were the simpleminded nature worshipers like Harold Bell Wright, whose widely popular novels of the 1920s presented the natural world as beneficent and kind. Sandoz had known the fury of nature herself and watched drought and snow drive neighbors mad. And there was the easy presumption that people would be compelled to do nature's bidding. Sandoz departed from any strict environmental determinism. The great danger in fact was a cultural (not natural) force that was spreading itself throughout the world. The cultural drift of modern times never taught and even denied this interdependence that she perceived in the past.

If communicating the precarious interdependence of human beings in nature was one difficulty, another problem was nostalgia. Simpleminded worshipers of all things past could misunderstand the role of memory. She talked in 1940 about a mid-America "trying to evade the implications of the present through the glorification of the past."[55] She wrote in an allegorical novel about fascism that as "the future became less promising, the past increased in importance."[56] While glorifiers of the past subverted the radical potential of memory, on the one hand, the emerging standards of professional history deadened the possibility of re-creating society through the imagination, on the other. Historians were repulsed by her use of invented dialogue. She insisted that the words she gave to her subjects were dictated by the context, which she knew in excruciating detail. Her method demanded an attitude of attention to the oneness of sensory and intellectual sources. Her last book, *The Battle of the Little Bighorn,* published posthumously, drew on all the best "professional" tools of the historian: on archival documents, on verbal recollections (some of which only she, with her long contacts and her homesteader childhood, could coax from privately minded individuals), and on her commitment to balancing different versions and including the point of view of the Sioux. But the deeper truth of the story came to her with tools not usually admitted in such a kit bag. Twice, she had camped at the site of the battle, once for nearly two weeks. In a letter she described the experience. She had with her "a bundle of notes and maps" from the government records and from Indian oral histories. "But what I got seemed outside and beyond the words — something that was in the June sun, the June moonlight," she wrote.[57]

This is where she would send us as well, into the moonlight and sunlight. It is a more complex recommendation than Horace Greeley's famous "Go West, young man"; and it is different too from the whispers that reached young Mary Fehr's ear in Switzerland.

Some critics understood. Her fellow western writer Wallace Stegner applauded her purpose and method. "I found myself comparing Crazy Horse with Hector, which makes you automatically Homer," he told her.[58] Sandoz believed presentation was key. She describes the apprenticeship of a band or clan historian in a children's novel, *The Story Catcher.* The elder Oglala tells his student he must learn to "see all things, know how they look and how they are done. . . . The picture is the rope that ties memory solidly to the stake of truth."[59]

The use of a word picture that evoked sight and sound and

smell was the rope in Sandoz's hands. With it she hoped to fix in the collective memory of humanity the waning experience of citizenship. Whether the memory would eventually lead to change was not something she would predict. But the tool of words on land gave her hope. In the end she was as stubborn as her father, unwilling to yield to narrow definitions of the appropriate. One Christmas Old Jules again ignored his ill-clothed family's need for shoes. Instead he used a windfall inheritance to purchase a phonograph player and hundreds of records. "Frozen feet heal!" he exclaimed to the people who came for miles to crowd the living room. "What you put in the mind lasts!"

I now live in a modestly urban neighborhood in Salt Lake City, Utah. I left the walks around Barden Reservoir in Rhode Island for the same reasons many Americans move from place to place: a job. I began to teach history at the University of Utah in 1992. We don't even keep egg-laying chickens anymore. In my backyard vegetable garden there are two rusty roosters made in Mexico out of recycled tin.

Our street is graffiti spattered but in a typically Utah wholesome way. While the teenagers tag the alley garages with spray paint, prepubescent girls turn the sidewalks into a swirl of pastel color using fat chalk they carry in large buckets. Mountains rise up from the desert floor as if the earth had only yesterday jawed them upward. It's a good place to feel human in — good in the sense of truthful, the jarring and much-altered ecology a metaphor for what counts as agency, as action, in the hugeness of history and time.

Words on words on land are difficult to defend as social action. As they should be — if you see words as different from deeds. The question of whether the divide between mental and physical action should be overcome has to be answered, I believe, equally with yes and also no. In this conclusion, I concede — readily — that living on land produces different experiences than a lounge chair's reading of settlers. And furthermore, there is still a desperate need for the physical promises of homesteads; for the political will to provide the start that the nineteenth-century homestead was imagined to be. It is horrible to be willing to abide frozen feet for children. Or for adults. In a better world, we would imagine both shoes and music as necessary. I would choose differently than Jules Sandoz. His daughter too had a tendency to demand extreme sacrifices of herself. In her stories and articles, she occasionally revealed an almost sadistic desire for hard times that would return people to the awareness of mutual need.

At the same time, though, the consciousness of culture's shaping influence is no small lesson from a geographic embrace. To get a glimpse of how very complex, subtle and deep are the interrelationships between the past and the present, between the being and the occurring, is to peek at a great mystery. There is power to be taken from this source — and maybe even hope.

Mari Sandoz was not optimistic, not in the foreseeable future, that is. She expected that dollars as big as cartwheels would triumph and that goodwill would be caught and held in the bunchgrass. In a mystical way, though, she was almost wildly hopeful. For her, there was a truth to which the rope of a word picture could be tied. She believed in what she once called a "deep racial memory," by which she meant the human race.[60] In such a view of a common human consciousness, wisdom over the ages can combine and grow. Hers was a modernist conception. My postmodern hope is a different one. For Sandoz, experiencing memory (not "having" a memory but interacting with it) brought her into contact with a single, eternal humanity. Instead I see many humanities — fractured, not organically cohered. What human beings share arises over time; changes, disperses, becomes something new. What links human beings across very different cultures develops and fades away like an idea does. There are landscapes out there — memories that became as rocky and hard as the earth is. Then upheavals came and prairie grass grew. And these too faded away. Each one of these moments had the cachet of reality. Each one of those moments seemed to encompass all that is possible; all that is imaginable. And then something else arose. Great forces — the power of elites to massage the truth, the distribution of money or military might — all these forces beyond individual control help to create each of those rocky, grassy or fiery landscapes. That we can tie a rope with words to those "various social hegemonies," as Foucault called them, is an immense power. With it, we can imagine change.

A common "racial memory" is a faith that Sandoz acquired in her time. Enough for me is the possibility of relationships, not direct, but linked via word pictures (of sensation and mind) to the insubstantial feel of place that is another time — the cap and mittens we cannot take off. My view befits a vagabond whose inclination is to see communication between, for example, aging North Berwick selectmen and a young reporter as precarious at best. My view seems to be a product of the (limits of) the imagination of my own time, a sensibility that has produced chaos theory to supplant ecology; a fractured self negotiating among its parts to replace the coherent personality theories of modernist psychology; and dissipated democracies, their voters disengaged.

We are farther down the road than Sandoz foresaw. The possibility of change is about as grand a hope as I can muster.

There is a great deal of power in believing that we can influence not only *what* we think but *how* we think — to believe that the beastily insubstantial thing we call culture might one day offer words that refuse to divide personal knowledge from expert, abstract punch lines; that unites social justice activism with intellectual labor; that might resist our current convention of separating experience from book learning; that might instead bind such opposites as body and mind, nature and society, self and other. The power to change the imagination is what makes words on land as powerful as land itself. And yet the power of the imagination is not necessarily a force that naturally develops in the direction of sustaining life or creating a better world. A faith in progress, even at the subtlest levels such as in Sandoz's work, is one of the casualties of other words on land of the depression era, as the next chapter discusses. The radical imagination holds as much promise to me as a homestead did for Jules Sandoz. In other words, it is just as likely to fail. But somewhere, maybe located not "in" only my "mind," this hope still makes sense to me.

CHAPTER FOUR

Back to a New "Family Farm"

*Josephine Johnson and a
Politics of Abundance*

In a field in April, a far-off dinner bell clangs. A man stands with the wind-kicked grit in his eyes. The ground does not want to be plowed, not by him, not by these worn-out tools. He walks back to the house where his new hired man stands awkwardly wait-ing for him, already hovering at the door as if those young legs could sprint still, another mile or five, fetching things, doing the work. Together, they step inside and the women's voices drop suddenly silent.

That morning, when his wife and eldest bragged of a treat to welcome the new help, the man had snapped with suspicion at the extravagance. "Who's buying peaches?" he wanted to know. But the peaches had been their own, homegrown ones. He had not understood that they still owned a last, hoarded jar. Now at mealtime, he sees the pickled fruit sitting in a bowl on the table, gold-shiny in their juice. He takes a half peach in a single bite. Imagine it: cool from its cellar storage, sweet-sour and syrupy on his parched tongue. The peach tastes like a first kiss right about now. He offers a mute apology, chewing there, with a vinegar grin.

Luxuries are relative, anthropologists teach us. Beauty is in the eye of the beholder. But how elective is a can of peaches, a kiss?

Walt Whitman once imagined a world that was "complete but cheap, within reach of all," and this world depended on "millions of comfortable city homesteads and moderate-sized farms, healthy and independent, single separate ownership."[1] So much lies tangled up in this dream: so much hope that the earth will provide; so much certainty that sacrifice today will mean reward tomorrow. If you have to give up peaches one year or five or one whole generation even, the next one will thank you. They will collect the well-earned rewards.

But what if the earth does not provide? What if the world is not as certain as the equation that if you waste not, you will want not? Where, then, is the line between subsistence (food) and luxury (sweet things, an extravagant love)? When is a life too cheap of pleasure, too chary of beauty in the name of future rewards?

Asking for pleasure — now, not later — is risky in a book that purports to be about social justice. Economic fairness begins with food, shelter, clothing. Or does it? Could there be a right to happiness lurking somewhere in our beliefs of what we want to demand for each other? The pursuit of happiness is such an impossibly vague notion, an absurd phrase to find in the Declaration of Independence. My father, a deeply rational man, initiated a conversation one Christmas dinner on this quirk of American political rhetoric. An immigrant scientist from Germany, he paused between passing my mother's good food and turned to John, the first-year law student who was my sister's just-announced fiancé. How is it, my incredulous father asked, that Americans could actually demand the right to pursue happiness? We all cringed in embarrassment, my sisters, brother and I. Dad was being so weird, so unlike "normal" people in our Chicago suburbs — the ones we presumed discussed football at supper. I was a self-conscious teenager then, but even now I have to push myself through a thicket of inhibitions into this topic. My resistance comes from many directions. My mother, who rarely joined such dinner table debates, nevertheless had an equally strong opinion: one might seek to offer happiness to someone else. To be indulgent toward others was perfectly okay. But to safeguard or even aggressively promote one's own, selfish pleasure? To do so in private would be questionable enough, but I seem to be about to suggest it as a legitimate public policy goal.

As a political dream of a better world, how can one admit to demanding present-day rewards of sweet pleasure? The answer tends to be that you can permit yourself the *simple* pleasures. And simple pleasures come from the land. In this long tradition, agricultural rather than manufactured products are less egregiously a selfish wish. Whitman's family farm offers a middle ground: on the one hand, it demands hard labor, but on the other, it extends the balm of simple pleasures that you may rightfully take and enjoy. Finding the balance is part of the symbolic task of the "family farm."

To help think through the relationship of selfish pleasure and social justice, I want to introduce you to a writer named Josephine Winslow Johnson. It is from her rarely discussed but Pulitzer Prize–winning book of 1934, *Now in November,* that I drew the scene about the peaches.[2] I rephrased it some, though not unfairly, because the whole book is a plea for sensuality in some ways, and that plea is always spoken, or revealed, in experiences with the land. In the story, the father whose first thought is to scold at the sign of peaches later plows under the wild phlox, a flower with a fireworks of pale blue petals. A daughter goes mad in the book — not the narrator, Marget, the middle child, but the eldest, Kerrin, who reveals her agony by disappearing nights into the woods. She comes back with her hair wild as if she had lain on pine needles or in a haystack. She escapes outdoors for her pleasure too. Sexuality forces the issue of pleasure to the foreground, where the stakes are life and death, or certainly health versus insanity.

Johnson was born in 1910 at the tail end of the time when agriculture was a normal part of most daily life. In *Now in November,* written when she was in her early twenties, she delivers a destitute family out of the factories and back to the land. In one of the many profound depression-era reappraisals of the dream of utopia attached to the family farm, Johnson finds the problem of self, of pleasure, of justice completely unsolved in the land. Between that first book and her last significant one, *The Inland Island* (1969), she crafts a new family farm. It is a homestead where Johnson and her second husband, Grant Cannon, pledge to allow the wilderness to return.[3] Scrub reclaims the pasture, a forsythia becomes a wild overgrown wicker cage, and Johnson walks in the field while she thinks of the bombs bursting over Vietnam. The contradiction of selfish pleasure and vast social ills is at the heart of this book that Edward Abbey labeled a "hymn of love and wrath."[4] In that book, Johnson finally makes a peace between the person of conscience that she is and her own desire for beautiful sanity.

I live on an island of sanity: the island of this place. I am fortunate. I no longer ask why. The small animals, the birds go about their ancient and patterned ways. They do not enlarge their territories or change their patterns in order that they may kill and die more quickly. They do not care about us one way or the other. They do not know what we are doing. They do not know what we have done. I come before them, a five-foot five-inch shape, giving off what particles of warning smell I do not know, but I am not a shape of known guilt to them. I do not stand for anything that man has done to man. Of that they know nothing.[5]

A family farm dedicated to preserving wilderness is an appropriate symbol with which to end the twentieth century. An "inland island," in Johnson's telling, is a complex and fractured answer to the question of how and whether to pursue happiness in an unjust world.

In this chapter I tell you more about Johnson's ideas than the theme precisely warrants. I ask you to forgive this extravagance; to be patient and to read the tangents. I want to help correct the lack of familiarity with her name and ideas. Many of her works are no longer in print, and much that I have studied will only be read by researchers. I want to take advantage of her work and her pleasure because she represents a tradition that gets erased in the (self-fulfilling) accounts of the "mainstream."

Josephine Johnson's work is a good guide because she was a careful, smart thinker and a terrific writer. And also because she was given to depression. She struggled with the self's aversion to itself, a microcosm of humanity's aversion to itself. In a century of genocides and environmental mutilations, hating humanity can be easier than celebrating it. At an interior, private level,

Johnson lived out the same conflict. Disgust and dismay were familiar companions. Having sympathy for herself was difficult. Here is part of a note she hammered out to herself, key by stubborn typewriter key. It was among her papers kept in archives at Washington University in St. Louis. I am hoping you will feel a certain sympathy and laugh with her as she laughs at herself. I quote the original spelling to protect the unadulterated quality of this glimpse into her personal life.

> Stop being so gllomoomy
> Stop talking about your age.
> Act cheerful. Stop being gloomy.
>
> Think about other people more. Not just The Poor, but
>   cheerful people.
> . . .
> Choose the brighter of two prospects. It might come true.
> Pretend you are wonderful. Pretend you know what you are
>   doing. Sometimes you do.
> Be satis fied.
> Act to other people like you lkike them to act to you. (ie —
>   cheerful. Not gloomy.)[6]

Notice how the opposite of gloomy reads like an American self-help manual: Appear cheerful. Have self-esteem so that you can be pragmatic, organized, productive. This is the Dale Carnegie school of dealing with the travails of the world. Think positive, it says. In the following pages, I weave something as personal as mood and mental health with a definition of liberalism exemplified by Johnson but forgotten by history and historians. What emerged as mainstream liberalism instead played more on notions of virility than on anything like Johnson's self-searching.

There is a larger social fabric that I mean to pull with this corner piece about the self's right to happiness versus the nobility of hard labor. There is a family of ideas about the temptations of consumption versus the obligation of restraint. The larger picture builds on a notion of time. Condemning indulgences derives from a philosophy of progress over time. Each sacrifice now produces nothing less than the pinnacle of civilization in the long run. Johnson's rebuttal of that dream was the beginning of her social philosophy.

On the family farm, you reap what you sow. Each action builds to a harvest; every wasteful moment betrays the future. Frittering away a lifetime on casual sensuality — wasting peaches — does not make Whitman's comfortable homestead.

Mixed into the foundation of the family farm symbol is a worldview about time. It counts on a steady, progressive advance. Biologist and essayist Stephen Jay Gould divides the history of Euro-American time consciousness into two dialectical themes. Drawing on the differing arguments of scientific and religious authorities from the seventeenth to the nineteenth centuries, his book *Time's Arrow, Time's Cycle* describes the gradual intellectual triumph of the progressive "arrow" of evolution.[7] In the earlier, cyclical view of time, the days melt into one moment to be changed only at the return of God's grace. The past, present and future are like seasons that appear, reappear and disappear. Moral time is more important than economic time. Time is a circle: human effort does not ascend; any moment is like the next in the context of the eventual cataclysm of God's judgment. The contrasting view, of progress, was not so much a new view as a long-held subsidiary one. By the 1830s, however, it had wrestled its main competitor to the ground. Scientists, many moralists and certainly capitalists began to trade on the assumption of estimable futures. For them, time builds: like rungs on an evolutionary ladder, like stages of mud to clay to brick to skyscraper, like money in the bank, "progress" is a belief system with a heavy moral boot.

Put those tuppence in the bank, young man. Avoid the temptation to go fly a kite. The demands of civilization that the movie *Mary Poppins* gently criticized correspond to the progressive sense of time. The arrow of time also corresponded to a sense of place. Evolution begins in dark primeval wilderness and moves out from this backward state forward to the paved streets of Europe.

The ideology that I am describing, obviously, is deeply imperialistic. To best portray the sensibility, then, I turn to one of the British Empire's most thoughtful critics: Joseph Conrad. In 1899 Conrad wrote a novel of a white man who was late. Kurtz, Conrad's famous soldier of European ivory fortunes, does not return to his company's base. At the appointed hour, the narrator, Marlowe, is sent after Kurtz, only to discover that Kurtz has fallen into primitive sin. The primeval jungle is at history's beginnings. Marlowe understands the sound of its screams, its desires — he recognizes its heart of darkness from his own inner urges. Away from the "solid pavement" of civilization, he sees with a kind of ironic consciousness how much is denied; how much is paved over. Conrad's writing builds on an imagination of black (primeval) and white (advanced) continents. It is a paradigm he is at pains to criticize. But there is more subtle geography at work. There is an earthly humanity and a heavenly one. The earth is a place to "live" in. To transcend the earthly home requires something other than life or even a denial of life. "You may be such a thunderingly exalted creature as to be altogether deaf and blind to anything but heavenly sights and sounds," Conrad writes. "Then the earth for you is only a standing place. . . . [T]he earth for [most of us] is a place to live in."[8] Ivory merchants marching across the jungle live with sights and sounds and terrible temptations. The passage continues: "And there, don't you see? your strength comes in, . . . your power of devotion, not to yourself, but to an obscure, back-breaking business."[9] Restraint makes Progress. Conrad is speaking here about the ivory business, about captaining a ship, about disciplining yourself to the plow. This is a moral trade; in exchange for commitment to some obscure, backbreaking business, there is success over primeval humanity.

Evolution is a kind of time. But it is also a kind of place — a symbolic landscape, the physical manifestation of progress. Time's arrow travels from dense jungle to London streets. The landscape is a moral testing ground of restraint winning out over indulgence. Desire, indulgence, beauty became a kind of backwardness in this imagining of civilization.

The family farm symbolically offered a solution to the extreme choices of primeval versus civilized humanity. It represented a microcosm combining both progress and pleasure. I am speaking here strictly of the symbol, not of reality. The family farm was a place of civilization, like London, and yet also its antidote, like nature. A valley of family farms was a magic place that could be imagined in Africa or New Jersey, in the northern or southern hemisphere, in black or white. It could soothe the antithetical choices that Conrad's novel makes so stark.

In the 1930s, as the Great Depression slammed the door on the indulgent 1920s, family farms pop up everywhere in literature, film and documentary sagas. It was a heyday of sorts for the symbol. Between 1920 and 1945, all the farm-based novels add up to what critic Roy W. Meier has argued is a distinct genre similar to the proletarian novel of the same period.[10] I believe that the family farm may have been a popular symbol precisely because the symbol has a history of representing the fulcrum between subsistence and luxury. This historical moment (as Josephine Johnson leaves childhood and becomes an adult novelist) is, worldwide, a convulsive moment in the debate of restraint versus indulgence. Ever since, the disciplined life has been less securely righteous.

The convulsion of the Great Depression was, in some ways, the end of a long transition during which a "culture of consumption" took hold. This is what many historians have concluded.[11] They argue that the balance between restraint and indulgence tipped in the advice columns, the sermons, the advertisements, the "prescriptive literature" of the 1920s and 1930s. As is typical of such cultural upheavals, the promotion of a culture of restraint remained a major theme in many other sermons, editorials and novels. But the weight shifted. The historians of this school juxtapose this consumer orientation to the earlier Victorian culture that valued the unpopular choices of a man of "character" rather than the popular appeal of a man of charisma or "personality." To Victorians, such a charismatic man was a "rake." To them, Babe Ruth with his women and cussing and charm would not be a hero. A man of character resisted temptation and held to his ideas regardless of popular disapproval. The assertion that a shift occurred toward a culture of consumption is an argument that is emphatically about cultural messages, not necessarily lived realities. The advice to consume more freely was, of course, in the interest of mass manufacturers whose business depended on mass consumerism. All those Model Ts, toasters, vacuum cleaners must be consumed.[12] But historians are not usually satisfied with the brutally reductionist suggestion that Capitalism Made Us Do It. People made choices in part on the basis of newly emerging belief systems. Here is one example of an earnest prophet of the notion that an indulgent, consumer-based capitalism could ensure justice for all. Bruce Barton, an advertising magnate, wrote a book about Jesus titled *The Man Nobody Knows,* in which Christianity endorses modern capitalism. In Barton's book, Jesus was the first business executive; the biblical proverbs were advertising slogans in disguise; and water turned to wine to keep a good party going. It may sound ridiculous, but the book was a best-seller. Consumerism wasn't evil; restraint wasn't righteous. Instead the tables were turned. Barton promoted a belief in the moral righteousness of a consumer-driven economy.

In *Now in November,* Johnson would reject the older, Victorian "culture of character" down to its most private restrictions. But she would not be satisfied with the alternatives that emerged in midcentury. Then, from a perspective gained after having lived through two world wars and then Korea and Vietnam, she would write her solution. In *The Inland Island,* she urged her own version of a culture of consumption. "A great, triumphant cry of self is needed. The will to live, and to have life more abundantly," she wrote.[13] This is a version of a new moral logic that is related to a new landscape, a new kind of family farm. Her wild family farm, like Whitman's vista of comfortable homesteads and Conrad's *Heart of Darkness,* exists in a time and place. Her "island of sanity" is a refuge from arrow and cycle both. It will be quite difficult for her to find.

Rebutting the sense of progress built into the symbolic foundation of the family farm was a task Johnson took up with regret.

She began with the wish that the family farm would work. Her family history predisposed her to appreciate the potential benefit that a private acre of land could bestow. In fact, when she was to write an autobiographical book, *Seven Houses,* later in life, she placed herself in a long tradition of franklins. The old English term "franklin," which was also her mother's maiden name, refers to landowners of free but not noble birth with fervent attachment to specific pieces of land.[14] Her father's family members were among the first white settlers of the St. Louis, Missouri, area. She grew up in a rural landscape, but rural does not mean wild country in this context: she lived on the country estate of her parents in Hillbrook, Missouri, in a deliberately well managed landscape.[15] Seated atop a hill with a view of rolling hills and a still pond, the Johnson house was filled with books, art (some painted by Josephine herself) and sisters. After the early death of her father, it was a completely feminine household presided over by her mother. Living in a bucolic setting was a pattern well established by her relatives. Her maternal grandparents were Irish immigrants who moved up from indentured beginnings to a country house, one staffed by servants. From her hillside childhood home, Johnson also visited less genteel rural settings, including her socialist uncle's dairy farm and her unmarried aunts' kerosene lamp–lit cottage.

Johnson's beliefs about what constitutes a good, just society developed out of her literal landedness. But when she focused on the family farm, the hallowed symbol of fairness, she found "uncertain and shifting ground." In the opening pages of *Now in November,* the Haldmarnes return to the rural place where the father, Arnold, had lived as a boy. The barns are "year-rotted," and Arnold reveals the secret that the land is mortgaged and so is not, after all, an unencumbered sanctuary. They are fleeing a world "all wrong, confused, and shouting at itself" — the depression — and would not have come to this place if Arnold's job in the lumber factories had not vanished. As the character Marget tells it, looking back eleven years later, they expected in the family farm a life that "was no less hard and no less ready to thwart a man or cast him out, but gave him something, at least in return."[16]

Johnson begins with the hopes traditionally associated with the family farm. Then she takes apart the Jeffersonian ideal piece by treasured piece. First, a farm cannot guarantee a comfortable economic life. Second, it fails to create democracy in miniature, something it cannot do because the "family" in "family farm" is traditionally undemocratic. Finally, there are no building blocks for "progress" in farms or farmers because the human mind on which the entire formula is based is itself on "shifting and uncertain ground." Much better than this shorthand, however, are the actual scenes and situations that Johnson develops to make these points.

The tone of Johnson's evaluation of the family farm ideal is not bitter, or triumphant, or cynical. It is gloomy, sensitive, beautiful. Later she would call this deeply shattering book a "realistic idyl," but the idyllic part is hard to find in its pages.[17] While most reviewers at the time praised the book as poetic and lyrical, one dissented, hearing instead the "prolonged accent of Irish keening."[18] The problems were as "new and old and stale and important as the weather," as Marget thinks during one argument between Grant and her father.[19]

The story shatters for the reader any sense of economic security guaranteed by honest labor in the soil. This was a truth being repeated everywhere during the depression. A coroner, attending the death of the eldest daughter, accepts a second piece of cake, commenting, "You farmers have got stuff to eat anyway. That's something, ent it?"[20] He doesn't realize the cake has the last of the family's molasses in it. At one level, the failure of farms to feed families is the result of a twisted national economy. Here is the familiar story of the farmer reaping little because of economic forces beyond local control—the price of corn, the market for milk. The first hired hand quits the place in midseason to join a road crew, and Arnold, the father, bursts out, exasperated, "A farm ought to pay as good as a road. No road's going to feed a man!"[21] This theme echoes through the book, and the lack of economic security is contrasted with the presumed correlation between land and wealth that is codified even in the tax laws. At the end, an assessor values the farm for its buildings, not seeing the empty space in the silo.[22]

The distant national and worldwide economy is one reason why the family farm is a disappointment. But the problems are homegrown as well. To puncture any naive hope in a better local solution, Johnson's story of the family farm includes the neighbors. On one side are an African-American tenant family, the Ramseys. The Ramseys are equally good farmers, facing the same drought. The Haldmarnes have accepted help from them. But a landlord forces the Ramseys from their home, feeling free to target them first because of their race. And the Haldmarnes, though sympathetic, can do nothing but stand helplessly, hopelessly, by. Meanwhile, the neighbors on the other side are the Rathmans. They have no mortgage; their land is rich, and they have grown sons to help with the work. But the elder Rathman falls and breaks his hip. By then his sons have left the farm for better-paying work, and in the end, the Rathmans too find security an illusion. Not even nature protects life from such insecurity. The opening narration of the book looks back on the eleven years on the farm and describes the land as "something both treacherous and kind, which could be trusted only to be inconstant, and would go its own way as though we were never born."

The hope of franklins, of independent landownership, proved wanting first of all because it did not, in fact, produce enough freedom from want. Family farmers could not make a living; had not been able to for a long time and, on closer inspection, did not even in the once-upon-a-time days. But Johnson's inquisition did not stop there. Even if the farm could be a viable economic unit, strong enough so that the household could turn its back on the rest of society and live "independently," would the family farm represent a moral social order? That depended on the family.

Arising in the context of the depression and in one of the more obvious convulsions in the rural economy, family farm literature is easily assumed to be a *cri de coeur* over the prospects of the small farm. But it is as much the family as the farm that was the problem. Injustice built into the family itself became a main theme in the most well known family farm novels of the period. The solutions presented in these novels varied widely, as can be quickly demonstrated by comparing John Steinbeck's *The Grapes of Wrath* (1939) and Gladys Hasty Carroll's *As the Earth Turns* (1933), two of the best-selling farm novels of the times. In the first, Steinbeck creates perhaps the most famous matriarch of American literature. Ma Joad's charge is to keep the family together, even if under new management.[23] Meanwhile, *As the Earth Turns* taught that the old patriarchal family was as underappreciated as all folk or rural life was. The pleasures of the turning seasons are enough for the good daughter and her benevolent father, Mark Shaw.[24]

Johnson's prize-winning novel takes an extremely hard look at the "family" in the family farm symbol. The sexist division of labor has high costs in the book. The frustration of being confined to girls' tasks precipitates the eldest daughter Kerrin's slide toward madness. The father resolutely imposes restrictions based on separate spheres for males and females. Kerrin turns her intelligence toward the selection of crops, but the father won't listen, ridiculing her suggestions.[25] Kerrin plays at boys' games, learning to throw a knife, but when she attempts to demonstrate this competence to her father as a birthday gift, he knocks the knife from her hand. The blade, flying wild, strikes the family dog, who bleeds terribly before he must be shot dead. Kerrin's precarious sanity and her striking intelligence make her more vulnerable than her sisters to the cost of having her competence so rigidly contained. Merle, the youngest, simply reacts with matter-of-fact contempt.[26] She doesn't much look forward to the arrival of the hired hand, Grant Koven — even though it is the only change in years on the farm. "We'll find him no different than any other [man]," she predicts. "They're like as ponds. Seem to think that just being born sets them apart as gods!"[27] But Merle ends up surprised: Grant offers to help her with the laundry, a woman's task. Marget watches Merle stare at Grant squeezing the laundry practically dry. "She thought him a little mad, I guess," Marget comments, "but hoped he'd finish before the spell passed over."[28]

The daughters and some of the younger men reject the undemocratic family in *Now in November* but not the elders.

The sense of generational disjuncture comes out most clearly in Marget's observations of her mother. Her mother sees marriage as "a religion and long giving." The daughters chafe under the limits of separate spheres. The gift of faith seems to insulate the mother from these knotty questions. Marget envies the mother her certainty, a conviction that the world is put together for the right, but believes it is something to be born with, like hair color.[29] In other books Johnson widens this point to indicate a larger social order jarred by this generational divide. In the autobiographical *Seven Houses* (1973), she sees in a photograph of her parents and grandparents a world in which people had their places. "In the year before I was born the family sat to be photographed on the front porch. Each person clearly him or herself. Aware of their role in life. Their *place*. There were places then."[30] These places include the position of maids, like the dark-haired Native American house servant, her race like her gender establishing steps in the hierarchy.[31]

Injustice within the family was a common preoccupation in the reassessment of the symbol of the family farm. To the extent that there was an orthodoxy on which family farm writers could draw in reframing the family, it was to center the home around the companionate marriage. Joined by love, husband and wife could work together, sharing tasks in a trope of a "comradely ideal," as historian Barbara Melosh has phrased it.[32] The comradely ideal, revealed in depression-era art, fiction and film, showed husband and wife laboring side by side in the fields. It was just this notion of the family that Johnson herself set up and knocked down in *Now in November*. Johnson's narrator, Marget, falls deeply in love with the hired hand. They might make just such a comradely pair, given Grant's willingness to do laundry and otherwise share responsibilities. But Marget is physically plain as well as introspective and shy, and Grant wants only to be her friend. The eldest sister, Kerrin, also loves Grant, and she throws herself at him clumsily, embarrassing the reserved Marget. Grant loves the third girl, Merle, but Merle does not love him, not out of meanness or intended rejection, but simply because of the seeming randomness of the heart's affections. Love does shimmer as a hope that could give meaning to the labor of their lives, regardless of how that labor might be divided. But like so much else, love proves unreliable, inconstant, unpredictable — too often unrequited.

Rather than a romantic comradeship, the most realistic solution to the family economy at the core of the Jeffersonian dream for Johnson is a jury-rigged combination of adults. The replacement for the nuclear family in her novel is two sisters, Marget and Merle. They are not inexhaustible matriarchs; they are stumbling, tired women carrying the weight of the mortgage. This is the realism of the novel that turns my heart every time I return to the book. For Johnson, there is no essential strength in women that makes it possible for them to do what the men could not. The mother burns to death in a desperate attempt to save the farm after road crews inadvertently (and stupidly) set fire to the drought-dry fields. With the mother dies a whole world, and the father, sapped, becomes the land he intended to conquer. Their identities merge in the author's descriptions of the father as "old and querulous and able only to shell beans in the sun" and the farm as like "a querulous sick old man whining for attention every hour."[33]

The disappointments of the family farm begin to add up. The ideology fails by assuming that labor in the soil will feed a family. It falls from the standard of equal justice for all by its treatment of women. And deeper still than the thwarted talents of girls and women, there is a failure to reckon with pleasure. Pleasure is downplayed partly *because* it is something for which the women stand. The division between pleasure and restraint takes on a gendered cast, one that Johnson reproduces subtly in her book. It is the father's determined economies that confine life to the round of feeding, washing, clothing. It is the daughters and the mother who try to educate him to yield to the "intervals and things stolen between." The undervaluing of momentary pleasures occurs because it appears as women's judgment. Even more darkly, the denial of pleasures in general coincides with the denial of women's sexuality. The "intervals and things stolen between" spread from losses in the land — from the pretty phlox — to small consumer pleasures and, most damagingly, to a frustration of sexuality.

Johnson is gently incisive. She is not an angry feminist at this point in her life but a pained one. Marget, our interpreter, is more thoughtful than accusing, and she is sympathetic to her father. The mortgage shrouds him in a fog of worry, and this makes him hold to a frugality so intense that Marget does not dare buy him a birthday gift, knowing he would only see "the farm sold under our feet for the sake of a ten-cent tie."[34] Seeing his intent, she hates and loves him for his meanness. "All the time I would feel us there on his shoulders, heavy as stone on his mind — all four of our lives to carry everywhere."[35] His refusal to let his daughters be "sons," to work the farm with him and share the responsibility, is one cause of his desperation. His fear becomes stubborn, relentless economizing. The mother tries to loosen him up, but he won't give. "It would have taken so little to make us happy. A little more rest, a little more money — it was the nearness that tormented," Marget says.[36]

The pleading for beauty is modest: for ten-cent ties; for an end to accusing looks when the mother opens the last can of peaches for Grant's first meal with them; for a few hours off. *Now in November* is hardly an embrace of rampant consumption, of crass consumer goods like the neighbor Rathmans' son's pursuit of a fancy car, nor is it an abandonment of sacrifice for the sake of material rewards. Still the weight shifts, that these small indulgences may be the only respite in lives so laboriously lived.

At another level, however, the demand for pleasure is not modest but a matter of life and death. The stakes are not just happiness. The risk is a denial of life itself; of healthy life. Freudian ideas about the relationship of sexuality to sanity seem to have influenced Johnson's work. The father not only denies Kerrin's competence in daily life but also refuses to acknowledge her sexual "maleness," her sexual desire that causes her to roam late into the night.[37] Kerrin is the suffocated woman in the culture of character; the frustrated woman in the Victorian attic; the wanderer in thunderstorms. Rather than serenely removed by womanhood from the gusts of sexual temptation, Kerrin is "restless and savage," unsatisfied by the meager courting of farm boys. She rides out in the dark, sometimes going foxhunting with men, sometimes walking alone and coming back frost-rumpled and with her hair wild. It is not made exactly plain what Kerrin does at night; only that she has no right to do it. "'Where's Kerrin?' Father would keep on asking, would read a chapter and go peer out into the moonlight. 'Why don't you keep her home, Willa?' he'd say to Mother. . . . 'No girl ought to be out at night this way!'" In the character of Kerrin, Johnson takes the pained feminism of undervalued household pleasures a step farther: what is it that women have no right to? What pleasure is denied them? When, in the end, the father mistakes Grant's cautionary touch of Kerrin's hand as an embrace, Kerrin strikes out at her father, throwing a knife at him and missing. The girl can have no claim to passion. Even when she takes her own life at the end of the scene, her father cannot understand her desperation. "He could not believe she had killed herself. A raw, unnatural thing. A thing no girl had a right to do."[38]

Even further, Kerrin's suicide, though tragic and terrible, is the healthier of alternatives. When the saner Marget bids good-bye to Grant, she wishes silently that she could forget everything else and throw herself at Grant the way mad Kerrin had done.

> There was the awful love, the desire shut back, sick in the throat. . . . Let me go — let me out! — O God please! . . . and the mind sitting there cold and hard and yet fearful: You can't do this . . . you can't do it . . . you can't. — It's a lie the body is a prison! It's the mind, I tell you! — always the cold, strong mind that's jailer.[39]

And so again, how sane is the absence of peaches? How do need and luxury separate? Passionate desire is delicious when it is greedy, hungry. Grabbing, insistent, demanding. What has happened to the franklins, the landowners who rely on order to create a good life?

The mythic family farm sets up a host of false assumptions. But Johnson is not content to enumerate the naive economic for-mula of Jeffersonian agrarianism, or to attack the Victorian fam-ily or to insist on the need for pleasure. Underneath all these ill-conceived assumptions lies a core conviction that is also false: in the certainty that a reasonable person can sort rationally between luxury and subsistence.

Land again becomes the litmus test, proving that a reasonable person — proving that human reason — is itself on "shifting and uncertain ground." The mind proves various. Reality, even of the most certain thing of all, the land, is relative.[40] Johnson's characters have emphatically different relationships to the land. For Merle and Marget, the land was "a thing loved for its own sake, giving a sort of ecstasy and healing."[41] For Kerrin, though, the land is "only a place to stay in, lonely as peaks or islands."[42] The father loved the land "in a proud, owned way, — only because it was his, and for what it would mean to us."[43] The young man Grant takes neither security, nor healing, nor escape in nature. He relies on human invention; on mechanics. "Don't trust anything natural, Marget," he warns her when they search for his lost pocket watch. "Only the little wheels."[44] Marget is herself aware of these contrasting perceptions and enumerates them.[45]

One needs a mind to sort, cleanly, between wasteful indulgence and rightful claims. But individual perception muddies the task, and so does the unconscious. Marget learns of this other part of the mind — in herself as well as in others — by watching Kerrin. She sets up a sense of dual reality in the early pages of the book that continues throughout. On page 33, Marget observes:

> And there was the double life, the two parts not within each
> other nor even parallel. The one made up of things done
> day after day with comfort and soberness . . . the saucepans
> and heavy dishes . . . The open life and the one that was
> greater of the two, calm, prosaic . . . rational. And there
> was the inner walking on the edge of darkness, the peering

into black doorways. The unrevealed answer which must be somewhere . . . this under-life which when traced or held to was not there, and yet kept coming back and thrust up like an iron dike through the solid layers of the sane and understood.

Marget watches her sister Kerrin's queer behavior, her troubled sleeps, and feels fear — "fear that life wasn't safe and comfortable, or even just tight and hard, but that there was an edge of darkness which was neither, and was something which no one could ever explain or understand."[46]

For the narrator Marget, the seeker of meaning, struggling on a search for mature faith, the unaccountability of the mind proves intensely frustrating. Awareness burdens Marget and she cannot sleep for the effort to understand. "Every new thought seemed to open a door, but when the mind rushed forward to enter, the door was slammed shut, leaving it dazed outside."[47]

Perhaps the scale of the problem can be made clearer by placing the previous sentence in a social-historical context. Set aside the character Marget for a moment. Think instead of the widespread collapse of confidence in humanity seen in European literature after the terrors of World War I. Think of the many expressions of the fundamental modern sense of "shifting and uncertain ground." The center cannot hold. Abstract modern art was offering a different sense of reality, in the fractured planes and disjointed human faces. How was one to be idealistic and realistic? "Every new thought seemed to open a door, but when the mind rushed forward to enter, the door was slammed shut, leaving it dazed outside."

Faith in the human mind lay underneath the worldview that

invented the "family farm" as a symbol of utopia. This faith was compromised in twentieth-century books like Johnson's *Now in November* by the role of the unconscious and by awareness that the perception of reality depends in part on the predispositions of the viewer. What died in family farm novels like Johnson's was the Enlightenment and its convictions in a rational, ordered and progressive universe.

Faith in God could not mitigate these qualms about human reason. For questioners like Johnson, a return to God could not assuage these doubts. All of Johnson's books wrestle with agnosticism, including her first, which finds the narrator constantly wishing she could participate in the various faiths, such as those she observes in her mother, in Grant or among pious neighbors. Marget exclaims, "[I] wanted something outside myself," but she needs a "faith that would *fit* life, not just hide it."[48] The great dilemma, both for faith in human reason and for faith in God, is the manifest suffering of people in the here and now. If you were willing to look in the face of this suffering, to know it and refuse to turn away from it, there were no easy answers.

> Perhaps if we could have been cut off from all seeing and hearing of those rare safe ones who had no need, we could have begun to blame it on God and be at peace. Knowledge is a two-edged knife, all blade, with no handle for even the owner to strike out with.[49]

Johnson cannot "blame" the reality of human suffering on God and "be at peace." Instead she is left with the two-edged blade of knowledge and nothing to hold on to. Reason has failed her — it is uncertain and shifting ground. And so has blind faith.

The disillusionments of the symbolic family farm added up to a potentially paralyzing despair. Without a formula for economic fairness, without a building block for democracy, with only a jury-rigged combination of adults who cannot themselves, with any certainty, find rules to impose on the local or large world — how then is a good society imaginable? From this depth of despair about the human prospect, what kind of conscious political program is possible? What kind of actions could one throw oneself behind? Here Johnson's life is a better guide than her "keening" novel. For some time after Johnson's first book, she remained a vocal participant in the debate. Matching the step of like-minded intellectuals of her time, she flirted with communism with her next novel, *Jordanstown,* published in 1937. She cannot quite give up, though, on the franklins: on the belief in private property. A piece of proletarian fiction, the novel offers a thinly veiled comment on the political programs of the New Deal, especially the Works Progress Administration. A character, Anna, wants more than make-work solutions. She complains that it is not enough to "dig ditches no place and change creeks to go some place else — and nothin' in the end. Nothin' for ourselves. Nothin' to take pride in. No place to talk in. No place to live in. Black ants scuttling on othah people's piles." Instead the abused workers want their own place — "something of ouah own . . . something of ouah own."[50]

Long-term hope, in other words, still lay somehow in ownership. In her nonfiction writings of this same period, Johnson said that the more radical New Deal community programs were on the right track. In a journalistic piece about the Southern Tenant Farmers' Union, she took the side of the embattled strikers. She was arrested during her attempt to report their side of the story. The tenant farmers needed more opportunities like the one provided by the nearby experimental La Forge community, where homesites were being parceled out by the government. There, Johnson wrote, "100 families are coming to know the meaning of security, of actual comfort, of hope in the future for themselves and their children."[51] She argued that a "large-scale program of rehabilitation" would repeat this experiment many times over. Such was indeed the hope of La Forge's parent organization, the Rural Resettlement Administration (RRA), and its predecessor, the Division of Subsistence Homesteads, but support for the programs collapsed by the early forties.[52] The RRA plan was the kind of political program toward which Johnson, with her attachment to place, was drawn. Like others, she did revise the traditional setpiece: in *Jordanstown*, the property that provides the sense of ownership, of having a stake, is communally owned. In fact, *Jordanstown*'s emphasis on group ownership showed Johnson at her farthest left inclination. During this same period, she contributed to the *New Masses;* in the entry she sent to *Twentieth-Century American Authors,* she urged the general abolition of the "profit system."[53] When, however, she became specific about where hope lay, she always returned to a deeply American tradition, the Jeffersonian connection between place, property ownership and democracy.

Despite all the doubts she raised in *Now in November,* Johnson yielded to the temptation to put her faith back in family farms. The depth of despair that she had written into the mind of the novel's narrator did not, in fact, destroy Johnson's own capacity to act in the world. She paired the dark feeling of her award-winning first novel with an extremely active life in the mid-1930s. She published five books in as many years; did some reporting; wrote sympathetic portraits of patients to help a cancer hospital for the indigent raise money; pursued an interest in art and painted murals at a school for "Disabled and Delinquent Negro Children"; traveled to Europe; took two dancing classes at a time; served as president of the Consumers' Co-operative in St. Louis and on the board of the St. Louis Urban League; and married the regional attorney for the National Labor Relations Board, her first husband, Thurlow Smoot.[54] In this period in her life, she was a vibrant, committed woman, with an alter ego — a cast of alter egos that included Marget, Kerrin, the easygoing Merle and the novel's union organizer Grant.

The profound, deeply philosophical problems she had uncovered in *Now in November* were not going to vanish, however. Only much later would she commit to paper a hint of how she resolved her love of land with her sense of conscience — of knowing how unjust the world was. The result shows her coming to some kind of terms with being gloomy. Reckoning with hopelessness is a problem that is personal and also historical. It took a while for me to understand Johnson's solution.

History does not readily admit to moods. "Depression" is a term used only in economic contexts. Not many writers will refer anymore to a "zeitgeist," the German term denoting the spirit or feeling of an era. Assigning a mood to a time period offends current sensibilities. Historians by and large learn from their research that race, class, gender, religion and many other factors dissipate any "zeitgeist" thesis into hundreds of contradictions.

My own intellectual training tells me also that mood is an inappropriate concept to mix with culture. Cultural swings derive from a vast ecology of factors: an interrelated system of powerful economic, political and social forces. The danger to avoid is a too-close comparison of the psychology of an individual with the psychology of a group. And yet there is something to learn from moods, from depression in the psychological sense, from the self's aversion to itself. Humanity's aversion to humanity has been a common enough theme in modern thought. Salves have been applied; solutions sought.

Depression is a mood "disorder"; a state of being drunk with insight about the limits of the good. Depression can derive from observation of the world as easily as from the hard scrutiny of — a brutal honesty toward — the self. For Josephine Johnson, war was the inescapable teacher. She was seven years old when World War I began, and at the age of fifty-nine she looked back and declared: "Every woman of my generation is sick of war. Fifty years of war. Wars rumored, wars beginning, wars fought, wars ending, wars paid for, wars endured."[55] Equally, she was disheartened by the destruction of nature: "I have had a love for the land all my life, and today when all life is a life against nature, against man's whole being, there is a sense of urgency, a need to record and cherish, and to share this love before it is too late. Time passes — mine and the land's."[56]

The limits of goodness in the world have fueled many political platforms. For example, the religious thinker and moral activist Reinhold Niebuhr preached a "conservative realism" after World War II. He saw the necessity for discipline and restraint in response to the fundamental (i.e., "original") sinfulness of humanity. Johnson would take a different path in *The Inland Island*. Instead of a renewal of vows of discipline, of noble suffering, she said what we needed was "the will to live, and to have life more abundantly."

The will to have life more abundantly is a political program that is morally much more comfortable to urge on others than on oneself. Especially in the state of disgust over one's own weakness, suffering seems like a more appropriate reward than pleasure. Johnson was an expert on the limitations of her own goodness. She observed herself under February's glare. "I know myself in this terrible white light. One's a coward. One's timid and therefore treacherous. This is important to know."[57]

Tormented by her lack of wit or wisdom — by her aversion to herself — she sought comfort. She tried to find it in "the heart's image of the wild free fox." Many days she searched for a sight of those elusive animals. At last she met the mother fox face to face.

> In the long looking, I had seen her as she really was — small, thin, harried, heavily burdened — not free at all. Bound around by instinct, as I am bound by custom and concern. And so, although I saw the grey foxes again that summer coming close to the kitchen door at night for food, the heart's fox vanished forever that evening in the woods.[58]

Private depression and societal despair are kin to each other, and this deep tie between the personal and the political takes center stage in Johnson's landmark *The Inland Island*. A moody book, it shifts between her own search for comfort and angry outbursts at war, racism and inequality. Her exploration corresponds to my larger question of what right to happiness can be demanded when basic needs remain unmet. The dilemma of grabbing an abundant life translated, for Johnson, into a question about whether she ought to have any right to her most frequent desire: to walk in the fields. She found such pleasure in nature but she did not want to be a "weak woman birder."[59] In her moral quandary, she needed to reject the notion that if she were a person of conscience, she would leave the land she loved. Part-time protest was not enough. She imagined a reproving God who commanded: "Get back to My work, which has no deer, no mink, no woods. Which has only people and suffering forever and ever and ever."[60]

Punishment is easier to dispense than abundance. There is an equation, handed down in many varieties of religious and moral traditions, that bad behavior counteracted by self-inflicted suffering will add up to rectitude. What the world needs is a good spanking. Or at least to go without our supper — without whatever pleases us. Then we might shape up.

The urgent call for a will to have life more abundantly, including for herself and her pleasure in the land, was part of a larger journey of discovery that Johnson recorded in the diary-like book. In it she explores ideas about human nature and comes to the conclusion that a person "does not change to marble under pressure." Instead people's characters form as conglomerate rocks do — pebbles and boulder clumped together, some clay mixed with beautiful crystals, all of it "waiting to be interpreted."[61] For her, humanity was not by definition sinful. In this conglomerate image of the soul, Johnson saw "the refused, the ungiven, the undone" lying inside the mass like a fossil insect. The rock took its shape from undissolving memories: "Love, failure, hate — or that lost ice-cream soda on the streetcar ride."[62]

Johnson's journey toward a politics of abundance began with a vocabulary of mental health rather than of sin or salvation. Desires even for ridiculous lost ice-cream sodas shaped the soul. So it goes. She did not reject or disapprove of this conglomerate nature with its lumps of feeling. She despised instead the urge to "tidy, tidy, tidy, tidy — lives, leaves . . . trees . . . emotions . . . minds."[63]

Sanity in a world gone mad was worth something. The sanity began with forgiveness for the self's lack of progress. Instead of a steady march toward civilization, Johnson observed her own soul in its convulsions. In the book she had written at age twenty-four, she despaired over the jagged motions of humanity. "The earth turns in great movements, but we jerk about on its surface like gnats," the narrator Marget concludes at the end.[64] With fifty-nine years and her own disappointments and jerky motion behind her, she observed herself and the world with the same cutting insight but something like loving acceptance instead of despair. She made room for the crowd inside her.

> All the undisciplined, poorly organized pack of women and children who live inside me. Self-indulgent, easily tired, short of intra-span [*sic*]; longing to clean house, watch birds, read books, paint pictures walk in the fields, walk in the fields, eat in the fields . . . die in the fields. And some of them want to save the world, clean up the cities and rivers, tear down the Pentagon.[65]

In the world, she also lived differently with the manifest disorder around her. Playing on the title of her earlier work, at the end of her career she writes that "now in November" she sees a great formlessness that "means both disaster and freedom. Many of the young will be freed, many lost. Freedom is no guarantee of anything. It is only defined today by what it is not. What it *is* takes forms strange and of infinite variety — bizarre as in a masquerade."[66]

Sanity, a kid of mental health, was the model that shaped the political aspirations of this reflective book. In her walks on their wild, overgrowing family farm, she sought self-forgiveness, and she also sought natural beauty. The simple pleasure of beauty in nature was by itself a version of indulgence for this woman from a landed background. It was her particular choice of luxury. As in the work of nature writers such as Annie Dillard, Terry Tempest Williams or Barry Lopez, her book soaks up the beauty she sees. Entries in this catalog of walks include experiences like this one: she "stroked a fallen log covered by moss as though it were a green living thing."[67] This act of being in nature comforted her. The same healing is a feature of Marget's inner life in *Now in November.* Marget is fortified by the "small and eternal things — [. . .] things like the chorus of cicadas, and the ponds stained red in evenings."[68]

Responding to the madness of the world by walking in the woods made her happy. It also led Johnson to find conscience. The book is filled with metaphors for the discovery of an internal moral capacity. She watches a larvae become a beetle, marveling at how "one infinitesimal life-struck cell" becomes a new creature though the process of "disintegration and re-forming."[69] Likewise, her own process in the book is disintegration and then rebuilding. She learns to see her own faith: what separates humanity from the fortunate birds, insects and stones is "something inside." She says that she finds herself, indeed, without protection in the mad world and yet still not alone. "What's there with you?" she asks, staging a dialogue with herself. "A black smouldering thing." She commands herself to name it. The answer: "Integrity. Conscience."

The naming of the human capacity for conscience is where

her preoccupation with the world's injustice and the diary-like inward explorations converge. Conscience must come from attention to the self. Rather than become selfless, Johnson's politics require a redefined selfishness. Conscience emerges out of the cry of the self. In this context, selfishness was noble.

A natural setting was the luxury that gave Johnson sanity, and in the selfish indulgence of it, her mind also refound a faith in humanity. The mood disorder of hopelessness righted itself by conscience-raising. Like a beetle re-forming itself, war and despair drove Johnson into a cry of self, and in turn, the self delivered up a new awareness of hope. War was suicide on a global scale. In the face of this insanity, she struggles with but ultimately refuses the assumption that her sacrifice now will result in greater good for a greater number later. Instead she calls for a conscious selfishness; for the will to live, abundantly. Now.

It is important to note that in Johnson's work, nature was a setting for the discovery of conscience but not a Bible itself. Nature could not help in distinguishing good from evil. Instead of a scripture to be read in the text of nature, it was a redefined selfishness that would have to act as moral guide. Out of the cry that arises from lumps of feeling — even lost sodas — a willingness to have life arises. And this willingness to have life is the power that we can harness to counter the sacrifice of life — in war or on the home front as well.

Johnson was well aware of the long historical tradition of looking to nature for a blueprint to a good society — of what I have called the geographic embrace. Occasionally, she would fall into this habit of thinking. All life is against nature, she exclaimed as she began the book. But more often she urged herself and her readers to remember that nature was much too various to substitute for human conscience. In nature, starvation is as natural as winter. Spring, the Great Mother, is matched by winter, the old king.[70] Nature is mother to all events, "All-Mother," not just mother to human life and not even favoring it. Johnson began to articulate this view of a "treacherous or reckless giving" in describing the drought in *Now in November.*[71] She wrote of it also in her poetry and short stories of the 1930s, particularly "Winter Orchard," in which the "white and awful indifference" of winter is contrasted to the "warm magenta stain of birth" in the branches.[72] Any blueprint drawn from nature would be utterly relativist, changing literally with the wind. Right and wrong would have to come from the self's examination of itself.

Land was a setting for contemplation, not a substitute for self-discovery and the naming of conscience. Johnson rejected nature's role as moral touchstone and was left with the self in part also because of her agnosticism. "For the true believer, great arms held the world together. For *this* believer, those iron arms have dropped away," she confessed. But the drive was still there. "We need forgiveness. It is cold out here in the chapelless world. I'm no druid either. No hawk, no snake, no great tree is going to forgive me. Whatever there is of God is in me."[73] The theme of finding faith without being able to anchor it in religious conviction remained a profound fact of Johnson's life. She was eloquent about the discomfort of this absence and spoke for others of her ilk. "The state of my soul reminds me of a spring camel. My agnostic soul. Half-raw pink skin. Half-ragged rolls of decaying wool. The old shedding beliefs itch. The raw new skin exposed, lacking its old wool, is cold, cold."[74]

The self is the center of Johnson's explorations. God is not available as a guide. Nature is a faulty touchstone. Instead, the origin of goodness comes from the will to live. The desire for abundance is the cry of the soul for light.

History may not admit easily to moodiness, but "disorders" of the soul can change the outlook one has on history. From this angle, which is not cool or detached but disintegrating and reforming, land and the indulgence of its beauty is part of the process of discovering hope.

In the preceding pages, I have gleaned a coherent philosophy that actually is not a feature of *The Inland Island.* The book itself is a conglomerate: pebbles of thought clumped in a day's reflections. The chapter titles are months of the year. Some of the paragraphs are elegant. Some read like a furious letter to the editor, dashed off in the middle of the night. With the tools of logical dissection, one can find all kinds of contradictions in the ideas. I did so when I wrote a dissertation that included Johnson's lifework. Why do I now present a picture of the thoughts arranged in a sensible way? The answer has partly to do with the purpose of my book — the genre within which I write is devoted to the exposition of ideas. And yet I am aware that the pattern I now see in *The Inland Island* is something I only learned through my own experiences of gloom.

In 1996 I found myself at a breaking point. The extremity of my anguish took me by surprise. Until then I had kept myself busy enough to sweep aside the accumulating debris of my life. After leaving Maine for a sensible professional course, after the exertions of graduate school, I had landed the assistant professor job that brought Mark and me to Utah. It was an immense stroke of luck — only a few such jobs open a year. There are literally hundreds of qualified Ph.D.'s for each one. We left rural Rhode Island for the urban West without even a hint of a job for Mark. On his ring of keys, there was only one left — for the car we had crammed full with our big dog and our most precious things. Almost instantly he got the job he ideally wanted, and we began a new pattern that by all rights ought to have been perfect.

Part of the problem was the sheer pace of linear, progressive time today. Typically, I would rise before daylight and drink my tea in the car on the way to work. I would pull into the deserted parking lot, slip through the darkened hallways, and behind the office door that my unemployed friends so envied, I would scribble away for a couple of hours at the new novel that was taking shape inside me. Then, at an appointed moment, I would switch to this book, my academic one, the book that would secure my economic future with this professional position. After that, classes would begin and meetings and student conferences and so on, often until well after dark. I generally worked weekends. The novel got short shrift. Mine was a fairly typical schedule, however peculiar my own ambitions are to my individual self. We work hard today.

One morning, toward the end of a generous nonteaching "leave" devoted to finishing this book, I found myself climbing a mountainside in the middle of an ordinary weekday in late spring. Weekdays were sacrosanct work time. I never played hooky. On the way to the trailhead, I wept. I can't give you clear reasons why except maybe to hint at the tension between the indulgent desire to become a novelist and the rational, deliberate march to security and status that is a professor's life. I am, as Johnson wrote, a conglomerate of "lost ice-cream sodas" as much as of legitimately hard conflicts and pains. Did I have the courage to grab hold of my own "wild and precious life," as poet Mary Oliver called it?[75]

Questions about the meaning of my own life didn't fit well in the schedule. Ascending through the dark passageway of pines on the wet trail, I carried hot cocoa in a thermos, a gift to myself, and my delighted and somewhat bewildered dog clambered up with me. My discipline wasn't the only thing cracking up. When I came to where the snow was too deep to walk farther, I sat. It was then that the daze I was in finally really dawned on me. I stared into an icy, brittle rain at the pungent green around me as if life in the present were an unfamiliar thing. Far in the distance, there was movement in the brush. A pale frothy blur tumbled out, headfirst it seemed, into the snow. It scampered right. It was a coyote puppy, delicate as a first breath and just as strangely noisy in the mountain stillness.

Soon I had to face that I was having trouble getting out of bed — me, of the 5:00 A.M. alarm. My body revolted — flus knocked me over two or three times a month, my brain dulled, I couldn't digest most foods. Earthy and rational universes were mingling inside me, and confusion was the order of the day.

The solution to my dilemma came, like Johnson's, out of an acceptance of confusion. When I returned to reread Johnson's *The Inland Island* after taking lessons from my own gloom, I recognized different truths. Johnson's journal of discovery resonated, I believe, at some unconscious level with me. Johnson once determined to be a great writer "at all costs."[76] The ambition to write became only one of the fractious selves in the book and had to share space with the walker in the fields, the Pentagon marcher, the coward seen in the noon light, the housewife, the thinker paralyzed with guilt over her own good fortune. To love humanity in this desultory combination of shapes — its weak aspects as much as its honorable ones — is a compassion I now seek to nurture. The cry of self is a defense against the sometimes too-easy willingness to accept punishing circumstances. And punishment comes as readily from obvious evils as from vaguely unseemly ones — from shame over some fossil insect hidden inside, some tar amid the crystals or even some old pink bubble gum hardened to the whole. Feelings don't seem to me to have much discretion.

Also like Johnson, I had extraordinary good fortune. The crisis in my own life did not lose me my job. As in the substantial comfort of her family, I had good health benefits, accommodating colleagues and then, suddenly, much more choice than I ever imagined I could have. A chunk of money from an unexpected family windfall made it possible for me to decide to become a full-time writer.

Guilt over her undeserved island made Johnson wonder out loud about her obligations. She knew the world ought to be different than it was. How to make it so? She struggled with the inherited idea that her own happiness seemed to be subtracted from the greater good. Unearned happiness seems as bad as unearned misery. A reproving God said, "Get back to My work, which has no deer, no mink, no woods." Feeling guilty might have made her shut up. It might have made me shy away from this topic. Those who can afford to indulge themselves with walks in the woods ought to have the decency to at least avoid naively advocating a public policy built on an ideal of happiness, however defined. In fact, the indulgence of beauty, and the defense of space and time for a local wilderness, can be seen more generally as a rich person's political preoccupation. But

Johnson did not accept the terms that divide the human cry for "extras" from the demand for "necessities." The things stolen in between — the pleasures promoted by the women in *Now in November* — stood shoulder to shoulder with the economic burden symbolized by men.

As I do, Johnson struggled to find the courage to speak out against injustice at the same time that she enjoyed and did not give up her inland island, her desultory walks in the woods. What my study of her helped me to realize is that our inhibitions are partially themselves the cause of the world we endure. She let her cry of self be heard — to not silence, with shame, her desire of wanting life more abundantly. How can a politics of abundance be spoken about? There are so many alternatives, louder ones, in which the sacrifice of goods and services sounds so much more important than anything else.

Johnson's politics of abundance is hard to hear. Her views disappear historically. Instead, a liberalism that defined itself in terms of virility ascended in the fifties. Instead, an environmentalism that separated the defense of nature from the defense of humanity triumphed. But there are other choices, which Johnson's work can help reveal.

Oh, to take a contract out on the taskmaster that is linear, progessive time; to "seize the day" instead of to go obediently to work. A friend once reprimanded me: everyone she knows is too busy at the office, taking the kids to the dentist, stopping for groceries on the way home and booting a stray cat from the kitchen to "seize the day." Or there is my onetime neighbor, now homeless, who careens from crisis to crisis, lost jobs and unpaid rents and unpaid hospital bills and unpaid child care chasing her like an evil wind with her name on it. "Seize the day" is an absurd wish to impose on harried humanity. It is unrealistic. Cruel, even.

Subsistence and beauty can so easily seem to be stacked in a neat hierarchy. Work is the bottom, the base, the really real, inescapable requirement of life. Be happy if you get a little icing now and then. Keep your priorities straight. There are all kinds of philosophical traditions wrapped up in these homely adages. One of those traditions sometimes gets labeled liberalism, for example, when mid-twentieth-century social observers such as Richard Hofstadter and Louis Hartz looked backward and saw a continuous "liberal tradition" stretching backward to the Constitution.[77] In this definition of American liberalism, the basic assumption is that people will act in their self-interest, and political systems should be designed accordingly. The key decision, however, is to assume that self-interest is economic — not spiritual, cultural or even some messy combination of motives. Mental sanity does not define one's self-interest; the physical body's survival does. And they are separate. This way of thinking is still profoundly influential in political theory. The "tragedy of the commons" is a phrase that calls forth a more contemporary version of that same philosophy of the self. Based on a 1968 essay by Garrett Hardin, the phrase is both a critique and a reassertion of that nineteenth-century economic liberalism.[78] Here is Hardin's argument, which arose in response to environmental issues: As everyone will act in his or her self-interest (there it is, again, the key assumption, self is *Homo economicus*), and as everyone has a right to common places such as national parks, the common places will inevitably become filthy and overpopulated as people maximize their self-interest. Privatizing land is the only way to protect it because only then will the individual feel the cost of, for example, overgrazing.

What is the tragedy of the commons within an individual's life? Or, to speed to the point, how can it be avoided? How can the duty to be fed, housed, watered — how can the economic, the "really real" requirements of life — be kept from overrunning the beauty?

The first step would be to avoid assuming that self-interest is "naturally" the father's bundle of obligations and rights in *Now in November* — the "provider's" contract. The "natural" self-interest, viewed from the 1930s, viewed from the pained, precise noon-light perception of Johnson's character Marget, has more variations. "Natural" self-interest exists on uncertain, shifting ground. In her newer liberalism, a liberalism that fights the gendered priorities of the "father's" role, self-interest includes peaches, a kiss. For sanity's sake.

The divide between work and seize-the-day play, between subsistence and beauty — this divide is like a color filter in the language I read, I speak, I hear. Once, on public television, I saw a show about an experiment that involved people spending some time upside down. After a short time, their eyes and brains adjusted. The world looked normal to them. The conviction that needs are hierarchically arranged with economic ones as the bottom line is like standing right-side up in modern life. Johnson swung upside down.

She had very little company. Many of her ideas did not fit the times.

At the end of the 1940s, when Johnson moved to Ohio with her beloved second husband, when Harry Truman began to serve the last term of an era that had begun with the New Deal, liberalism was at a moment of redefinition. Arthur Schlesinger, Jr.'s, 1940 book, *The Vital Center,* became one of the most influential texts in this trend.[79] Schlesinger sought to steer a middle course between the failures of both the right and the left. In this vital center, he urged politicians to accept the social welfare state without succumbing to pie-in-the-sky visions based on underlying faith in human perfectibility. The right needed to abandon its obsequious relationship with big business and return to a responsible conservatism, dating back to Hamilton, that favored a strong government promoting honor, valor, self-sacrifice and public responsibility.[80] For its part, the left had to give up its utopian inclinations and, armed with a new Niebuhrian pessimism, be willing to compromise pragmatically.[81] Schlesinger measured out equal parts of impatience for the right, where greed and the extremes of the House Un-American Activities Committee lay, and for the left, where radicals seemed too content to criticize from the sidelines and never accept the burden of power and accountability.

Like Schlesinger, Johnson sought to reconfigure the direction of liberalism in the middle years of the century. They agreed on some issues, especially a distrust of science. But the fit beween Schlesinger's vital center and Johnson's ideas, while superficially similar, disappears.

Schlesinger's admirable hope for a strong and compassionate government ultimately lay in the reclaiming of virility by the right and the left. The book is laced with language that indicates this theme. The false conservatives were men "without juices,"[82] the progressives had the "weakness of impotence"[83] and were too soft and sentimental,[84] the too-easy faith in working people came from a "somewhat feminine fascination with the rude and muscular power of the proletariat."[85] It was war and the specter of liberal pacificism that propelled Schlesinger toward this masculine rhetoric. In fact, he reserved his worst invectives for Henry Wallace, the modestly pacifist, deep-thinking New Dealer and labor hero whom FDR reluctantly abandoned for Truman in the selection of a vice president in 1944. The masculine rhetoric did much more, though, than allay mainstream liberals' fear of their more pacifist wing. Truman used similar words to harden the Democratic party against unions, once spitefully calling old allies "effete union leaders" and accusing impoverished strikers of "living in luxury, working like they pleased."[86]

War might have been the excuse for the clutch toward greater, firmer masculinity. But other choices also were being made by this definition of the center as the martial middle. Johnson's critique of liberalism parted from the emerging mainstream. Tutored in the gendered discriminations of the family farm, she was the right person to examine the values that lay deeper.

Johnson's politics of abundance emphasized the "softer" skills. She enthroned the housewifely virtues — the willingness to clean the dishes again and again, and to provide a steady diet of unconditional love. The epithet "sentimental" did not sway her from the difficulty of pressing love through the "sieve of words."

Now I speak about a right to happiness built on a commitment to love — to love of self and love of others, generously extended. I feel very much out on a limb here, and clearly Johnson did too. Most of her work at midcentury is busily defensive. She says more about what is wrong with other views than about what she sees as right. Still, inside her critiques lies this vision of a politics of abundance.

Johnson condemned shallow liberal compassion. In *Invaded City,* an unpublished tale of pacifism and homegrown fascism that she wrote in 1941, it is both a man and a woman who demonstrate this weakness of meager generosity. The strutting liberalism of the newspaper publisher, around whose family the action revolves, is pure show. The man and his wife pride themselves on their "cosmopolitanism," expressed in the foreign origins of their household staff, but it is a very safe open-mindedness. "There were no Jews, no refugees — nobody untrained and rawly new, nobody who had seen a world invaded and blown to bits. Their accents, if any, were vestigial remnants — sometimes carefully cultivated like exotic flowers."[87]

The insubstantiveness of this liberalism was rooted in a heedlessly stingy love, a theme that Johnson took up in *Wildwood,* published in 1945. The story describes a middle-aged couple who agree to adopt an orphaned relative. The girl, Edith, proves to be much older than they had imagined, much less cute, and she grows to adulthood under the shadow of their disappointment. The parents' goodwill proves only a shell as they busy themselves with naturalist hobbies — gardening and bird-watching.

The incomplete, weak version of liberalism coincided, in Johnson's view, with escapist uses of the environment. In all of Johnson's middle years, she struggles to reject the wrong use of nature. Gardening and bird-watching were injurious when they were used as alternatives to facing human conflicts. By comparison to the escapism of the parents in *Wildwood,* Johnson had in her mind's eye the Dutch gardener in *Invaded City,* who becomes a martyr to pacificism. It is not the act of gardening that is escapist; it is the attitude of the gardener that is the test.

Liberal goodwill was often thin, and it also was made to seem misguided. In *Wildwood,* as Edith becomes a young woman, she seeks good causes and thinks of throwing a party for African-American children. (As noted above, Johnson herself was involved in her St. Louis days with a school for African-American children.) But Edith's father admonishes her, saying she only wants to see herself as generous and kind. She wants to play "Little Lady Bountiful."[88] Johnson seems to call into question the possibility of good intentions, unable herself to fend off the "Little Lady Bountiful" charge. But at the same time, she cannot join a seemingly sophisticated cynicism toward idealism. She had taken up this topic first in *Jordanstown* by pairing off the young, vibrant reformer with a father who is mockingly cynical. The subject remained a conundrum for her, and in the 1954 title story of her collection *The Sorcerer's Son and Other Stories,* she reprises the conflict. An artist, illustrator of children's books, drinks himself into a stupor to feel like a real man. He is burdened by his belief that the world he creates on paper — a world that includes angels as well as dragons — is not really an adult vision.[89] To compensate for his gentle visions, he hardens himself with drink.

Liberalism at midcentury wanted a more manly outlook than idealists' pipe dreams. Johnson understands, for her own reasons, the problems with idealism. Like Schlesinger, she disputes the faith in reason and science as an alternative. Characters in *Invaded City* and *Wildwood* cast the scientific impulse as highly vulnerable to immorality. Matthew, the adoptive father in *Wildwood,* uses his interest in science as an excuse to withdraw from the world. The novel is set in the U.S. Midwest during World War I. The war has no bearing, Matthew says, "on the eternal verities, the search for knowledge of the wing, the position of the breastbone, the plumage of the tail."[90] When news of the war becomes intolerable, he takes his hat and stick and goes out by himself to dine with friends or to a nature club meeting and there restores himself and sees himself reflected as a man of knowledge and dignity, a scholar and writer in his cronies' eyes.[91] In *Invaded City,* the young son of the publisher is drawn toward science. The plot follows the boy, Johnny, as he chooses between the moral instruction of the Dutch gardener, a pacifist, and his father, who becomes the head of the local fascist vigilantes, the Citizens, a group dedicated to rooting out traitors on the home front during World War II. One of the major turning points finds Johnny experimenting with a pigeon in his room. He has become something of an expert on pigeons and now extends his study to how to kill one. Scientific curiosity has its evil side and is related to a will to power. Later Johnny "kills" Heilie, the Dutch gardener, in the same way, finding out what will happen when he turns over evidence of the old man's unpatriotic pacifism to his father's Citizens. Heilie has a heart attack. The scene is observed by the narrator, the maid Elsa: "All of her life she would see that look in Johnny's eyes when Heilie fell — the child's mad horror changing into the mild fanatic look of triumph — the delight of the scientist in his task brought to completion, the fanatic's reverence of power."[92]

Unsure herself of the role of idealism but equally suspicious of self-righteous charity and of science, Johnson's greatest difficulty during this middle period was in articulating her hopes. The problem was succinctly staged in the "Story Without End," a piece that was reprinted in *The Best American Short Stories* in 1946. A father enthralls his daughter and son with the tale of a village devastated by the regular assaults of a dragon.

The king of the town purchases his own safety by granting the dragon free rein. Out of the woods comes a hero bearing a magic sack. When the dragon arrives to smite the villagers' crops, the young man hurls something from his magic sack and the dragon is slain. But what is the something? What is in the magic sack, the listening daughter wants to know. The storyteller father has no answer.[93]

In the 1930s unions and collective action had beckoned as magic weapons against the "dragon," but Johnson finds the commitment to solidarity short-lived. In "Glass Pigeon," a 1943 short story, Johnson shows a large, clumsy grandfather and longtime union organizer visiting his grandson. The grandson, who has lived with his mother's family since the death of the father, had already absorbed the manners and convictions of the in-laws who cast the lower-class grandfather as uncouth. "Each generation is born a congenital idiot," Johnson wrote later in *Wildwood,* implying that the values of pacifism and cooperation always needed to be learned anew and then were often abandoned.

Unions had also beckoned as an institution that would knit the races together, a vision that Johnson developed in *Jordanstown* in 1937. But soon racism began to seem more and more intractable to her. In the 1947 short story "Christmas Morning in May," a white girl plans a Christmas party in the spring, inviting an African-American neighbor to their gathering. Later the black child's family silently returns the gift to the white family's stoop. The white mother can understand her neighbor's reticence. A small yard separates the two families, but "at times one is overcome by the grotesque and monstrous size of that little yard, the unreality, the myth which has become by terrible nurture the reality."[94]

Though pessimistic, Johnson did have some ideas of what could be in the magic sack. She tentatively held up her faith in love and mutuality. She always mixed that faith with doubt that people would hew to it. As in *Wildwood,* her characters are frequently cheap with their capacity to love. "It is by our own will and blindness that we walk the lonesome valleys, that we *make* the lonesome valleys, the valleys without voice and light," the character Edith observes.[95] Ill will, narrow notions of beauty and other standards for naming those deserving of love, "terrible nurture" — all these stand against love that is ready for the asking. Love, by contrast,

> grows in sand. It grows in mud. It thrives in loam and lead alike. It thrives on nothing more than tears, it flourishes in rains and storms, it adapts itself to the desert, and furnishes water to the dying. There is no holding it, no cataloguing it, no saying Love is thus-and-so, or Love needs thus-and-so to live, and by these seed-germs is it born, and by this poison shall it die.[96]

She is very careful about how she upholds love as a solution. As in *Now in November,* romantic love remains unrequited in *Wildwood.* A more general kind of love, expressed by the Dutch gardener in *Invaded City* as the desire to protect and nurture all life, invites the retribution of the militaristic Citizens.

Johnson hesitated but always returned to the difficult task of talking about the "sentimental" virtues. Her last novel before she turned to autobiographical books, *Dark Traveler* (1963), describes a family's warming toward a schizophrenic cousin named Paul. Paul, near suicide at the end, withdraws from the brink when his younger cousin needs him. As a Simon &

Schuster editor noted, it is "a book about weakness which must be loved for the hope that it will turn into strength."[97] In this, it very much foreshadows the culmination of her ideas in *The Inland Island*. Throughout her fictional work, Johnson's characters struggle and often fail to recognize and embrace their capacity to love.

It is with feminist insight that she finally could name hope. One notable successful version of this conflict over how to express love came in her 1951 short story "Penelope's Web." A story about mothering, the first-person narrator in this gently humorous tale finds herself pursued by dirty dishes and the twin tyrants of "boredom and introspection, the occupational diseases of housewifery."[98] By the end of the story, the woman discovers that her wish to have all the dishes done, the job completed and behind her at last, misses the point.

> In the nature of life there was no finishing. None of the unknown and vanished wives before her in this house had ever "gotten done." . . . It was not due to some defect, within herself some inner weakness or sin, that she could not keep a dish or a house clean for more than a day. . . . The solution was to do and redo and be the faithful Penelope wedded to life, and the web woven and torn and rewoven, and the realization that the tearing and the raveling was, after all, the purpose of the weaving.[99]

The character realizes that the ordinary housewifely tasks are, in fact, the purpose of life.

Johnson's politics could be upbraided as "soft." Gendered terms — a whole language that corrals attributes into female and male categories — made it harder to expect "Penelope's Web" to be taken seriously. Johnson took her own shots, deploying this gendered vocabulary. Her feminism turns angry in *The Inland Island*. She blames men, in particular the ones in the Pentagon, as the cause of a culture of destruction. In the book and a widely published article, she pointed the finger below the belt. The need was "to stop killing and being killed, for the old men and their mad old fears and their musty old way of life."[100] Pissed off, Johnson blamed warmongering men for the absurd horror of Vietnam "in which we blind, burn, starve, and cripple children so that they may vote at twenty-one."[101]

Johnson's tentatively upheld notions of love and mutuality, the source of her pacifism and of her passion for equality, were losing the battle in the world around her. In her personal life, she had found the requited love that she had realized in her fiction was unpredictable. She unabashedly told a feminist reviewer that marrying Grant Cannon was the "most significant choice" of her life.[102] She saw little reason for hope, neither politically nor professionally. Her manuscripts either moldered unpublished or drew only small numbers of readers.

Then came environmentalism.

A cry of self that arises from walks in the fields, from a woman wealthy enough to own a family farm turned wilderness, from a woman whose own marriage was a rare, sustaining kind of love — a cry of self that emerges from such conditions of luxury can be hard to imagine as anything but indulgent. But the difficulty in seeing Johnson's journey as a path to social justice may come out of a failure of imagination that is historically shaped. Johnson's was a politics of abundance linked to a call for nature preservation. As such, her ideas could easily disappear in the stereotype of escapist environmentalism.

Liberals in the 1950s took the road most traveled: the cold war road of "virility," of hard calculation versus soft compassion. From our perspective at the end of the century, it is hard to remember a sense of environmentalism that linked nature love to human love. Like the Vital Center liberals, the leaders of the accelerating environmental movement in the 1950s represent only a portion of what could have been. What becomes the mainstream tends to wash out other alternatives that once flowed by its side. David Brower led the Sierra Club to save the Grand Canyon from damming. The goals of clean air and water drew leaders out of the fold. Their attentions betray very select (and noble) intentions: to preserve, to conserve ecologies. But what about to nurture fairness, to sustain life in abundance? Now, in retrospect, it often seems that defenders of nature have always meant to protect nature *rather than* humanity.

As if Thoreau hadn't also been a war protester.

The expectation that a politics for nature is therefore not a politics for humanity has some good history behind it. As Johnson's own self-doubt revealed, it was quite possible to retreat into nature. One could escape political realities in wilderness. This readily available alternative of escapism in recent years has become a more passionate antihumanist philosophy for some people overcome with the insight about the vulnerability of the planet. For some Green extremists, humanity is despicable and nature should be protected at the expense of humanity.[103] In response to these kinds of statements, some critics have deplored nature activism in general, grouping all varieties of nature writing together with escapism and ignorance about social justice issues.

While mainstream environmentalism and its extremist off-shoots can in some instances divide nature love from a politics of fairness to human beings, there are also other alternatives. One can find, in history and in the present, all sorts of activists whose intentions merge concern for nature with concern for a good society. In fact, a newer school of thought in environmental history tries to wrest the origins of the environmental movement from John Muir and the other nature mystics and instead root the movement (and thereby seek to bring it back to its roots) in the activities of public health workers in the mid- and late nineteenth century. Robert Gottlieb, in his 1993 book, *Forcing the Spring,* upholds heroes like doctor-activist Alice Hamilton, whose concern for public health helped launch the cleanup of rivers. He reminds readers of the existence of environmental movement founders such as Bob Marshall, identifying him as one of those who combined social consciousness with a sense of a "green utopia."[104] He ends his history with the Love Canal–protesting housewives whose environmental actions refuse any easy antihumanist labels. He argues explicitly that the backward glance at the origins of environmentalism has traditionally suffered from a hindsight that sets women's social activism outside of the mainstream. As in the history of liberalism, a gendered retrospect that forgets to reckon with the activities of women or of ideas stereotyped as effeminate or soft becomes a self-fulfilling prophecy. The writing of history helps to create the mainstream it purports to describe. Rather than assume, therefore, that a devotion to environmentalism somehow "naturally" leads away from social justice concerns, it is important to hear what has been drowned out.

The land, from generations back, has offered itself like a page to be read. Thousands have studied it. I wish nature would speak as Johnson's character Allen does in Johnson's *Jordanstown:*

> I believe that suffering is a perversion, and not a necessity. . . .
> I believe that there are enough of all things for every man,
> and we shall not give up or be quiet. We shall not stop talk-
> ing and give you peace. We shall go on planning and protest-
> ing and building until we see the earth again a great altar
> where the fruit and grain wait as communion for all men.[105]

But nature does not speak this message. Conscience does.

With Johnson, I see a liberalism in the margins. In the islands of thought. It is a creed of conscience in which we declare our independence from the fate of suffering. Nature is not a common heaven ("a great altar where the fruit and grain wait as communion for all men"). Nor is nature hell, a riotous den of people with viciously selfish instincts set loose on each other.

Women do not, by nature, understand the need for moral conscience. Men are not, by nature, warmongering. But history adds up, patterns get hard to break, language shapes what we see as possible. There is something peculiarly painful about selfishness for girls, counseled as we so often are to sacrifice. Fighting-back feminists were not on the bookshelves of my early home, or even later when I chose plenty of books for myself. A reviewer of an early version of this book commented on the depressed tone of the draft, wondering where everyone from "Wollstonecraft to Woolf" was. What I learned, with Johnson, was a self-tested feminism; a self-tried environmentalism; a self-enjoined social commitment.

Nature is not the source of society's ills, nor can it be handily blamed. Nature did not make us do it. Our choices determine much of our suffering; we have been choosing very badly. The world around us brims full of shallow goodwill, hardened hatreds and entrenched elites. What we need are paths to consciousness; to conscienceness. For Johnson, these paths wound through woods and forsythia cages; through introspection laced to observation.

Johnson's liberalism is a kind based on neither eternal cycle nor confidence in progress. It is the island of sanity built upon the sense of time under confinement; it is a housewife's round of unfinished chores. At best, time pollinates. It carries companionship to you in fulfilling the primary obligation of all: to name conscience. Integrity. Perhaps you do this in landscapes without people; perhaps you read nature writing to come to awareness.[106]

Let us see if we can't turn upside down; if our eyes and spirits won't adjust. An inland island can be imagined as a retreat from reality; as an escape from humanity and its choices. What if we were to see islands in time, where selfishness brings about a rebirth of joy and inspires cries of conscience, as a politics of sanity? Arising out of the shattering honesty of the self's aversion to itself, this use of land as a therapeutic resource is one path to social activism. Josephine Winslow Johnson's work exemplifies this possibility.

In the next chapter, I take a different path out of the mire that surrounds the self when faith in progress dies. There are many ways, it turns out, to live with humanity's aversion to itself, as those who have fought the long wars against racism can attest. Islands of community add up to a shifting, changing, unpredictable force in the civil rights activism of Ella Baker. But rather than expect evolution or predict the end-station of civilization, the sheer motion is itself the myth I make with Baker's help. Acting locally, thinking globally is the movement that Baker's civil rights philosophy embodies.

CHAPTER FIVE

Acting Locally,
Thinking Globally

*Ella Baker and a
Politics of Identifying*

In Maine there is a story that makes the rounds of newcomers, many of whom are desperately anxious to shed their suburban or urban pasts and be accepted as locals. In it a pair of back-to-the-landers — old now and taxpayers in the town for decades already — venture the hope that at least their children will be considered natives. An old-timer corrects them: If a cat had kittens in the oven, you wouldn't call them muffins, would you?

The message of this little piece of folklore, the accusation almost, is that place really does matter. This view can seem outdated. Given the rate at which Americans move from place to place, there just are not, statistically speaking, many "native" sons and daughters left. And even if your roots are firm in one particular ground, the distinctiveness of your locale is less convincing when the (WalMart) stores, the (Starbucks) coffee, the (Barnes and Noble) books and the (fast) foods are the same in Arundel, Maine, and in Anaheim, California (or in Warsaw, Poland, for that matter).

The insistence that *who* you are fundamentally derives from *where* you and your ancestors lived may, in fact, reveal more of a deep longing than any reality. Even a century ago, the determining experiences of life seem to have had much more to do with whether one belonged to the Yankee elite of that small town in Maine or whether one was a girl millworker, a freed slave, an Abenaki Indian, a farmer plowing mortgaged land and so on. A town's shaping influence, in other words, seems less important than race, class or gender.

Before the Industrial Revolution, perhaps, the accident of birthplace had greater effect, but the sweep of history for better or worse has been a gradual thinning of the significance of place. This view has much truth to it. Communications expert Joshua Meyrowitz drives the point home. Satellite dishes perched in cow pastures on a remote Indian reservation pulling in Brazilian soccer matches has made culture "essentially placeless," he says.[1] In the United States, in particular, many thoughtful observers believe there is a cultural bias against place. "The American mind always has a suitcase packed," quips Mick McAllister, juxtaposing Indian cultures.[2] A taint of nostalgia hovers above those who cling to localism. But, as British Marxist historian Raymond Williams once gently pointed out, "Only other [people's] nostalgias offend."[3]

The nostalgia for a small community where people have known each other for generations contains within it the seed of a noble myth, a vision of human possibility: at the local level, we might act better toward one another. To be local means to be a member of something like a clan — a human family that claims its own and cares for its own. Who would want to be an outsider, a muffin instead of a kitten, in that case?

The vision of human possibility encapsulated by the nostalgia for the "local" community converges with a larger tide — the conviction that small is better. To the embarrassment of the left and the right, their words chime together on this topic.[4] They yearn differently but with the same building block. Size. Scale. How can the lines be better drawn on the round earth? The small town beckons. Sometimes the yearned-for smallness is technological, to return to some more organic relationship to the world outside. The ideas spin around each other and are not easily separated.

A whole raft of literature describes the simple, the small, the self-sufficient life. Essayist, novelist and small farmer Wendell Berry offers classic arguments on the "*propriety* of size and scale."[5] Writing often about small-scale agriculture, Berry demolishes the presumed advantages of huge-scale agribusiness. He defends the small farm as more ecologically and also more economically sound over the long haul. Underneath this commitment to a stewardship economy is a deeper moral economy. Small is better for a host of ancient, organic reasons. Whereas Berry's books make the case with political argument and invective, others simply reiterate the beauty of the hope. And do so beautifully. In one of the more recent manifestations, Paul Gruchow returns to the farm of his youth and relives what life among neighbors in a tended place might have been like.

> Nostalgia, we believe, is a cheap emotion. But we forget what it means. In its Greek roots it means, literally, the return to home. It came into currency as a medical word in nineteenth-century Germany to describe the failure to thrive of the displaced persons . . . who had crowded into that country from the east. Nostalgia is the clinical term for homesickness, for the desire to be rooted in place.[6]

Urban activists have their own version of the small-is-better formula. Neighborhoods represent the small towns of the city. Community is easier to envision and to organize when it is attached to tidy geographic units — the area clustered around a parish, or around an art deco shopping district or a local park, for example. Neighborhood action groups, sometimes inspired by the philosophies of famed organizer Saul Alinsky, occasionally manage to reclaim local control from the maw of the city.

Sometimes the lure of the small scale is simply that a human being can grasp the social whole in miniature — can physically see the feet of the social worker marching up to Crazy Mary's door; can visit on Saturday with the local butcher who sells meat at a high enough markup to pay for a water-ski boat at the nearby reservoir; can attend the ecumenical service and feel the goodwill and also the sniping among the differently faithful. This is the utopia of Garrison Keillor's Lake Woebegone. Conflict isn't banished. People don't all love each other. The women may be strong and the children above average, but the power struggles remain. The feeling of comfort is a literary trick. The irreconcilable differences and stubborn injustices become digestible, shrunk to sweet-spicy jerky.

But the "local" represents more still than the left's or the right's rallying cry or the fictional town of Lake Woebegone or an urban lever for neighborhood unity. The "local" is a landscape that calls forth a vision of democracy in action. The local level is a place for realizing the dream of genuine democratic government. The local represents a how-to guide for enlivening the power of ordinary people. This version of the local was a politics that was applied, concretely, in the American civil rights movement.

In this chapter I offer an example of a "localist": someone who developed a twentieth-century philosophy of community that began "where" the people are. She aimed unabashedly high: for democracy in day-to-day life; for democracy globally; for democracy even at a psychological level. Her method played upon some long traditions: the backward glance to self-sufficient, small towns where people can rely on each other for aid; the commitment to local politics as the schoolhouse for democracy; a fundamental distrust of big governments rather than a Vital Center liberal's confidence in the system. She played upon these themes like a jazz musician, repeating them and changing them for the sake of a powerful feeling for humanity. Here is what we want to find out: Can land help solve the problems that lead us to quarrel? And especially: What are the proportions that matter? Is size (the beloved small community) as significant as it appears?

· · ·

> Periodically, Miss Baker would stop whatever [we were] doing and probe with a series of questions. . . . "Now let me ask this again, what is our purpose here? What are we trying to accomplish?"
>
> *Mary King,* Freedom Song

Historians, journalists playing catch-up and even an institute in her name now celebrate Ella Baker, tireless organizer for the National Association for the Advancement of Colored People (NAACP) (1941–46) and a key figure in the founding of the Southern Christian Leaders Conference (1957), the Student Nonviolent Coordinating Committee (SNCC) (1960) and the Mississippi Freedom Democratic party (1964). In the 1950s and 1960s, the media anointed Martin Luther King, Jr., as the great leader of the civil rights movement. Miss Baker, as she was respectfully called, worked from within the shadows.[7] Happily, as a saint of self-sacrifice should.

Miss Baker sometimes publicly accepted that shrinking violet stuff. But it's not her story. Not really.[8] In a letter to a friend, she joked about this "race saving business" she was in. Her feet hurt. But "who am I to weary of the noble task of molding the destiny of 13,000,000?"[9] Is that modest? Ella Baker took up a banner and walked down Main Street after Main Street. The force of her conviction led her to ask one person, then another, then the next, to lead their neighbors out-of-doors. She called from a public phone booth sometimes. She got paid by the NAACP sometimes. Always she organized and she taught others to organize. She polished her skills quite deliberately, thought hard and well about what to do and when, and was not overcome.

She had a very black face, a skinny small body. A deep powerful voice.

She got her values in a small town, many people want to say. Born in 1903, she grew up in very rural Littleton, North Carolina, and many like to make a shiny coin of this rural start. She had Christian parents. Her father worked away from home, waiting tables on the ferry between Norfolk and Washington. Her grandfather did, it is true, help establish a self-sufficient community of former slaves. They owned land, grew food, shared in hard times.

Was this the source of her greatness?

She tells the blessed community story again and again, but she also tells this part, which others leave out: that one white family owned the town. Her small town was embedded in another, which was embedded in another. Local awareness led to an understanding of larger social issues, she believed.

I have had 40 or 50 years of struggle, ever since a little boy on the streets of Norfolk called me a nigger. I struck him back. And then I had to learn that hitting back with my fist one individual was not enough. It takes organization. It takes dedication. It takes the willingness to stand by and do what has to be done when it has to be done.[10]

Miss Baker once said that people in the "so-called leadership roles were subject to questioning, not so much in terms of beating them down but finding out 'what it is you do — how do you go about it? How do you go about this?'"[11] I recruit Miss Baker in what she dubbed the "so-called" leadership role. Therefore, she is subject to questioning. What is it exactly that makes the local better? Why was she a "localist," as one of her biographers dubbed her?[12] Eventually I will want to know especially how or whether territoriality fits in. "Territoriality." The *OED* offers this example of the word's use by one E. P. Evans in 1894: "The consciousness of what might be called common territoriality tends to bind together."[13]

. . .

> To me, I'm part of the human family. What the human family will accomplish, I can't control. But it isn't impossible that what those who came along with me went through, might stimulate others to continue to fight for a society that does not have those kinds of problems.
>
> *Ella Baker, quoted in Ellen Cantarow and*
> *Susan Gushee O'Malley, "Ella Baker: Organizing for Civil Rights"*

I listen to the gridlock of hope that closes around "small is better" and draw this conclusion: The fascination, the infatuation with scale, translates to a long-running wonder and puzzlement about what the right relationship is between the local and the large. Beneath "small is better" lies a stream struggling to run uphill. Because you cannot have only the "small." Small is relative to something else. In society, the local is not all there is. Has probably never been all there is.[14] Is not where Ella Baker came from. She arose out of relationships between the local and the large.

Relationships carry action verbs. Love. Marry. Rule. Fight. Correspond. Mix.

Communities carry labeling nouns. Our town. This race. That religion. Ethnicity. The labeling kind of localism is the politics of identity. Ella Baker's was a politics of identifying. Her verb was *to organize*. The action itself of organizing created community. Enacted it. If community were a verb, perhaps it would be *organize*. I endeavor to speak plainly, but the ideas are complicated and require first of all changing what I am guessing are your expectations. In defining the local and the large, the habits of language encourage us to favor snapshots over the blur of motion. The habits of language encourage us to turn communities, towns, cities into proper nouns. Into the grammatical subjects and objects of sentences.[15] Notice these metaphors for the relationship between social spheres: organs of a corporate social body; integral parts of an organic whole; towns and states and nation-states nested like Russian dolls. Organs don't change daily; the small doll stays two inches tall. These are still lifes.

I mean to force a different literary trick. I will keep twisting words out of their driven tracks. For example, remember that *culture* is also a verb. One can culture penicillium in a petri dish. Ella Baker cultured community. Forcing an active use of the word *culture* requires that you abandon a current assumption that culture is a thing or collection of things (a system of beliefs — made manifest in rituals, behavior and so on, according to one of the founders of modern anthropology, Bronislaw Malinowski). Try to imagine culture, instead, as a form of action, as a choice of movement toward or away; as the daily election to participate. The *OED* notes that the use of *culture* as a verb today is chiefly poetic. This strikes me as an advantage: poetic versus linear, metaphorical logic as against other kinds; the creation of new ideas by association on the same page.

Let us start with what Baker wants the people to *do*. She wants them to organize. Organizers raise resources: nickles and dimes. This is what they do. But more than that, they create leaders, other organizers. It is in the act of leadership begetting leadership that community momentarily appears. Creating community is the end goal. Organizing is the means. Community is a moment of mutual identifying. Mutual identification. As simple as "making a connection." This is a very ordinary human experience.

Listen, you can be "religious," can't you? What if you can be communalist? A person given to the practice, the practicing of community. Such a person is an organizer, in Baker's theory. Ideally the border between the organizer and organized breaks down. Release the freeze on the frame and the once-organized becomes in the next moment the organizer. As Baker said,

> There're some people in my experience, especially "the little people" as some might call them, who never could explain the NAACP as such. But they had the knack of getting money from John Jones or somebody. . . . Now, somewhere in the process . . . [a neighbor woman] may learn to articulate some of the program of the Association. But whether

she does or not, she *feels* it. And she transmits it to those she can talk to. And she might end up just saying, "You ain't doin' nothin' but spendin' your money down at that so-and-so place." She may shame him. Or she may say, "Boy, I know your mama." . . . See, somewhere down the line this becomes important to them.[16]

How to start the chain of action; how to "culture" community like a force that spreads uncontrollably from one host to the next? When a person organizes, she or he needs to start "where the *people* are," Baker said once plainly. "On what basis do you seek to organize people? Do you start to try to organize them on the fact of what *you* think, or what they are first interested in? You start where the *people* are. Identification with the peo-ple."[17] It makes a good mantra, a good slogan to nod agreement to. "You start where the people are. Identification with the people." That's where you find them, this ephemeral thing, this conjured reality, a "people." Where are the people? In the act of identifying.

Organizing draws in the broadest sense on where the people live. This can mean where they live in place. It can mean where they live in time. The local prospect. Local means what you are first interested in. The issues that are close to home.

Maybe you would start with some simple thing like the fact that they had no street lights, or the fact that in the given area somebody had been arrested or had been jailed in a manner that was considered illegal and unfair, and the like. You would deal with whatever the local problem was.[18]

The politics of identifying creates community on the fly, in the midst of ever-changing needs. In territory and history. Neither the name of the organization founded by the leaders/the led, nor its predetermined bylaws, nor the name or nature of the foe deserves to be emphasized. You do not start with the goal. You start with the motion, the local commotion. One person leads another, and that person leads another, and they lead others to the city council, to the state legislature, to the minister. They lead each other to whoever the historically specific power broker is.

The local is difficult to grasp because it is extemporized. Spontaneous. Not fixed. And understanding this philosophy gets harder still. Pay attention now, because even the "large" won't stand still. (One style of motion will be relative to another style of motion.) You start local, where the people are: a place that is never frozen in geography but depends entirely on circumstance and the people in it. Then where do you go as a people identifying with each other? Is there a larger community toward which you should build? Is there a right *-ism,* a not-simple thing toward which we could aim? A government that finally fulfills the hopes of democracy? Surely, there are bureaucracies to complain to, police stations where the billy clubs fly, Pentagons and Smithsonians. The local could be paired off against the (evil) large. Plenty of experience justifies this conclusion. But what if the "local" and the "large" are two levels of invention, two moving pictures instead of two still lifes?

Ella Baker learned about communism as did anyone paying attention in New York in the 1930s. She knew that hope. She was there also when "black power" arose from the street actions and bookshelves of certain local organizers. She did not, though, distinguish between the different big organizations, between different accumulations of power, population, presence. Starting where the people are is good because of the freedom they might conjure up. But even that place is not a still picture, not a frozen-in-time "city on the hill" — a utopia. It too is a form of doing. "I was never working for an organization," she said. "I have always tried to work for a cause. The cause is the drive of the *human* spirit for freedom, ... to grow and to develop to the fullest capacity with which [God] has endowed us."[19] Another day she put it this way. She wanted everyone to share in equality and worth. "By worth, I mean creativity, a contribution to society."[20]

This is a small woman, older than was fashionable in sixties social movements, eccentrically dressed with a pillbox hat and a formal purse. She stayed after the famous had left, stayed when the discussion degenerated into bitterness and bickering, asked again what is our purpose here. There is a *lack* of vision in her, a lack of answers formulated ahead of time. Instead there is a faith in humanity most peculiar for someone with a lived background in racism. Instead there is an openness toward the big picture of humanity's potential. Instead there is conviction in an unnameable set of possibilities.

I do not think her point of view makes any sense. Which is to say again, it is not based in reason, the age of reason. Enlightenment thinkers planned progress. The slaves of Jefferson were put in their place by what was called reason. They were labeled, like botanical subjects, by what was called science. Their hope for freedom sang up from Baptist revival meetings, from rushing feelings in direct contradiction to any hope that reason might unearth. The proof of any faith is nonstatistical, nonlogical; a leap away from the part of the mind that adds one plus one. It relies on the exceptional, the miracle, the single step forward.

It believes *despite* the evidence. The civil rights organizers sang: "I've got the light of Freedom." In the prime of the twentieth century, Baker built her lifework on these lessons: Faith invents humanity in progress (the large); organizing invents community on the fly (the local). To understand, you have to get used to motion; to nothing staying the same for long.

Baker taught organizers what to do. Now we have come to the question of what organizers should do *about what,* to the question of identifying or organizing or coming together *for what.* The answer turns out to be very fluid. She does not say to organize for a smaller society based on principles of self-rule. She does not say to organize for communism, for socialism, for any - *ism.* As civil rights historian Charles Payne put it, for Baker, "'leadership should be a form of teaching,' not powerbuilding."[21] Organizing is the end in itself. Only through the act of organizing or of culturing do the goals of the moment arise, Baker says:

> I think the nearest thing to an answer [is] having people understand their position and understand their potential power and how to use it. This can only be done, as I see it, through the long route, almost, of actually organizing people in small groups and parlaying those into larger groups.[22]

Perhaps I am exaggerating Baker's commitment to means over ends. I do not know how much. Sometimes she did name a cause. An end to hunger, an end to joblessness, an end to humiliation, to racism, to oppression. Honestly, I cannot measure how much she meant to emphasize these over the processes, the verbs, that I have singled out. Clearly she exercised her own judgment. All groups, all local interests, are not good ones: she did not travel south to help organize the Ku Klux Klan. She began with commitments, to the struggle for freedom and specifically the freedom of oppressed African Americans.

To begin with ideas ahead of time — a commitment to fight against racial injustice — only establishes a direction in a very general sense. Imagine a cause that moves you. For me, the huge disparity between the economically secure and the abjectly poor in this productive world comes immediately to mind. Naming a cause is not the same as knowing where to begin. Start "where the *people* are." Begin with what the people are first interested in. That was Ella Baker's solution. That was how she connected dreaming and action; faith and concrete purpose.

When I err, I probably do so by not going far enough. I must learn to think very differently than the upper-middle-class child who got stars on her report card for moving, letter by letter, toward the end of the alphabet. From Brownie to Girl Scout, from beginner to intermediate *Classics for Moderns* piano book, from playful childhood to a competitive career adulthood, my entire life reads like a testament to setting goals.

The more I am educated to history, the less and less I extrapolate from my experience as an individual, especially one with such unusual control over her destiny. Instead of step by deliberate step, the past moves toward the future as ice does across a pond. A cluster of crystals grows; it twists right. Far right. Elsewhere, meanwhile, it zigzags. The pattern of time grows inevitably from past to present, that much is certain. Ice meets ice from the other side of the pond, closing over the whole. But goals are strikingly irrelevant — strikingly, at least, to a person of my background. Those of us insulated by privilege find it very difficult truly to absorb how rigged the game is; how far outside the reach of planning and intention.

In having to consciously shake off a kind of day-planner approach to political change, I am not just part of an economic class but also a time. The day-planner approach to politics came about through the efforts of that reasoned group of upper-middle-class reformers at the end of the nineteenth century called the Progressives. "You are all secret Progressives," charged a professor to a lecture hall full of more than three hundred Brown University undergraduates. I listened as a graduate teaching assistant. Leaping nearly Olympically from one side of the lecture stage to another in his enthusiasm, political scientist James Morone described the machine politics of nineteenth-century New York. Immigrants traded their new currency — their votes — for a job, a turkey on Thanksgiving, a place in the local baseball lineup. A council member could give such perks away. We were mesmerized. Disgusted. We knew corruption when we saw it. In debates students playacted a change of heart, arguing for the sake of the exercise that "particularistic" politics could be seen as democratic. To rise in this system you would swing from limb to limb of an extended, clannish political party, gathering advantages one by one. The fruits of your labor in this network drew on social skills and the human capacity for loyalty. If you too feel offended, pause and judge the results in comparison to the elite-controlled politics of the Progressives: in machine systems, virtual nobodies got the contracts to build roads, bridges, lives. The "universalistic" politics of the Progressives, by comparison, established civil service tests to quash patronage. And, of course, the more educated scored higher, and the new immigrants with their faulty English and the poor with their lousy and intermittent schooling lost out.

A politics of democratic faith is a kind of third way, something that resembles neither the day planner of the efficiency-minded Progressives nor the personal-address-book approach of machine politics; neither the metaphor of a rational mind nor the loyal servant. It is very hard to describe a faith without saying a faith *in what*. Here is how Baker attempted to explain. She said the cause was to realize the "drive of the human spirit for freedom." Does that narrow the picture? If so, she corrects you:

> Tomorrow, if every vestige of racial discrimination were wiped out, if all of us became free enough to go down and to associate with all the people we wanted to associate, we still are not free. We aren't free until within us we have that deep sense of freedom from a lot of things that we don't e'en mention in these meetings.[23]

I can hear her emphasis in the contraction "e'en mention," an effort within grammar by the transcriber of this interview to catch her meaning. Why don't we mention them? Because some of what holds us back, we can't name or know: "People cannot be free until they realize that peace is not the absence of war or struggle, it is the presence of justice."[24] She talks about what justice might look like, right then and there, in the United States of 1964. She talks about the millions going to bed hungry every night, about able-bodied men without work. But then she returns to the theme of the internal struggle: "The only group that can make you free is yourself, because we must free ourselves from all the things that keep us back."[25]

The local: to organize. *For what?* To be free. *Of what?* The answer will change. Freeing yourself is included in the picture.

A style of doing links the local and the largest ambitions, links the streetlights to the Light of Freedom. I drew on Payne's words when I identified Ella Baker as a "localist" for this style.[26] In a later interview, he reiterated that she was "practical, hard-working, effective and, most of all, local."[27] What strikes me most profoundly about this version of "small is better" is its fluidity. Other thinkers dwell on local character or spirit of place. They conjure a genie from the teapot of local politics, a down-home personality recorded somehow in the surroundings. What they fear is the sweep of consumer culture, international business or other large-scale forces blowing apart this local spirit. In Baker's theory, the people do not add up to a thing, however ephemeral. A locality does not add up to a culture. Local places are not miniature nations. The preservation of local identity is not the central plot line for Baker. The recovery of strength is. Finding courage is. Conjuring the capacity for identifying.

Focus on the method. Some label it democratic populism, grassroots democracy, strong democracy.[28] A better label would be jazz. The musician identifies with a traditional melody, responds to a group, finds a distinct voice that changes with the next phrase, song, constituency. This is the practice of antiphony, says British cultural theorist Paul Gilroy. It is one of the root gestures of a legacy that he calls black Atlantic culture, a geography not bound by land but emphatically unbounded — characterized by sea travel, by oceanic geography, by hybridity and creolization. The music is one expression of a (often not "written") social theory tradition.

> This [tradition] spreads out in discontinuous, transverse lines of descent that stretch outwards across the Atlantic from Phyllis Wheatley onwards. Its best feature is an anti-hierarchical tradition of thought that probably culminates

in C. L. R. James's idea that ordinary people do not need an intellectual vanguard to help them to speak or to tell them what to say.[29]

Ella Baker *performed* leadership. Joseph Road, another analyst of "Circum-Atlantic" traditions, of an "oceanic interculture," described the action this way:

> The social processes of memory and forgetting, familiarly known as culture, may be carried out by a variety of performance events, from stage plays to sacred rites, from carnivals to the invisible rituals of everyday life. To perform in this sense means to bring forth, to make manifest, and to transmit. To perform also means, though often more secretly, to reinvent.[30]

Ella Baker performed community. Do not make the mistake of confusing improvisation with lack of intent, training or careful discipline. Jazz musicians practice. Baker helped to create citizenship schools, leadership training seminars. The difference is that the performance itself, not the recording, is the definition of success. The difference is that empowerment is the sought-after result, not even any particular use of that power. That the people decide how to use the power. A good performance on the part of a leader turned the audience into musicians. "My theory is," she said once outright, "strong people don't need strong leaders."[31] Another time she put it this way: "The idea got around that there was no strength unless the people who were under the hammer knew something about how to keep themselves from getting killed under the hammer."[32] She rejected the star system because she knew stars burn out. Energy for social change comes from those "under the hammer." She said this was her favorite saying: "The butterfly upon the rose speaks contentment to the toad, but the frog beneath the harrow knows where the nail point goes."[33]

"The struggle is eternal," Baker is famous for saying. It was not a sorrowful prediction. It was a celebration. The struggle is eternal. Thank God. That is what humanity is capable of: struggle. Music to her ears.

. . .

> So, I hoped that inside of me there has always been the concept that the whole is greater than the part — that is the concept of the value of developing a movement that involves people to the extent that they become knowledgeable about their own condition and were activated to do something about it or understood what could be done.
>
> *Ella Baker, quoted in Lenore Bredeson Hogan,*
> *"Interview with Ella J. Baker"*

So what might territoriality mean in the context of a community that does not correspond to a colored shape on an atlas but instead appears as a jazz performance does? "Now let me ask this again, what is our purpose here?"[34] What would it mean, for example, to "act locally, think globally" in the context of such a fluid, moving shifting sense of the local and the large? You might think it is impossible to fit "territoriality" or any sense of place with a politics of identifying. It is not impossible, but it is extremely difficult.

A weather map might be the best way to represent symbolically how a fluid sense of community still attaches to the physical earth. Communities are as fleeting, and as constantly familiar, as clouds. Clouds are unique and ordinary at the same time.

Each moment of cloud formation depends manifestly on local conditions. On where the people are; what they are first interested in. Being communalist in this sense means learning to study the local signs — really knowing the local topography of feeling and precipitating action accordingly.

Another way of describing how "territoriality" feels inside the fluid perspective of Baker's kind of localism is to consider nomads. To think like a nomad is to sense the world as a set of changing patterns. Space is highly textured to the traveler who must heed specific local clues for a sense of direction. Knowing how to read the local signs requires relationships — between you and your fellow nomads and between the moving caravan in its territorial place. A nomad understands how to act locally, that is, with a profound commitment to a specific place (and then the next specific place) — to define community on the fly, in motion, in commotion. It means taking comfort from a sense of direction rather than from staying put in place. The direction comes from the cause of human freedom and from the local conditions that define what that cause might be in this moment. Direction does more to define — to invent — the sense of community than do lines drawn on the earth. The nomad's sense of place is completely unlike the one symbolized by the farmer who stakes the four corners of a field; a farmer whose field is one section inside a grid of other pieces of land. A nomad senses the local environment in terms of wind and weather; a nomad is prepared for change.

A weather map and a nomad's fine-tuned sense of local conditions are images that suggest powers beyond the control of the mapmaker or traveler. The world is already rigged: existing patterns have built up confluences here, desert there. By contrast, an atlas claims control over territory: it imposes order on a once-blank sheet. The nomad travels in a world that is already inhabited, not "free" of history or detail. The sense of place I am describing heightens the attention to local and yet fully anticipates that nothing stays the same for long. The local is not the setting for an authentic essence. It is not valued for its quaintness or Otherness. Instead local conditions are useful for determining how to live now and where to go next.

The radical re-visioning of geography — to a weather map from a land atlas or to a nomad's rather than a farmer's perspective — is literally difficult for many of us to imagine. As a person who has probably moved at least once, try thinking of your culture as deriving from "where you are between" rather than "where you are from."[35] There are some philosophers who work at this dramatic revision of geography, for example, the French theorists Gilles Deleuze and Felix Guattari. Historian of philosophy Edward S. Casey summarizes these philosophers' efforts to open up or recognize different ways of being in space by foregrounding their distinction between "striated" or "sedentary" space and "smooth" or "nomad" space. As I have done, those philosophers also constantly rely on images to explain what they mean by "nomad" space. For them, the oceans, the arctic ice fields and the steppes are better landscapes to evoke this worldview, as compared to farmland. The contribution of those philosophers' formal vocabulary to our discussion is partly to confirm that we really are in tricky territory (the difficulty of imagining space from so outlandish a perspective is real and imposing). Their ideas are also useful in emphasizing that what we are seeking is a change in the maddeningly insubstantial, living thing called culture. How to behold the local? The striated (farmer's) view "is always from point to point, hence from one countable simple location to another."[36] But in smooth or nomad space, the view from inside the beholder broadens to include much more geographic information. "Here one moves not only in accordance with cardinal directions or geometrically determined vectors but in a 'polyvocality of directions.' . . . On the high sea, or in the windswept desert, one *listens to* direction, *feels it,* as much as one sees it."[37]

To understand the "local" in terms *other* than as a fixed community in a bordered square of earth requires a massive reorientation of perspective. But there is help to be found. The change in geographic perspective that I am describing is analogous to a shift occurring in perspectives on the self. In this analogy, the sense of the local encapsulated by Baker's example corresponds to a "decentered" sense of self. The traditional perspective, which is so very hard (but not impossible) to overthrow, is a "centered" perspective. Here is how the comparison unfolds. Imagine, for a moment, that the physical location of a town, from the railroad tracks on one side to the river on the other and then to a dotted line that runs through a farmer's field — that wonderfully touchable, point-at-able location of the town — is like the body of a person. Like a heart or soul centered inside a body, the community "exists" inside the territorial body. This imagination of a body (territory) with a self (community) inside is the "centered" view and is very familiar and comfortable to a person of my background. What I seek to understand is what the decentered perspective would be.

The imagination that pins the "local" to a spot on the land belongs to the same worldview as what theorists call the "centered" self. The U.S. political system categorically assumes the existence of this kind of self. It assumes that all of us have a self-interest inside us like an organ that pumps information to the mind. Literature, philosophy and religion all combine to create this notion of a self that looks inside to find its desires, knows itself by its difference from Others and can discover, within itself, an essential core that is the true Self. This is the theory of the human subject common to Alexander Hamilton, James Fenimore Cooper, Andrew Carnegie.

Theorists of different stripes have fired questions at this assumption of a distinct, sui generis self. These critiques include civic republican historians who target the "natural" prizing of selfish interest; feminists of the school of Carol Gilligan who theorize a gendered, early psychological production of the self-in-relationship-to-others; and postmodern activists who question the whole business of owning a self, substituting instead a series of selves that take (and change) shape depending on the context (or language game) of the moment. As legal scholar Jerry Frug quipped in an essay in which he too sought to summarize the alternate "decentered" senses of self: "Much of twentieth-century thought belongs in [the accompanying] footnote" on the philosophical assaults on the centered self.[38] As he did a fine job surveying this literature in succinct fashion, I will quote his words at length.

> The literature about the decentered subject does more than merely reject . . . a notion of a stable identity for the self. It provides many different notions about what a decentered self is. . . . One way . . . emphasizes that the self is formed only through relationship with others. As Kenneth Gergen puts it, "it is not individual 'I's who create relationships, but relationships that create the sense of 'I.'" . . . For a post-

modern subject, by contrast, the subject's efforts to build a community reenacts a performance, a game, a role in a publicly created system. The domain of politics, Michel Foucault argues, lies in examining and challenging the ways in which such a performance, game, or system creates the notion of the individual. Thus Angela Harris, citing the work of bell hooks, Patricia Williams, and Zora Neale Hurston, has argued that black women — not uniquely but in poignant and striking ways — have articulated a multiple consciousness. . . . "We are not born with a 'self,'" Harris says, "but rather are composed of a welter of partial, sometimes contradictory, or even antithetical 'selves.'"[39]

As the decentered self has already many manifestations in theory and in action, let us use them to imagine what the world looks like when it is made up of decentered communities. On this kind of map, everyone belongs to several different groupings. Simultaneously. All of those communities of interest are fluid. A town is not a place but a geographically based group. Rather than arise out of the contractual agreement of individual selves, decentered communities are groups of people who come into being in relationship with other groups. To paraphrase Gergen, it is not individual "communities" (one town vis-à-vis another) that create relationships but relationships that create the sense of "a community."

Making the world a more just place requires some concrete things to do, you might legitimately protest in the face of all this theory. "Acting locally" was such a comforting admonition. It means staying put where you are, learning your ecological *and* sociopolitical environment and participating. And I am offering something quite different. By my way of thinking, Baker was a "localist" even when she traveled. She went from town to town in the South. As an NAACP organizer, she taught how to set up local branches. She taught method. "You were not a person who came in and gave a speech and left. You believed in staying and helping to develop grass roots leadership," she said of herself.[40]

Acting locally, thinking globally is a different rallying cry when taken from the civil rights movement of Ella Baker than from the environmental movement. Acting locally means listening for the human cry of freedom that begins in local concerns like malfunctioning street lamps or polluted well water. Acting locally means believing that the ordinary day-to-day concerns of people will add up to the "large," the worthy efforts to make us free of things we can't "e'en mention." Acting locally is an act of faith in democracy, in the rule of people. It is not a faith in local place as much as local people. The environment is not viewed as a still life, a background, a setting apart from the people who happen to inhabit it. The local landscape is a reflection of local desires—a welter of partial, sometimes contradictory or even antithetical selves.

To me, the decentered community seems to offer a better hope than drawing borders. But we have all been around enough to know how ideals can kick you in the face. And it is not hard to anticipate where the kicks might come from. This lovely philosophy—of communities that are more like clouds than staked soil; that are more like verbs than proper nouns—this utopia that discovers (and rediscovers) its direction by local people's interests—the decentered community method could work as well for white supremacists as it did for SNCC. Again, though from a different sense of space, "small is better" devolves into something that the extreme right could champion as easily as the left. Any cause can become the cause du jour, depending on the local people. On where the people are.

"Small is better," even in a decentered version, really trusts local people to be good people. To have good intentions. Or does it? Quoth Baker: "To me, I'm part of the human family. What the human family will accomplish, I can't control. But it isn't impossible that [others with our experience] might stimulate others to continue to fight for a society that does not have those kinds of problems." In other words, it is not impossible that a decentered community would be good. It is amply possible that acting locally could abet evil in the world. Nothing in the theory prevents it.

In the ideal, acting locally is a method that draws on a psychology of social action. When you start where the people are, they become empowered. Once that happens, who knows what the human family will accomplish. The method might free the militia members to overwhelm their own leaders — who knows. Baker's was not the Progressives' faith. She did not count on positive change. She did not trust in evolution. She developed faith in a very human process of discovery.

Empowerment, not expertise, is the source of this faith. The hedged bet of the civil rights version of "acting locally" is this: who knows what people will do if they are empowered. It could easily be bad but it could also be good. But this hedged bet eases my worries more than other alternatives. If we solved the problem of bad people by setting universal goals we could all agree on (that we all, even, voted on), we would be back inside the Progressive imagination. We would be imposing a grid of ideas on the landscape of human possibility. We already know the problems with the Progressive view. We already know the problems of trusting a specific version of the large, even when it is "universalistic" democracy. Nothing in that theory prevents the ethnocentric from masquerading as the universal.

Another drawback in the ideal of the decentered community is that it might appear to loosen the ties to place. In a long-term trend of exponentially escalating environmental damage, many theorists might object that people need to know and protect their fixed point more than ever before. This version of "small is better" hopes that by staying put people will intimately learn the consequences of using the earth in certain ways. But the method of organizing — of communitizing — can still be decentered, even if this geographic intimacy is the goal. If what the people are interested in is clean water, then empowerment will help them to realize that goal. The worldview of "smooth space," of the "nomad," is a perspective from which to perceive the possible and the impossible. It requires discovering direction, not assuming that nature or ecology points out your direction for you. In fact, the beholder who listens for direction, not just sees it, may be more attuned to the needs of ecology, needs that are themselves constantly shifting and changing.

What would be the advantage of rebuilding institutions to accommodate this more decentered worldview? Dare I speak as if I am naming a utopian hope? I do because it "is not impossible," as Baker hedgingly wished, that you would see the same problems I do: the injustices born of the fact that national borders presume to separate one nation's poor from another's, one nation's rich from another's. The first and third world divisions depend on striated space; depend on acting locally in the sense of fixing what is at home, in a fixed point in place. I despise that a line on a map between an urban county and a suburban enclave can separate resources as if "naturally." This kind of "local" has many negative side effects. But to examine how feasible, and also how commendable, a decentered sense of community would be by comparison requires a more historically specific discussion. A more localized one.

. . .

> She would make you think through what you were about to do, let you decide your tactics, then educate you to history. She would never say anything was impossible but would gird you for disappointment.
>
> *Ivanhoe Donaldson, quoted in Jacqueline Trescott,*
> *"The Voice of Protest"*

I am myself a vagabond, at some deep level. I can see this orientation especially when I look back in time at my family history. I always knew my parents were immigrants — that they had grown up on the wrong side of World War II, leaving Germany for the United States in 1955. In the fourth grade, some classmates chased me home through the tree-lined suburban streets of Chicago, yelling "Nazi" while they coincidentally fell down to check if such a foreigner wore underpants or not underneath her school dress.

Being a nomad of sorts myself, though, comes ironically in contradiction to my ancestors' motions. It is true that my parents transported themselves across continents; and that their parents also moved from the equivalent of one country to the next. But they moved and then settled into a deep loyalty to their nation. On my father's mother's side, in particular, there were the Jews who gained political rights as German citizens in the mid- to late nineteenth century. It was an extraordinary leap forward, to be allowed to claim basic civil liberties, including the right to own property. These Jews then became Christian at the turn of the century in order to assimilate more smoothly into their new homeland of Germany. My once-Jewish, German ancestors were deeply loyal to their nation, so much so that when Hitler's anti-Semitic decrees began to target them, they apparently never even considered fleeing for their lives. One relative, I understand, said something like you don't leave the ship of state when it is in trouble. The fact that I am bewildered by their nationalism was the first hint I had that my way of being in place differs at some profound level from the traditions from which I come. What they did made sense to them, to their world.

Fatherland is a word that fails to resonate as it once did. This is true not just in the context of German atrocities, but the dissonance is part of an emerging historical moment of which this book is a part. Take the long view of history for a moment, before even the nationalism of my German relatives. When Shakespeare wrote *Hamlet* in 1600, the loyalty of son to father was one and the same as loyalty to the crown. The crown symbolized the country, and love of country mingled inseparably with filial devotion. "Fatherland" in this prenationalist era was a literal conception: the place was a person. Hamlet defended Denmark when he rose to avenge his father. All the way down the line — from Hamlet to his friend and nobleman Horatio to the servants guarding the gates — the emotion of familial love fired their patriotism.

When I imagine a "decentered" geography, when I dream a little of "acting locally" in a fluid, nomadic sense, I do so from a background of severed emotional ties to the state. I grew up after the extraordinary extremes of German nationalism entered the pages of history; I came to adulthood when Vietnam renewed

the question of whether or how much to support your government "right or wrong." My patriotism is more divided: multiple
selves contending and negotiating and insisting on a morality
that is not univerally applicable but situated in a specific context.

My complicated patriotism is several steps removed from a
sensibility of the fatherland. After the monarchical period, in the
wake of democratic revolutions, the word *fatherland* emphasized land more than the father. The nation in its modern conception inscribed a line around territory and said, here, inside
this space, here is the community. This is what you should love,
like you once loved the monarch: this beautiful country of fields
and forests.

The deeper groundwork undergirding the nostalgia for the
small town is patriotism. In the worldview that corresponds with
the geography of the modern nation-state, devotion attaches to
land. And lands seem "naturally" to require fixed borders. The
small town is the nation in miniature. The "centered" geography
gives substance to the insubstantial, vaporous thing called community by fixing borders around lands.

Nationalism appears so natural, so inevitable. And yes, place,
like blood or kinship, often is a glue that binds people together.[41]
The fact that nationalism appears so natural is another way of
saying that nationalism is a worldview — a way of seeing the
world. And worldviews change. In fact, the nationalism of my
German-loyal ancestors and of the period after the monarchies
represents a distinct kind of relationship to place. As a substitute
for the loyalty once directed to a person (the monarch who
embodied the crown or country), the physical borders of land
became more and more significant. Benedict Anderson, who has
written one of the preeminent histories of nationalism, described

the difference. He contrasts modern nationalism with the earlier European monarchical system, which was geographically organized around religiodynastic centers: "In the modern conception, state sovereignty is fully, flatly, and evenly operative over each square centimetre of a legally demarcated territory. But in the older imagining, where states were defined by centres, borders were porous and indistinct, and sovereignties faded imperceptibly into one another."[42]

Modern nationalism, the kind to which my once-Jewish ancestors pledged allegiance and the kind that underlies the current maps and the deeper conceptions that give sense to those maps — that kind of nationalism is actually a relatively recent construction. Historians differ in their explanations for why and when modern nationalism came into being.[43] Anderson argues that it was imaginatively conjured into existence through print capitalism and the experience of exile. Other theorists root its growth in industrialization. A common conclusion is that nationalism only overcame imperialism as the world system (and as the hegemonic imagination of community) at the end of World War I.

Modern nationalism is a worldview that has seemed "natural," it turns out, only relatively recently, perhaps definitively only since the end of World War I. The corresponding emotional attachment to a bordered place is also a historical phenomenon, that is, one that arose in time. Remember the definition of *territoriality* that I cited near the beginning of the chapter. The *OED* quoted its example, significantly, from the year 1894. "The consciousness of what might be called common territory," the writer hesitantly advances, tends to "bind together." The point is that our consciousness of what binds together may change.

Worldviews change, and with them vocabularies die and arise. As do jokes. The Maine native's rejoinder that ties to place go deeper even than birth — that kittens cannot, by virtue of just being born in an oven, be therefore joined to the muffin clan — is a joke that would make no sense at all except inside the modern sense of territoriality. Act locally, think globally might someday be a rallying cry that means more than concentrating your efforts inside predefined borders. It might mean ignoring the borders and joining together in other ways.

When I peek over the edge of my fathomable universe and articulate a geopolitics that is more like a weather map than a land atlas, I am only foreseeing the end of nationalism. And of course this is already being anticipated in all the talk of transnationalism. The demise of the modern nation-state seems at least plausible. The next generation might claim its passports at the head office of Microsoft or Mitsubishi. Given that the top transnational corporations now command annual budgets larger than many countries' GNPs, this makes an at least imaginable future. Or suppose that the residents of what Saskia Sassen termed the core cities band together in some new, as yet unimagined kind of community — Hong Kong, New York and London rivaling, say, Singapore, Tehran and Zurich.[44] In response, Malaysia, Tex-Mexicas and all the Trenton, New Jerseys, of the world unite. Stranger things have happened, and sometimes quite suddenly. Remember the Soviet disunion.

Our nations are "imagined communities," in Anderson's often-cited phrase. He did not mean that, by contrast, monarchies or tribes were real, concrete communities and nations illusory or contrived. He needed to emphasize that nations are invented facts of life; that the idea of pledging allegiance to such gossamer creations came about in time. Thousands upon thousands of ordinary messages every day reinforce the natural, inevitable aura that surrounds a nation, surrounds indeed the whole system of imagining the people of the world in national groupings.

It might give you reason to hope — the extent to which imagination explains how the world divides. We might, in concert, imagine something better. But hope, in the end, will not come from reason. The evidence will not add up to faith. The nation-state is an "imagined community" that actually serves particularly well the interests of transnational or of nonterritorial capital. Nations are as convenient to corporations as cities are to national sports franchises. The transnational capitalists can play one nation against another for the favor of its jobs and investments. These corporations gain strength precisely by freeing themselves from geography. They dominate by multiplying markets beyond regional and national boundaries. Baker "would never say anything was impossible but would gird you for disappointment."[45]

The evidence defies hope. There are powerful interests who are well served by the "imagined community" of the modern nation-state. The long view of history encourages the intelligence — a kind of covert certainty — that change is around the corner. Eras do give way. New communities materialize. Drastic change happens. A new transnational sense of community could arise. But the opposite certainty is also legitimate. In the homeless shelters, the impoverished schools, the trenches, who dares look far into the future? Power structures melt into an endless sameness as different faces serve up the same diet of humiliation, hunger and agony again and again. Close up, suffering does not seem to alter in any significant way.

The impossibility and the inevitability of change have to be swallowed together. Poets dare. Here is Seamus Heaney, from "The Cure at Troy":

> History says, *Don't hope*
> *On this side of the grave.*
> But then, once in a lifetime
> The longed-for tidal wave
> Of justice can rise up,
> And hope and history rhyme.
>
> So hope for a great sea-change
> On the far side of revenge.
> Believe that a further shore
> Is reachable from here.
> Believe in miracles
> And cures and healing wells.[46]

If we are to believe in a further shore, are we also to envision it?

Designing a more just world, detail by detail, was once a very popular entertainment. At the turn of the last century, Edward Bellamy's *Looking Backward* was a best-seller. Ordinary people read it despite the fact that its clumsy love story barely covered up a dry operating manual for Bellamy's utopia. In his vision, an industrial army replaced capitalism, ensuring everyone an income and plenty of leisure. Gone was the society in which the poor pulled the rich as horses did a coach. Gone would be the imagination that a society needs a permanent underclass staff.

Everyone could be fed and housed and granted the liberty to pursue their own lights (after three years' universal conscription at the jobs no one wants). Only those forty-five and older would vote, similar to the way the enlightened older alumni determine a college's destiny from the board of directors. Bellamy even planned the layout of shopping malls and so on.

This is a different era. The causes for our hesitation seem only to multiply. Grand plans for improving humanity remind us of Stalin. Our century paints chaotic pictures; splashes of color flung on canvases. Envisioning the right society is not quite the pleasurable crossword puzzle it was. It is very hard to model a future for which it is worth striving.

If writers and artists and intellectuals hesitate to envision a new utopia, democratic citizens outside the limelight also have reasons to crab sidewise from the task set forward by their constitutional forebears, who wrote democracy into law. "Where do ordinary people, steeped in lifelong experiences of humiliation and self-doubt, barred from acquisition of basic public skills, gain the courage, the self-confidence, the mutual trust, above all the hope to take action in their own behalf?"[47] Harry C. Boyte's answer to this question is local organizing.

Acting locally, as in the practical example of Ella Baker's civil rights organizing, offers a new territory for hope. We do not need to start with a goal. A complete utopia. We do not need a point on the horizon. We need to listen to the local conditions with a sense of direction. We have a cause in "the drive of the human spirit for freedom." We can't "e'en mention" most of what that freedom means yet. But acting locally will get us there.

Who *knows* what the human family will accomplish. Faith is not an intellectual enterprise. It cannot come from within a worldview that divides knowledge from conviction, mind from body, science from art, reason from soul. New combinations — bastards, monstrous unions — can help to defy the vocabulary to which we have become accustomed. "Actions speak louder than words" is an old adage. A politics of imagination, of abundance, of identifying allows actions to speak louder *with* words. In a new language, hope and history could rhyme. Dreams and reasons could combine. Myth and sophisticated realism could reproduce the past together, inspiring more than just the lyrics that imagine "all the people sharing all the world."

Epilogue

When I was eleven, my parents took us on the first of what would become three summer tours of the great American West. I was small enough to curl up and nap on a bed made of suitcases between the middle seat and the long back of our Ford station wagon. It was the summer of 1968, and my two sisters and brother and I roamed that interior landscape like it was the West itself, flinging ourselves over the saddle of the middle seat, counting VWs in the herds of passing cars, fighting for top spot between Mom and Dad. Every two hours, an egg timer perched on the dashboard would sound "ping." My parents stopped the car, the one who was driving walked around to the passenger side and they changed drivers. On this precise and sensible schedule, they would remain refreshed on what I now figure must have been about thirty-four hours of driving time with four noisy, active kids. Maybe they made the Chicago to Idaho run in considerably less than that: my mother loved speed. She loved the rules of camping: no electric rollers, jeans every day, a clean bra waiting in her suitcase like a Christmas present she would unwrap on some appointed day in her secret calendar. "You don't know what a pleasure this is," she said on one of those mornings, pulling on her womanly things in the dim light of the tent. I sure didn't, and I was fascinated. She unfolded, my mother did, on those camping trips West.

Traveling West as a preteen and teenager is part of the story of how I came to understand my place, my sense of place, in the world. Geography is a personal experience, and mine came in movements beween locations. In a larger sense, landscapes are metaphors for the role of personal experience in understanding the world. In this book, I have often used the word *landscape* on occasions when the word *culture* could also fit. In so doing, I have meant to imply that everything we see is shaped already by generations upon generations of influences, a geology of ideas, associations and frames of reference. And these generations are as specific as they are general.

My sense of place, for example, of the American West where I now live, comes from Western movies and other popular stereotypes that many of you also have seen. And yet I have a particular landscape too, one that my personal experience significantly shapes. My mother, who finds such freedom in the blue-jean and outdoors culture, grew up devouring Westerns by forbidden flashlight when she was a girl in Bad Mergentheim, Germany. (There is a famous German writer of Westerns, Karl May.) She would pull her sheets over her head, more or less literally while American bombs burst overhead and while her father, a Prussian soldier and doctor, operated on high-ranking officers in the Nazi forces. For his part, my father imagined (rightly as it would turn out) that American scientists would allow a smart young fellow to rise in the ranks much more quickly than the deferential German hierarchy would. Home was complicated. Distance helped. Coming West became a theme — they now live in New Mexico — and my sense of this place inherits much from their, and their ancestors', dreams.

This book has meant to emphasize the degree to which we invent the landscapes around us. There are many layers of invention: I began with a broad historical layer. During the last century or so, various larger social trends have combined to make geography the last certainty in an uncertain world. A classic example of the habit of embracing geography, I said, was the invented landscape of the West as "hope's native home." Somehow hope, which we cannot find or admit to elsewhere or otherwise, can arise by taking lessons from the red butte wilderness. There we claim some certainty about the direction to which we must turn as a society. This broader cultural training, a landscape created by words or conceptual signs, has twin effects. On the one hand, a fiction of hope's native home or, more generally, of nature's ability to guide society offers a safe place to combine conviction and reason; to mix statements of faith and arguments of intellect. Landscapes, given the cultural habits to which we become accustomed, are easy settings in which to debate political morality. On the other hand, the general assumptions about geography disable other types of awareness. Because we are trained to see the cosmic in landscapes, we are — at some deep, habitual level — disinclined to see the ordinary, political realities. We are disinclined to see who got what from whom. The vast government aid program that was the frontier disappears in histories of welfare or other types of government intervention in the economies of families.

The many layers of invention that determine what we see include broad historical trends like the geographic embrace that I described in chapter 1. But we react to such larger, geologic-like influences from within more specific circles of time, place and personality. In the remaining chapters, I undertook to examine the situations in which three specific writers and activists used landscapes for social justice purposes. Mari Sandoz created landscapes for her readers that she hoped would propel them backward in time to a different cultural geography. Her words on the land evoked societies complete with smells and spring bunchgrass growing up on the hills. In the power of the "biography of community," her books stake the outlines of a way of life that was being ground under by modernity. Rooted more firmly in the middle part of this century, Josephine Johnson had first to reject the hopes attached to the mythic family farm before she could invent her own solution, a place that celebrated sanity in a war-mad world. Her walks on the land offered a new selfishness, one harnessed to the demand for great abundance for all. Finally, in the example of Ella Baker, I explore a radically ungrounded sense of geography. The mythic landscape of the small town or "local" ideal links up to hopes of greater racial justice by being part of a much more fluid orientation in general. In Baker's case study, I look to a future history, one not quite yet envisioned on a mass scale, in which local loyalty is a spirit of trust in the people. Act locally, think globally becomes a rallying cry for a transnational democracy, when localism begins where the people are, in what they are first interested in. Changing like the weather, momentary as a jazz performance, communities become a moving caravan of people highly attuned to their situation in place and time. Communities no longer would be invented or imagined so strictly by their fixed geographic location.

My own experiences wove together with the stories I told about Sandoz, Johnson and Baker. In this epilogue, I mean to explain why details about my personal life became part of a book on American ideas that link land and social justice. In a general sense, you have read about me to emphasize the subjective influences on intellectual insights. I believe it is impossible to view landscapes neutrally; it is misleading to talk of cultures as if one were an outside observer. I have included information about myself because of deeply held convictions about the limits of objectivity. These scholarly objections to the detached or scientific viewpoint link up to the larger hope of this book, which is that historical knowledge can have more than an ironic tone. I have turned to novel writing in part because I find authors of fiction more willing to combine logical insights with emotional and even spiritual truths. When you read about me in this book, I hint at the frustrations that helped me to leave for my own personal "West."

The personal character of this book comes out of my preference for skilled subjectivity and also my sense of the dangers of omniscience. Democracy is a philosophical faith that people can govern themselves. But the citizens of the United States appear to be less and less certain that their input is necessary or wanted. The causes of voter apathy are many; one of the causes connects with the modern role of experts. I fear the gutting of the dream of democracy by the advantages of expert knowledge. "Objective" information generally comes from an educated, expensively trained, privileged class of people. The complex nature of truth disappears under the mantle of authority that drapes over the shoulders of experts. The specter of technocracy is a familiar enough danger. But, like their colleagues in the more technical disciplines, experts in literary and historical knowledge also offer a challenge to the wild hopes of democracy. In social theory, a significant body of work now seeks to illuminate the role of culture producers — book writers like me — in the maintenance of inequality. It is a subtle argument about the delicate coercions of knowledge.[1] The personal revelations in this book aim to counteract the privileged authority that clings to expert claims.

What I have sought to achieve with the personal tone of this book is not so much the absence of an aura of expertise but the presence of humility. I am aware that I cannot know the extent to which my sense of place influences the conclusions I have drawn from my wide reading. I have trusted that you readers may see what I can only gesture toward. You will invent my book with me, and you will have better tools to do so when I reveal something of the generations upon generations in my own cultural landscape. Instead of an omniscient thesis, I have written in a way that offers several prisms through which to perceive the history I am writing. In the Johnson chapter, these prisms include Johnson's characters, Johnson at different points in her life and me in different points of mine.

The humility that recognizes the extent to which an expert like me cannot know how we arrive at our conclusions is born partly of psychological insight. We draw conclusions with our conscious minds. But the unconscious confuses things. How much might my rejection of objectivity, for example, be rooted in my own struggles for authority within my family, my peer group or my profession? The answer likely is a paradox: my life is both unique and the latest in a pattern.

Instead of an aura of expertise, created stylistically with an omniscient narrator's voice, I have sought to recognize the presence of my humanity. And my humanity consists of many competing, conflicted selves, "a welter of partial, sometimes contradictory or even antithetical selves."[2] In these pages, I am an employed historian at the University of Utah, a student, a novelist-in-training, a lover of selfish walks in the woods, a guilt-ridden, obedient follower of routines, a child of condemned Christian Jews and of Nazis. I have also avoided, in other words, writing this book from a single, coherent personal voice. I am not a protagonist in the classic Aristotelian sense: a self emerging from conflict into coherence. The polar opposite of the omniscient expert's treatise, the first-person memoir, also fails to fit the view of landscape and culture that I meant to exhibit here. Instead I have created a composite of voices. I have tried to sneak up on honesty.

Finally, I also include the personal details of my life out of recognition of my gradually more tutored feminism. In the sixties and seventies, the feminists had a slogan: the personal is political. The "personal" ought not be exempted from political scrutiny, they insisted. Family life needed, desperately, a self-consciously political examination. "The personal is political" contained within it the seed of a larger critique, including a revolutionary challenge to the world of knowledge. In the humanities, for example, presidential politics is not enough anymore to tell the history of the United States; personal subjects, even to the most intimate histories of sex, are now more frequently included in textbooks. In literature, scholars now study novels once condemned as "sentimental" as among the canon of serious American literature.[3] The personal-is-political critique has changed the stature of kinds of knowledge once dismissed or undervalued for being gendered female. For people like me, coming up in the educational ranks decades after the initial chant, a further step appeared. The next challenge was to recognize the role of personal insight in the *production* of knowledge, not just the distribution of it. The reason I include myself in the story of landscape and social justice draws from these feminist insights, in addition to those from postmodernism and psychology.

The feminists who chanted that the personal is political had specific goals in mind, including the simple demand that women be recognized as present in history. Theirs was in part a compensatory labor. They reacted to the presence of obvious discrimination, the movement having risen up in the context when even civil rights activists discounted the contributions of women. As Stokely Carmichael famously said about the Student Nonviolent Coordinating Committee that fought against racism: "The position of women in SNCC is prone." Women's voices such as those of Mari Sandoz, Josephine Johnson and Ella Baker have failed to be included in the definitions of the mainstream in part because of that discrimination. I could say that I chose only women for this study *because* I wanted to contribute to the ongoing struggle against discrimination, but the truth comes in a more zigzag fashion. I chose those writers because their work resonated with me. My standards for selection drew on my wish to find myths I could uphold rather than analytically destroy. It is not a coincidence that the people I chose ended up being women, and though I am partially aware of the causes of that resonance, I would be pleased now if my choice of all-women examples adds to the long-running effort to include women in history.

My mother's West, where the old inherited rules of propriety give way to a freer spirit, is an invented place. What this book would ask you to celebrate, though, is the recognition that a "real" West — say, of Mari Sandoz's bitter home life — also invites you to dream a little. Implied in the bitterness is a vision of what a more just relationship within the home might be. I have leaned in to the habit of exploring human visions of possibility via landscapes. In geographic images — especially iconographic places like the West, the family farm, the small town or local ideal — even the super-educated like me may claim an inheritance of a freer spirit to speak about political morality. The alternative is to yield to the supposition that truth and knowledge and expertise are mostly helpful in learning how to be realistic. In the domain of realism, the evident failures of human beings to live up to their dreams destroy inspiration.

Honeybees also create their landscapes. Their eyesight permits them to see much more than blue sky. With their multifaceted vision, they perceive the angles of light cast by the sun on every particle of "sky." Then they dance this information to their fellows, in order to give directions to that day's field of ripe clover. The invention of what we see has a particularly human manifestation. Our human angles of light are internal. We have a thousand concepts of justice, and if our dance of direction fails to be certain, it nevertheless is what I find beautiful.

NOTES

INTRODUCTION

1. Donna Haraway, *Simians, Cyborgs, and Women: The Reinvention of Nature* (New York: Routledge, 1991), 3.

2. The comparison of language meanings to family resemblances is one of the many ways in which I show my indebtedness to Ludwig Wittgenstein. See especially Wittgenstein's *Philosophical Investigations,* translated by G. E. Anscombe (New York: Macmillan, 1958).

CHAPTER 1. A TALE OF FORGETTING

1. I was alerted to the existence of this letter by a reference to it in Paul K. Conkin's *Tomorrow a New World: The New Deal Community Program* (Ithaca, N.Y.: Cornell University Press, 1959), 104. The letter from Lizzie Crane is in the General Correspondence section of Record Group 96, Records of the Farmer's Home Administration (which

includes records of the Division of Subsistence Homesteads), National Archives, Washington, D.C.

2. In some of the homestead laws, estimates of fraudulent land claims are set *conservatively* at 95 percent — cheating on a "magnificent scale," as Marc Reisner wrote in *Cadillac Desert* (New York: Viking Press, 1986), 44.

3. Quoted in Alan Taylor, *Liberty Men and Great Proprietors: The Revolutionary Settlement on the Maine Frontier, 1760–1820* (Chapel Hill: University of North Carolina Press, 1990). Taylor adds: "In this view, the . . . frontier migration came at the worst possible time, when common folk, newly agitated by the Revolution, most needed elite counsel to calm their expectations" (94).

4. For a distinct statement of this position, see the *Congressional Globe,* 37th Cong., 2d sess., 1916.

5. Paul W. Gates describes the reformers' aims in *History of Public Land Law Development* (New York: Arno Press, 1979), 390–92.

6. Samuel Pomeroy's speech in favor of the 1862 Homestead Act is reproduced in the *Congressional Globe,* May 5, 1962, 1938–40.

7. *Report of the Public Land Commission,* H.Ex. Doc., 46th Cong., 2d sess., vol. 22, no. 46 (Serial no. 1923). The preface states, "But for this wise provision, the majority of those people would be homeless" (xxiv).

8. "The right to property was first of all a right to *subsistence,*" acknowledges even John Opie, whose larger argument is to point out the contradictions within agrarian philosophy between the right to subsistence and the right to wealth. See Opie's *The Law of the Land: Two Hundred Years of American Farmland Policy* (Lincoln: University of Nebraska Press, 1987), esp. 29.

9. John Taylor of Caroline, *Arator: Being a Series of Agricultural Essays, Practical and Political: In Sixty-four Numbers* (Indianapolis: Liberty Classics, 1977 [reprint of 1818 edition]), 37.

10. Morton J. Horwitz has described the transition from this early, agrarian-based conception of property to one responding to rampant economic development in chapter 2 of his *The Transformation of Amer-*

ican Law, 1780–1860 (Cambridge, Mass.: Harvard University Press, 1977). See especially p. 31 and footnotes.

11. In his "Four Freedoms Speech" to Congress on January 6, 1941, Roosevelt envisioned four freedoms that would give the democratic world the reasons to fight international fascism: freedom of speech and of religion; freedom from want and from fear. A copy of the speech can be found in Richard D. Heffner's *A Documentary History of the United States* (New York: New American Library, 1952), 290–97.

12. The dedication of government land for homesteads began earlier, with, among other programs, temporary preemption acts in the 1830s, and continued later, into the 1920s, with a last surge in land entries in part stimulated by the Stock-Raising Homestead Act. I bracket the time period more conservatively to indicate the highest level of commitment.

13. Robert Higgs, *Crisis and Leviathan: Critical Episodes in the Growth of American Government* (New York: Oxford University Press, 1987), 20.

14. James W. Oberly, *Sixty Million Acres: American Veterans and the Public Lands before the Civil War* (Kent, Ohio: Kent State University Press, 1990), 160–62.

15. See especially Paul W. Gates, "The Homestead Law in an Incongruous Land System," *American Historical Review* 41 (July 1939): 652–81. Allan G. Bogue and Margaret Beattie Bogue have recently collected some of Gates's other important essays in *The Jeffersonian Dream: Studies in the History of American Land Policy and Development* (Albuquerque: University of New Mexico Press, 1996).

16. Opie, *The Law of the Land,* 95.

17. "Senator Thomas Hart Benton on Manifest Destiny, 1846," from the *Congressional Globe* 29, no. 1 (1846): 917–18, reprinted in Caroline Merchant, ed., *Major Problems in American Environmental History* (Lexington, Mass.: D. C. Heath, 1993, 250–51.

18. Patricia Nelson Limerick's *The Legacy of Conquest* (New York: Norton, 1987) and Richard White's *"It's Your Misfortune and None of*

My Own": A New History of the American West (Norman: University of Oklahoma Press, 1991) are only two of the most well known works since the mid-1980s that revise U.S. western history. Peggy Pascoe's *Relations of Rescue: The Search for Female Moral Authority in the American West, 1874–1939* (New York: Oxford University Press, 1990) is among those that have influenced me most profoundly. For a quick review of the issues in the controversy over the New Western history, see the discussion of the tour cancellation of the Smithsonian's "West as America" exhibit by the exhibit curators, William H. Truettner and Alexander Nemerov, in *Montana: The Magazine of Western History* 42, no. 2 (Summer 1992): 70–76. For an especially good treatment of the uneven impact of agrarianism on white women, see Deborah Fink, *Agrarian Women: Wives and Mothers in Rural Nebraska, 1880–1940* (Chapel Hill: University of North Carolina Press, 1992), chap. 2.

19. Richard White's discussion of the Dawes Act in his western history textbook is a good example of this school's approach. See *"It's Your Misfortune and None of My Own,"* 115.

20. Theda Skocpol, *Protecting Soldiers and Mothers: The Political Origins of Social Policy in the United States* (Cambridge, Mass.: Belknap Press, 1992).

21. In *Protecting Soldiers and Mothers,* 66, Skocpol does mention "public distributions of land" as part of a list of "opportunities for economic advancement." In general, though, the book is written within the paradigm that includes primarily publicly funded pensions, unemployment insurance, health insurance, worker's compensation and sometimes education within the sphere of social spending.

22. Alan Dawley, *Struggles for Justice: Social Responsibility and the Liberal State* (Cambridge, Mass.: Belknap Press, 1991). For a reference to the revolutionary liberalism, see pp. 386–87. Another example is Michael B. Katz's *In the Shadow of the Poorhouse: A Social History of Welfare in America* (New York: BasicBooks, [1986] 1996). Katz's main contribution is to highlight the poor relief and public assistance programs that deny the existence of a "golden age of charity when neigh-

bors took care of each other without the help of government" (xv). And yet he does not include land giveaways even in his survey of types of programs.

23. For an example of this omission, see Richard Franklin Bensel, *Yankee Leviathan: The Origins of Central State Authority in America, 1859–1877* (Cambridge: Cambridge University Press, 1990). It is significant that the absence of discussion of the Interior Department was noted by a reviewer; see *Reviews of American History* 20 (1992): 187.

24. *Report of Public Land Commission,* 611–15.

25. Oberly, *Sixty Million Acres,* 162. For the long roots of land speculation, see Daniel Friedenberg, *Life, Liberty and the Pursuit of Land: The Plunder of Early America* (Buffalo, N.Y.: Prometheus Books, 1992).

26. White, *"It's Your Misfortune and None of My Own,"* 140.

27. See *Historical Statistics of the United States: Colonial Times to 1970,* 646 nn. 238–45.

28. Quoted in "Mortgage Deduction Obstacle to Tax Reform: Popularity of Relief among U.S. Taxpayers Makes It a Hot Potato," *Salt Lake Tribune,* March 30, 1998, A6.

29. See Stephanie Coontz, "A Nation of Welfare Families," *Harper's,* October 1992, 16. Coontz notes: "The richest 20 percent of American households receives three times as much federal housing aid — mostly in tax subsidies — as the poorest 20 percent receives in expenditures for low-income housing." In addition to the mortgage tax exemption, the federal government intervened dramatically to favor middle-class chances at home ownership by amending bank regulations during the New Deal. See Coontz and also Ronald Tobey, Charles Wetherell, and Jay Brigham, "Moving Out and Settling In: Residential Mobility, Home Owning, and the Public Enframing of Citizenship, 1921–1950," *American Historical Review* 95, no. 5 (December 1990): 1395–1422. Tobey, Wetherell, and Brigham argue that the New Deal's restructuring of the rules of home financing "made possible the implementation" of the "Lockean notion that citizens should have a property stake in society" (1395–96).

30. Fred M. Shelley, J. Clark Archer, Fiona M. Davidson, and Stanley D. Brunn, *Political Geography of the United States* (New York: Guilford Press, 1996), 20–21.

31. Shelley et al., *Political Geography of the United States,* 313.

32. Lani Guinier, *The Tyranny of the Majority: Fundamental Fairness in Representative Government* (New York: Free Press, 1994), 119.

33. See Gordon E. Baker, *The Reapportionment Revolution: Representation, Political Power, and the Supreme Court* (New York: Random House, 1966).

34. Shelley et al., *Political Geography of the United States,* 320.

35. Sometimes writing together, sometimes writing separately, Frank Popper's and Deborah Popper's thoughts on this subject have appeared widely in the popular press as well as in academic journals. See especially Frank J. Popper, "The Strange Case of the Contemporary American Frontier," *Yale Review* 76 (Autumn 1976): 101–21; Frank Popper, "The Great Plains: From Dawn to Dust," *Planning* 53, no. 12 (December 1987): 12–18. Although the buffalo commons idea found some supporters among Native American groups and the Poppers see evidence of it coming to pass of its own accord, the *Rocky Mountain News* (September 25, 1994, A3) noted that the general response was variously "ridicule, . . . denunciation, even a death threat."

36. See Conkin, *Tomorrow a New World,* chap. 5.

37. "Former HUD Official Proposes New Urban Homestead Act for Low-Income Citizens," *American City* 88 (November 1973): 12.

38. Michael Kelly, "The Mid-Life Crisis of Jesse Jackson," *Gentleman's Quarterly* 60 (December 1990): 281.

39. *Report of Public Land Commission.* Eldridge's comment is on p. 522.

40. Jacqueline Jones, *The Dispossessed: America's Underclasses from the Civil War to the Present* (New York: Basic Books, 1992), 14.

41. I am thinking here of the Housing Act of 1949. Title II extended the depression-induced federal mortgage insurance and Title III funded low-rent housing.

42. The spatialization of privilege is similar to what Peggy McIntosh has called white privilege: the aggressive advantages accruing to the white race that disappear when racism is defined only as prejudice against, not prejudice for; when black is a race but "white" is normal. See McIntosh's "White Privilege and Male Privilege: A Personal Account of Coming to See Correspondences through Work in Women's Studies," Working Paper no. 189, Center for Research on Women (Wellesley, Mass., 1988).

43. Richard White, "Trashing the Trails," in *Trails: Toward a New Western History,* edited by Patricia Nelson Limerick, Clyde A. Milner II, and Charles E. Rankin (Lawrence: University Press of Kansas, 1991), 37.

44. Edward W. Soja, *Postmodern Geographics: The Reassertion of Space in Critical Social Theory* (London: Verso, 1989), 6.

45. Literary critics and anthropologists are among the academics leading the rethinking of geography. See Trevor J. Barnes and James S. Duncan, eds., *Writing Worlds: Discourse, Text, and Metaphor in the Representation of Landscape* (New York: Routledge, 1992); Akhil Gupta and James Ferguson, "Beyond 'Culture': Space, Identity, and the Politics of Difference," *Cultural Anthropology* 7, no. 1 (February 1992): 6–23; and the special issue, "Place and Voice in Anthropological Theory," *Cultural Anthropology* 3, no. 1 (February 1988).

CHAPTER 2. A TALE OF REMEMBERING

1. This inspirational story of Walter Prescott Webb's early years is included in Joe B. Frantz's "Walter Prescott Webb: 'He'll Do to Ride the River With,'" an introductory essay in Walter Prescott Webb, *An Honest Preface and Other Essays* (Boston: Houghton Mifflin, 1959). The wealthy stranger was William E. Hinds. The quote regarding the "social complex" can be found in Webb's *Great Plains* (Boston: Ginn, 1931), 247.

2. I still find useful a classic treatment of this question by Arthur O.

Lovejoy and George Boas, *Primitivism and Related Ideas in Antiquity* (Baltimore: Johns Hopkins University Press, 1935), 452. For a more recent history of the normative uses of nature, see Neil Evernden, *The Social Creation of Nature* (Baltimore: Johns Hopkins University Press, 1992), esp. chap. 2.

3. Raymond Williams, "Ideas of Nature," in *Problems in Materialism and Culture: Selected Essays* (London: Verso, 1980), 69–70.

4. Howard Horwitz includes this point among many other fine examples of nature's "protean . . . service as the ground of values and argument." See Horwitz's *By the Law of Nature: Form and Value in Nineteenth-Century America* (New York: Oxford University Press, 1991), 3. His source for Payne's sentiment is the *Congressional Globe,* 29th Cong., 1st sess., App. 306.

5. In discussing these, I want to make clear what I have implied by interchanging the words *nature* and *landscape.* Nature, rather than the last, best place to access unchangeable truth, is a shifting, changing conception — a "scaping" or shaping of "land" or the physical world.

6. James T. Kloppenberg, *Uncertain Victory: Social Democracy and Progressivism in European and American Thought, 1870–1920* (New York: Oxford University Press, 1986), 25. One might consider the "West" as a popular culture form of the "via media," or middle way, which Kloppenberg argues preoccupied intellectuals such as Wilhelm Dilthey, Thomas Hill Green, Henry Sidgwick, Alfred Couillee, William James and John Dewey.

7. For a recent account of philosophers who tried to reharmonize religion and science, see Walter H. Conser, Jr., *God and the Natural World: Religion and Science in Antebellum America* (Columbia: University of South Carolina Press, 1993).

8. For a comprehensive discussion of this legacy of Progressivism, see James A. Morone, *The Democratic Wish: Popular Participation and the Limits of American Government* (New York: Basic Books, 1990), chaps. 3 and 4.

9. See Peter Novick, *That Noble Dream: The "Objectivity Question"*

and the American Historical Profession (Cambridge: Cambridge University Press, 1988).

10. The beginnings of the special assignation of the "West" as the direction of social progress might be traced even to Columbus. Stories of his journeys represent his westward travels as individual and collective progress toward salvation, as Joel Porte points out *In Respect to Egotism: Studies in American Romantic Writing* (New York: Cambridge University Press, 1991), 34. However, the American West came to take on the burden of exhibiting democracy in a special way. From the Louisiana Purchase through the various homestead acts in midcentury, legislators and citizens increasingly began to narrow the trial landscape of "nature's nation" to the "frontier" regions. While Turner in his 1893 address still spoke of the frontier as a movable feast once at home in Appalachia, definitions of "frontier" and the geographic "West" had merged through popular media like Buffalo Bill's Wild West Show and the first dime novel Westerns by the 1870s.

11. Frederick Jackson Turner, "The Significance of the Frontier in American History," reproduced in George Rogers Taylor, ed., *The Turner Thesis: Concerning the Role of the Frontier in American History,* 3d ed. (Lexington, Mass.: D. C. Heath, 1972), 27, 22.

12. This passage is cited by Jane Bennett and William Chaloupka in their introduction to *In the Nature of Things: Language, Politics and the Environment* (Minneapolis: University of Minnesota Press, 1993), ix.

13. Note also that in the same way that modern discourses of the body are built around a polarity of normal/deviant rather than the earlier virtuous/sinful conception, nineteenth-century Americans began to use a more scientific than moral vocabulary in the interpretation of nature's social messages. Rather than sort between republican virtue and selfishness, they identified evolutionarily advanced as opposed to primitive social relations.

14. Jane Tompkins, *West of Everything: The Inner Life of Westerns* (N.Y.: Oxford University Press, 1992).

15. Wallace Stegner wrote this phrase in 1979 in the introductory essay to a book of essays titled *The Sound of Mountain Water* (New York: E. P. Dutton, 1980), 38. He repeated the idea, calling the West "hope's native home" in an editorial, "Land of Hope, Land of Ruin," *New York Times,* March 29, 1992.

16. Stegner, "Land of Hope, Land of Ruin," 38.

17. By the way, Stegner was conscious of what he was doing. In 1955 he wrote, "The natural world is a screen onto which we project our own images." See Wallace Stegner, "The Marks of Human Passage," foreword to *This Is Dinosaur: Echo Park and Its Magic Rivers* (New York: Knopf, 1955), 15.

18. Martin Green, *The Great American Adventure* (Boston: Beacon Press, 1984), 161.

19. This is how Charles Miller describes the use of nature during the Enlightenment, echoing others who generalize that nature helped to destabilize the authority of the clergy between the medieval and Enlightenment periods in Europe. See Charles A. Miller, *Jefferson and Nature: An Interpretation* (Baltimore: Johns Hopkins University Press, 1988), 7.

20. For a discussion of women scientists' reactions to Clarke's views, see Rosalind Rosenberg, *Beyond Separate Spheres: Intellectual Roots of Modern Feminism* (New Haven: Yale University Press, 1982). Other relevant writings include Sherry Ortner's classic essay, "Is Female to Male as Nature Is to Culture?" in *Women, Culture, and Society,* edited by Michelle Rosaldo and Louise Lamphere (Stanford, Calif.: Stanford University Press, 1974), 67–87.

21. Giovanna Di Chiro, "Nature as Community: The Convergence of Environment and Social Justice," in *Uncommon Ground: Toward Reinventing Nature,* edited by William Cronon (New York: Norton, 1995), 298–320. See especially p. 311.

22. Hayden White draws on Northrop Frye for this definition of myth in his *Tropics of Discourse: Essays in Cultural Criticism* (Baltimore: Johns Hopkins University Press, 1978), 175.

23. See White, "Trashing the Trails," 31–35. The method of distinguishing between texts according to the dominant trope is developed extensively by Hayden White in *Tropics of Discourse.*

24. For an extended discussion of new efforts for politically engaged academic work, see Nicholas Bromell, "What Next? Thought and Action in Intellectual Work," *American Quarterly* 47, no. 1 (March 1995): 102–15.

25. Limerick recalls the story of the mushrooming media attention in Patricia Nelson Limerick, "The Trail to Santa Fe: The Unleashing of the Western Public Intellectual," in *Trails: Toward a New Western History,* edited by Patricia Nelson Limerick, Clyde A. Milner II, and Charles E. Rankin (Lawrence: University Press of Kansas, 1991). Two articles on a 1989 scholars' conference precipitated an "improbable rush of media coverage," Limerick says.

26. Marco R. della Cava, "A Showdown over Frontier Legends," *USA Today,* December 7, 1990, 1. Limerick herself, while frequently crowned the leader of the New Western historians, repeatedly emphasizes the blurred borders between old and new. See Limerick, "The Trail to Santa Fe," 61; and *The Legacy of Conquest: The Unbroken Past of the American West* (New York: Norton, 1987), 30–31.

27. Larry McMurtry, "Westward Ho Hum: What the New Historians Have Done to the Old West," *New Republic,* October 22, 1990, 32–38. Also titled "How the West Was Won or Lost."

28. The television miniseries *Son of the Morning Star* aired February 3–4, 1991, on ABC.

29. Limerick, "Trail to Santa Fe," 72.

30. Donald Worster, "Beyond the Agrarian Myth," in Limerick, *Trails,* 7.

31. For a related discussion, see Patricia Nelson Limerick's "The Trail to Santa Fe," 65–68.

32. The young McMurtry wrote in 1965 that Walter Prescott Webb had glorified ruthless race warriors such as the Texas Rangers. Reprinted in *In A Narrow Grave* (Austin, Tex.: Encino Press, 1968).

McMurtry's first three books, *Horseman, Pass By, Leaving Cheyenne,* and *The Last Picture Show,* are all set in West Texas and offer realistic narratives as antidotes to the West of myth. During his middle years, he sought to leave Texas and the burden of its myths behind. He'd sucked the region dry, he thought in "The Texas Moon, and Elsewhere," *Atlantic Monthly,* March 1975, 30. *Lonesome Dove* signals his return, twenty years later, to the West. *Lonesome Dove* was quickly followed in the next six years by several other Westerns, including *Anything for Billy, Texasville,* and *Buffalo Girl.*

33. McMurtry, "Westward Ho Hum," 38.

34. McMurtry, "Westward Ho Hum," 37.

35. McMurtry, "Westward Ho Hum," 38.

36. Donald Worster, *Rivers of Empire: Water, Aridity, and the Growth of the American West* (New York: Oxford University Press, [1985] 1992).

37. Worster, *Rivers of Empire,* 56.

38. Worster longs for an alternative moral and intellectual allegiance. In the 1985 preface to *Nature's Economy* (Cambridge: Cambridge University Press, 1985), xi, he draws on Max Horkheimer and Theodor Adorno to make a distinction between types of reasoning: "There is, on the one side, a dedication to freeing the human mind from its self-constructed mental prison to search for intrinsic value, order, ultimate purpose, the ends of life. . . . Reason devoted to liberation, to transcendence. On the opposite side of the dialectic is the drive for domination of nature."

39. Worster, *Rivers of Empire,* 11.

40. Worster, *Rivers of Empire,* 335.

41. Worster, *Rivers of Empire,* 335.

42. David Harlan offers a useful review of the epistemological challenges to historical methods, particularly as they have been launched from the philosophy of language and from literary criticism, in "Intellectual History and the Return of Literature," *American Historical Review* 94, no. 3 (June 1989): 581–609. Harlan's suggested solution is introduced on p. 604.

43. An in-depth discussion of these questions can be found in my Ph.D. dissertation, "Champions of Place: Politics and Landscape in the 1930s and 1980s," Brown University, 1993. See the introduction, in particular, for my discussion of methodology.

44. Donna Haraway, "A Cyborg Manifesto," in *Simians, Cyborgs, and Women: The Reinvention of Nature* (New York: Routledge, 1991), 176.

45. Note, for example, the central role of the question of agency in Haraway's work. In the introduction to *Simians, Cyborgs, and Women,* she speculates on how we might "refigure the kind of persons we might be" and argues that "we must have agency — or agencies — without defended subjects" (3).

46. Richard J. Bernstein, *The New Constellation: The Ethical-Political Horizons of Modernity/Postmodernity* (Cambridge, Mass.: MIT Press, 1991), 28.

47. The call for recognizing different kinds of history, rather than enthroning one as the legitimate or professional version, is also a suggestion I take from Harlan's wide-ranging essay, "Intellectual History and the Return of Literature." A different alternative to allowing several *kinds* of history to share the stage is to encourage the creation of histories that, within a single text, offer multiple philosophical moods. This is what is suggested by Hayden White's *Tropics of Discourse.* Calling the different orientations "tropes," White urges the combination of irony with romance (in the classical sense of heroic tales), of comedy with tragedy.

CHAPTER 3. THE WEST OF WORDS: MARI SANDOZ AND A POLITICS OF MEMORY

1. Mari Sandoz recounts the story of Mary Fehr and Jules Sandoz's meeting in *Old Jules* (Lincoln: University of Nebraska Press, [1935] 1985), 184–207. See especially p. 189 for the circumstances of Fehr's departure for the United States. Helen Winter Stauffer adds some

details to the story in her biography, *Mari Sandoz: Story Catcher of the Plains* (Lincoln: University of Nebraska, 1982). See especially pp. 18–21.

2. Mari Sandoz to Ralph Knight, Associate Editor, the *Saturday Evening Post,* February 4, 1958. This letter is among those published in a collection of Sandoz's correspondence, *Letters of Mari Sandoz,* edited by Helen Winter Stauffer (Lincoln: University of Nebraska Press, 1992), henceforth cited as *Letters.* See pp. 302–3.

3. See the foreword to James Fentress and Chris Wickham, *Social Memory* (Cambridge, Mass.: Blackwell, 1992).

4. "Mari Sandoz Discusses Creative Writing"; Mari Sandoz to Mrs. Eugene Thorpe, April 5, 1940, both cited in Stauffer, *Mari Sandoz,* 126.

5. See Stauffer, *Mari Sandoz,* e.g., 47, 56.

6. At the time of these events, her first name was still Marie. I have chosen to impose her later name for the sake of narrative consistency.

7. The incident is described in Stauffer, *Mari Sandoz,* 25.

8. *Old Jules,* 350–53.

9. Stauffer, *Mari Sandoz,* 28–29.

10. *Old Jules,* viii.

11. See Frederick Turner's interview with Pifer, recounted in his *Spirit of Place: The Making of an American Literary Landscape* (Washington, D.C.: Island Press, 1989), 198.

12. As one example of such a critic, see Robert Hughes, *Culture of Complaint: The Fraying of America* (Oxford: Oxford University Press, 1993).

13. See Stauffer's afterword to *Old Jules,* 429. See also the letter to Frank C. Hanighen, in *Letters,* 62.

14. *Letters,* 210.

15. *Letters,* 54.

16. Stauffer, *Mari Sandoz,* 54–55.

17. The actual phrase "plundered province" comes from the essay of that name by Bernard DeVoto, "The Plundered Province," *Harper's*

Magazine, August 1934. The idea of the West's economic subservience to the East was in broader currency by then.

18. *Letters,* 420, 330.

19. *Letters,* 13.

20. The extent to which landscape becomes a character in *Old Jules* is revealed even in the front matter, which includes a list of "The People" in the book. Subsumed under that heading are Old Jules, his sweetheart and four wives, the doctor, the cattlemen and so forth, ending with "the region: the upper Niobrara country — the hard-land table, the river, and the hills" (2).

21. *Old Jules,* 325.

22. These seasons, in more technical terms, are the archetypal tropes as Hayden White revives them: of "romance" or heroic humanity, of tragedy, of irony, and comedy. White argues that the best histories manage to juggle all four, whereas the more common ones dwell on one. See Hayden White, *Tropics of Discourse: Essays in Cultural Criticism* (Baltimore: Johns Hopkins University Press, 1978).

23. *Old Jules,* 422.

24. Primarily the irony emerges in the juxtaposition that Sandoz sets up between her father's words and her mother's bitter experiences of being beaten, disenfranchised and expropriated of her wealth. In addition, Fehr learns to talk back in her daughter's retrospect, sassing with some vinegar and even indulgence by the end. See, for example, p. 396 for the comment on not making tax money. On p. 399 of *Old Jules,* she comforts him as he gloomily recounts how farmers turned to the quick money of the potash boom, making more than he did in a lifetime. "'Ach, if our eyes were meant to see that far ahead we wouldn't need our padded hinders to fall on,' Mary said."

25. Michel Foucault, "Power as Knowledge," an excerpt from *The History of Sexuality,* vol. 1, *An Introduction,* translated by Robert Hurley; reprinted in Charles Lemert, ed., *Social Theory: The Multicultural and Classical Readings* (Boulder, Colo.: Westview Press, 1993), 518.

26. Stauffer, *Mari Sandoz,* 216.

27. Stauffer, *Mari Sandoz,* 88.

28. *Letters,* 450.

29. Mari Sandoz recalls this response from her mother in a letter to Walter Frese, January 28, 1963, in *Letters,* 404–5.

30. For a useful summary of the impact of this regionalist movement, see Robert L. Dorman, *Revolt of the Provinces: The Regionalist Movement in America, 1920–1945* (Chapel Hill: University of North Carolina Press, 1993). Dorman calls Sandoz the Cassandra of the movement, arguing that she was fated not to be heard because of her harder view of reality.

31. Mari Sandoz to Tyler Buchenau, April 30, 1934, in *Letters,* 79.

32. *Letters,* 251.

33. From "Mari Sandoz Discusses Creative Writing"; Mari Sandoz to Mrs. Eugene Thorpe, April 5, 1940. Cited in Stauffer, *Mari Sandoz,* 126.

34. Stauffer, *Mari Sandoz,* 171. Stauffer paraphrases from a letter from Mari Sandoz to Ralph L. Collins, Indiana University, April 4, 1946.

35. Mari Sandoz, *Slogum House* (Boston: Little, Brown, 1937), 336.

36. Mari Sandoz, *Crazy Horse: The Strange Man of the Oglalas* (Lincoln: University of Nebraska Press, [1942] 1961), 128.

37. *Slogum House,* 62–63, 68.

38. Mari Sandoz, *Capital City* (Boston: Little, Brown, 1939), 235.

39. Sandoz's re-romanticization of "primitives" as examples of democratic sophistication rather than as innocents coincided with similar shifts on the uses of the cultural Other in anthropology and other social sciences. Elsie Crew Parsons, for instance, had used ethnological evidence to criticize U.S. society by suggesting that on gender relations Americans were just as backward as primitives. By the time of Margaret Mead's work, starting with *Coming of Age in Samoa* in 1928, the argument changed. Mead's book also assaulted sex discrimination in the United States but did so by suggesting that Americans had, in fact, a great deal to learn from the primitives of Samoa. Rosalind Rosenberg

describes this shift in *Beyond Separate Spheres,* 231. The upending of the civilization paradigm in part on the issue of gender relations drew on the long-term assault led by Mead's mentor, Franz Boas, on the racism of evolutionary hierarchies. The promotion of racial and gender equality, advanced in Sandoz's narratives of *Old Jules, Crazy Horse,* and *Cheyenne Autumn,* was part of more general skepticism about Social Darwinism.

40. Sandoz describes this participatory democracy throughout the book *Crazy Horse,* beginning for example on p. 11. The period covered by the book does include the rise and then decline again of a council form of government, but even this representative form is under the continual watchful eye of the people who will support it only as long as they deem necessary.

41. *Crazy Horse,* 107.

42. Sandoz takes on an anthropological voice in *Crazy Horse,* describing kinship structures and in-law taboos. Women could set their husband's belongings outside the lodge to end a marriage. Such decisions, though, did not place individual rights (the woman's or the man's) above the group's needs. In one episode in the book, Crazy Horse and Black Buffalo Woman don't marry because of intertribal tensions. See, e.g., p. 234.

43. Note how the young "curly" feels himself a part of everything, *Crazy Horse,* 103.

44. See Mari Sandoz, "The Son," published in condensed version in *Reader's Digest,* May 1952, 21–24. Reprinted in Mari Sandoz, *Sandhill Sundays and Other Recollections* (Lincoln: University of Nebraska, 1970), 71.

45. See "The Homestead in Perspective," in *Land Use Policy and Problems in the U.S.,* edited by Howard W. Ottoson (Lincoln: University of Nebraska Press, 1963), 47–62. Reprinted in *Sandhill Sundays and Other Recollections,* 21.

46. Mari Sandoz, *Cheyenne Autumn* (New York: McIntosh and Otis, 1953), vii, viii.

47. Sandoz considered herself an expert on colloquialisms; see *Letters*, 328. She considered language a live instrument; see *Letters*, 355.

48. *Cheyenne Autumn*, 120.

49. *Letters*, 330. *Slogum House* was banned from the Armed Services Editions in 1944; her books were banned by the Riverside, California, library in the late 1950s.

50. *Crazy Horse*, 85.

51. See Bernard Devoto, review of *Old Jules, Saturday Review*, November 2, 1935, 5–6.

52. *Letters*, 201.

53. *Cheyenne Autumn*, vii.

54. Stauffer argues that Sandoz "was sure that the dreams and underlying symbols found in the human mind from earliest infancy revealed man's racial heritage." *Mari Sandoz*, 216.

55. *Letters*, 194.

56. *Slogum House*, 172.

57. Letter to Margot Liberty, Custer Battlefield National Monument, August 5, 1961, in *Letters*, 374–75.

58. Wallace Stegner to Mari Sandoz, December 2, 1942. The letter is quoted in Stauffer, *Mari Sandoz*, 161.

59. Quoted in Stauffer, "Mari Sandoz," Boise State University, Western Writers series no. 63, 1984, 44–45.

60. Mari Sandoz to editor Bruce Nicoll, June 14, 1964. Quoted in Stauffer, *Mari Sandoz*, 251.

CHAPTER 4. BACK TO A NEW "FAMILY FARM": JOSEPHINE JOHNSON AND A POLITICS OF ABUNDANCE

1. Alan Trachtenberg quotes Whitman's remark in *The Incorporation of America: Culture and Society in the Gilded Age* (New York: Hill and Wang, 1982), 73.

2. Josephine W. Johnson, *Now in November* (New York: Carroll Graf, [1934] 1985).

3. Josephine W. Johnson, *The Inland Island* (New York: Simon & Schuster, 1969).

4. Edward Abbey, "*Inland Island,*" *New York Times Book Review,* March 2, 1969, 8.

5. *Inland Island,* 128.

6. This page, parenthetically titled "Notes @ Self,"is among Johnson's papers kept at the Washington University Libraries in St. Louis, Missouri. In her real life, Johnson complained already in the 1930s to Bernard DeVoto of being afflicted by an "oblong and blurred unreality." In a personal letter to Johnson, DeVoto referred to a previous conversation about this sense of unreality. The letter is included in series 1 (1162) of the Washington University archives on Johnson. It is undated, but from the context and a reference to hopes for 1938, it would be sometime in 1937.

7. Stephen Jay Gould, *Time's Arrow, Time's Cycle: Myth and Metaphor in the Discovery of Geological Time* (Cambridge, Mass.: Harvard University Press, 1987).

8. Joseph Conrad, *Heart of Darkness* (New York: Penguin, [1902] 1973), 86.

9. Conrad, *Heart of Darkness,* 86.

10. Roy W. Meier, *The Middle Western Farm Novel in the Twentieth Century* (Lincoln: University of Nebraska Press, 1965), 3.

11. Warren Susman, with his book *Culture as History,* is widely recognized as the main founder of this school of interpretation. See also T. J. Lears and Richard Wightman Fox, *The Culture of Consumption: Critical Essays in American History, 1880–1980* (New York: Pantheon Books, 1983).

12. Stuart Ewen makes this argument in exaggerated form in the 1976 classic, *Captains of Consciousness: Advertising and the Social Roots of the Consumer Culture* (New York: McGraw-Hill, 1976).

13. *Inland Island,* 92.

14. Johnson's comment on franklins is cited in the biographical sketch of her in *American Women Writers* (New York: Frederick Ungar, 1980), 412, and also appears in *Inland Island,* 8. Her mother's maiden name was Franklin. A social column saved in the Washington University archives that appears to be from the *St. Louis Post-Dispatch* (date unclear) describes her father's family, enthusing that "her paternal ancestors (going back to her great grandfather) have lived in and near this little city [Bowling Green] for almost a century. Her ancestry reaches back to the Johnson family of Virginia, among whom was Richard Johnson, statesman of that state; to the Langfords of Kentucky, who trace back to Pochontas [*sic*] and to the Franklin and Fier family of old Ireland."

15. One journalist, visiting Johnson after her Pulitzer Prize in 1935, described the neighborhood as an area of "scattered farm-houses, fine residences and extensive, carefully tended grounds." *St. Louis Post-Dispatch,* May 7, 1935, 1, 5; no byline.

16. *Now in November,* 5–7.

17. Johnson, responding to the suggestion that she lengthen the book, wrote to Clifton Fadiman at Simon & Schuster in July 1934, "I shall try then, to expand it as much as seems possible and still keep it from appearing an unfinished attempt at a full-length novel — instead of what I want it to be — a compact and suggested impression — a sort of realistic idyl."

18. Ferner Nuhn was the dissenter; he titled his review of the book "Dark-brown Tragedy" (*The Nation* 139, no. 3612 [September 26, 1934]: 360). Among the promoters were Bernard DeVoto, who was acquainted with Johnson and considered himself something of an intellectual godfather; Edith H. Walton, "A First Novel of Fine Distinction," writing for the *New York Times Book Review,* September 16, 1934, 6; John Cheever, *New Republic,* September 26, 1934, 191; Alvah C. Bessie, "A Novelist to Watch," *Saturday Review of Literature,* September 15, 1934, 109.

19. *Now in November,* 117.

20. *Now in November,* 204. The character of a tramp makes the same comment, p. 50.

21. *Now in November,* 50.

22. *Now in November,* 220.

23. Indeed, in this book the women possess inexhaustible strength — an unfailing spring rather than a cistern in need of rain, as Johnson would later rebuke the idea in *The Inland Island,* 88. Critic Joan Hedrick in 1982 despairs at Steinbeck's substitution of an Earth Mother myth for Mother Earth. See Joan Hedrick, "Mother Earth and Earth Mother: The Recasting of Myth in Steinbeck's *The Grapes of Wrath,*" in *Twentieth-Century Interpretations of "The Grapes of Wrath": A Collection of Critical Essays,* edited by Robert Con Davis (Englewood Cliffs, N.J.: Prentice Hall, 1982), 137. Steinbeck's exploration of matriarchy may have been inspired by a reading of Robert Briffault's *The Mothers: The Matriarchal Theory of Social Origins* (New York: Macmillan, 1931), suggested A. Warren Mothley in "From Patriarchy to Matriarch: Ma Joad's Role in *The Grapes of Wrath,*" *American Literature* 54, no. 3 (October 1982): 397–411. Cited in Nellie Y. McKay, "*The Grapes of Wrath,*" in *New Essays on "The Grapes of Wrath,"* edited by David Wyatt (New York: Cambridge University Press, 1990), 47–70.

24. Gladys Hasty Carroll, *As the Earth Turns* (New York: Macmillan, 1933).

25. The father is depicted as generally impatient of advice from women, including his wife. When the mother suggests that Grant Koven might work as a hired hand, the father "shoved her suggestions away as though they were stupid thoughts that had come to him hours ago and been found of no use." But then, of course, he does find it a good idea, and hires Grant. *Now in November,* 51.

26. She "would have made a good boy," the father thinks. *Now in November,* 63.

27. *Now in November,* 86–87.

28. *Now in November,* 88.

29. *Now in November,* 139.

30. Josephine W. Johnson, *Seven Houses* (New York: Simon & Schuster, 1973), 41. Emphasis in original.

31. In recollecting "Miss Mack with her great black Indian braids. Outsize in that small Victorian world," Johnson cringes at the memories. "What did we think as children about Indians and the national acts of genocide?" she asks in parentheses. "I do not have the faintest idea. I am ashamed to investigate." *Seven Houses,* 47.

32. Barbara Melosh, *Engendering Culture: Manhood and Womanhood in New Deal Public Art and Theater* (Washington, D.C.: Smithsonian Institution Press, 1991). See especially chap. 2, "The Domesticated Frontier."

33. *Now in November,* 230, 134.

34. *Now in November,* 48.

35. *Now in November,* 52.

36. *Now in November,* 37.

37. "I knew that she wanted love, — not anything we could give her, frugal and spinsterly, nor Father's (having long ago stopped even hoping for it), but some man's love in which she could see this image she had of herself reflected and thus becoming half-true," Marget tells us. *Now in November,* 46.

38. *Now in November,* 201.

39. *Now in November,* 206. Ellipses in original.

40. Johnson's appreciation of relativity focused on the contrast between individual minds in *Now in November,* but she also was aware of cultural differences in perception. She took a course in sociology at Washington University, and in a college paper explained as a product of cultural misunderstanding the belief that Italians were slow to assimilate. The Italian women refused English classes because attendance would produce a reputation of neglecting their homes, she argued. As a whole, though, Johnson's fiction rarely focused on cultural conflict. Her college paper, dated July 24, 1930, takes on a general study of the Italian character based on research on an immigrant community in St. Louis. Johnson, age twenty at the time, seeks in the paper to dis-

tinguish cultural groups within the Italian community — the Sicilians versus other Italians, for example. The Sicilians do not fare well in Johnson's treatment: the paper is a mix of stereotype bashing and ethnic prejudice. The remark about the Italian women's attitude toward English classes can be found on p. 2. This and other of Johnson's college papers can be found in series 5 of the Washington University archives on Johnson, identification no. L10 M107 J1 C214.

41. *Now in November,* 35.

42. *Now in November,* 45.

43. *Now in November,* 35. Johnson employs unusual dash spacing.

44. *Now in November,* 103.

45. See especially *Now in November,* 35. In general, Marget's retrospective from the November of the title back ten years to their arrival on the farm is suffused with comments on the status of the mind. The opening page (3), for example, describes the mind as "a sort of sieve or quicksand"; later the mind is "a jailer" and so on.

46. *Now in November,* 24.

47. *Now in November,* 127.

48. *Now in November,* 142. Emphasis in original.

49. *Now in November,* 142–43.

50. Josephine W. Johnson, *Jordanstown* (New York: Simon & Schuster, 1937), 92.

51. Josephine W. Johnson, "New Year for the Sharecroppers," *American Teacher* 23, no. 5 (February 1939): 23.

52. For a history of these programs and their decline, see the still useful book by Paul W. Conkin, *Tomorrow a New World: The New Deal Community Program* (Ithaca: Cornell University Press, 1959). I have relied on Conkin's spelling of the La Forge community, rather than the Johnson article, which gives it as LaFarge.

53. "I believe in abolishing the 'profit system' and desire a true democracy — economically as well as politically," Johnson wrote in *Twentieth-Century Authors,* edited by Stanley J. Kuntz and Howard Haycraft (New York: H. W. Wilson, 1942), 729. From the context, it

appears that Johnson's entry was contributed sometime in the late 1930s and was revised for a supplementary edition in 1955.

54. "I ... am actively interested in co-operatives and in social and political reform," she wrote in the autobiographical sketch for *Twentieth-Century Authors*, 729.

55. *Inland Island*, 92.

56. *Inland Island*, 8.

57. *Inland Island*, 25.

58. *Inland Island*, 90.

59. *Inland Island*, 13.

60. *Inland Island*, 119.

61. *Inland Island*, 48.

62. *Inland Island*, 45.

63. *Inland Island*, 53.

64. *Now in November*, 226.

65. *Inland Island*, 117.

66. *Inland Island*, 138–39.

67. *Inland Island*, 43.

68. *Now in November*, 119.

69. *Inland Island*, 63.

70. *Inland Island*, 56.

71. *Inland Island*, 56.

72. Johnson's early stories were collected and published speedily after the warm reception to *Now in November*, in *Winter Orchard and Other Stories* (New York: Simon & Schuster, 1935).

73. *Inland Island*, 138–39.

74. *Inland Island*, 26.

75. Mary Oliver, "The Summer Day," in *New and Selected Poems* (Boston: Beacon Press, 1992).

76. *Inland Island*, 117.

77. Louis Hartz, *The Liberal Tradition in America: An Interpretation of American Political Thought since the Revolution* (New York: Har-

court, Brace & World, 1955). See also Richard Hofstadter's *American Political Tradition and the Men Who Made It* (New York: Knopf, 1948).

78. Garrett Hardin, "The Tragedy of the Commons," *Science* 162 (December 13, 1968): 1243–48.

79. Arthur Schlesinger, Jr., *The Vital Center: The Politics of Freedom* (Boston: Houghton Mifflin, 1949).

80. See Schlesinger, *Vital Center,* chap. 2, "The Failure of the Right."

81. See Schlesinger, *Vital Center,* chap. 3, "The Failure of the Left."

82. Schlesinger, *Vital Center,* 21.

83. Schlesinger, *Vital Center,* 41.

84. "The defining characteristic of the progressive, as I shall use the word, is the sentimentality of his approach to politics and culture. He must be distinguished, on the one hand, from the Communist; for the progressive is soft, not hard." Schlesinger, *Vital Center,* 36.

85. Schlesinger, *Vital Center,* 46.

86. Truman felt provoked by a railroad strike in 1946. His response, a draft speech that was nothing short of a diatribe, showed him as "angry as any American President in recent times," as James T. Patterson put it in *Grand Expectations: The United States, 1945–1974* (New York: Oxford University Press, 1996), 47.

87. *Invaded City,* 119, series 1, Johnson archives, Special Collections, Washington University Libraries.

88. *Wildwood,* 120.

89. The character, Evan, kills another man and himself in a drunken car crash. For the section on angels and dragons, see *The Sorcerer's Son and Other Stories,* 16. The story was originally published in *Virginia Quarterly Review* in 1954.

90. *Wildwood,* 105.

91. *Wildwood,* 102.

92. *Invaded City,* 173. The manuscript is included in the Washington University archives. Johnson had not settled on the names of the

characters in this draft. Heilie is sometimes called Hans, Peter and other names.

93. "Story without End" was first published in 1945 in the *Virginia Quarterly Review* and is reprinted in *The Sorcerer's Son and Other Stories.*

94. "A Christmas Morning in May," reprinted in *The Sorcerer's Son and Other Stories,* 53. The story was first published in *Harper's Bazaar* in 1947.

95. *Wildwood,* 149. Emphasis in original.

96. *Wildwood,* 100.

97. The comment is by Kerstin Larsson and is included among in-house editorial remarks as Simon & Schuster considered the book for publication. Washington University archives on Johnson, series 3 (1162).

98. "Penelope's Web," reprinted in *The Sorcerer's Son and Other Stories,* 61. Originally published in *Harper's Bazaar* in 1951.

99. "Penelope's Web," 66–67.

100. "Penelope's Web," 92.

101. "Penelope's Web," 47.

102. Barbaralee Diamonstein, *Open Secrets: Ninety-four Women in Touch with Our Time* (New York: Viking Press, 1970), 212.

103. For a good discussion of the antihumanist tendencies in some Green thought, see Murray Bookchin, *Remaking Society: Pathways to a Green Future* (Boston: South End Press, 1990). The book begins with Bookchin's horror at a Green meeting in Amherst in June 1987, when a California Green said it was "human beings'" fault that the world was in ecological crisis. Bookchin's main and good point is that such a view refuses to distinguish between types of societies and claims that the human species itself is at fault. He sees deep ecology and its anti-humanism as the twin of the view that says human beings need to dominate nature. Dave Foreman, a founder of Earth First! defends himself against Bookchin's charge in a book-length dialogue between

the two men: *Defending the Earth: A Dialogue between Murray Bookchin and Dave Foreman* (Boston: South End Press, 1991).

104. Robert Gottlieb, *Forcing the Spring: The Transformation of the American Environmental Movement* (Washington, D.C.: Island Press, 1993).

105. *Jordanstown*, 258.

106. In using the word *awareness* here, I mean to play on Scott Slovic's work, *Seeking Awareness in American Nature Writing: Henry Thoreau, Annie Dillard, Edward Abbey, Wendell Berry, Barry Lopez* (Salt Lake City: University of Utah Press, 1992). As should be apparent to experts in the field, I find Slovic's argument convincing, except for his "preference" to see awareness as a nonpolitical activity (see p. 18).

CHAPTER 5. ACTING LOCALLY, THINKING GLOBALLY: ELLA BAKER AND A POLITICS OF IDENTIFYING

1. Joshua Meyrowitz, *No Sense of Place: The Impact of Electronic Media on Social Behavior* (New York: Oxford University Press, 1985), 6, 317.

2. Mick McAllister, "Homeward Bound: Wilderness and Frontier in American Indian Literature," in *The Frontier Experience and the American Dream: Essays on American Literature,* edited by David Mogen, Mark Busby and Paul Bryant (College Station: Texas A&M University Press, 1989), 152.

3. Raymond Williams, *The Country and the City* (New York: Oxford University Press, 1973), 12.

4. For a comparison of right and left appeals for grassroots politics and against big government, see Harry C. Boyte, Heather Booth, and Steve May, *Citizen Action and the New American Populism* (Philadelphia: Temple University Press, 1986).

5. Wendell Berry, *The Gift of Good Land: Further Essays, Cultural*

and Agricultural (San Francisco: North Point Press, 1981), xi. Emphasis in original.

6. Paul Gruchow, *Grass Roots: The Universe of Home* (Minneapolis: Milkweed Editions, 1995), 7.

7. As the *St. Petersburg Times* noted in a 1992 retrospective, "When you read African-American history, you rarely find her name. She never made the cover of *Life* or *Time* magazines." Peggy Peterman, "A Leader in the Struggle," February 11, 1992, City Edition.

8. In several interviews, Baker spoke frankly about the inability of Southern ministers to accept a woman and especially an older woman as a public leader. In an interview with women's historian Gerda Lerner, she also noted the supportive role in which women are typecast and the unequal footing from which they work: "I don't advocate anybody following the pattern I followed, unless they find themselves in a situation where they think that the larger goals will be shortchanged if they don't." See "Developing Community Leadership: Ella Baker," in Gerda Lerner's *Black Women in White America: A Documentary History* (New York: Pantheon, 1972), 351.

9. Cited in Charles Payne, *I've Got the Light of Freedom: The Organizing Tradition and the Mississippi Freedom Struggle* (Berkeley: University of California Press, 1995), 85. Baker discussed her relationship with other civil rights leaders in an extended interview with Eugene Walker, Southern Oral History Program, #4007, G-7 (Baker), in the Southern Historical Collection, University of North Carolina Library, Chapel Hill. See especially p. 38.

10. Ella Baker made this remark in the documentary video *Fundi: The Story of Ella Baker,* directed by Joanne Grant (New York: First Run Films, 1981).

11. Lenore Bredeson Hogan, "Interview with Ella J. Baker," New York City, March 4, 1979. This interview is kept in the archives at the Highlander Research and Education Center in New Market, Tennessee. The quote is found on transcript p. 22.

12. Payne, *I've Got the Light of Freedom,* 101.

13. *The Compact Edition of the Oxford English Dictionary,* vol. 2, 1971 ed.

14. For a great overview of the history of ideas about community identity, see Akhil Gupta and James Ferguson, "Beyond 'Culture': Space Identity, and the Politics of Difference," *Cultural Anthropology* 7, no. 1 (February 1992): 6–23.

15. Theorist Michel de Certeau addresses a similar issue as he struggles to capture the action (the verb tenses) of life in the city from the physical traces of the motion. Talking of a "chorus of idle footsteps," he writes that in the city,

> footsteps are myriad, but do not compose a series. . . . They weave places together. . . . It is true that the operation of walking on can be traced on city maps in such a way as to transcribe their paths (here well-trodden, there very faint) and their trajectories (going this way and not that). But these thick or thin curves only refer, like words, to the absence of what has passed by. [Making those thick or thin curves visible] has the effect of making invisible the operation that made [them] possible. . . . The trace left behind exhibits the (voracious) property that the geographical system has of being able to transform action into legibility, but in doing so it causes a way of being in the world to be forgotten.

De Certeau, "Walking in the City," reproduced in Simon During, ed., *Cultural Studies Reader* (London: Routledge, 1993), 157–58.

16. Baker's comment can be found in Ellen Cantarow and Susan Gushee O'Malley, "Ella Baker: Organizing for Civil Rights," in *Moving the Mountain: Women Working for Social Change,* edited by Ellen Cantarow (New York: Feminist Press, 1980), 72.

17. Cantarow and O'Malley, "Ella Baker," 70. Emphasis in original.

18. Lerner, "Developing Community Leadership," 347.

19. Ella Baker's Address to a Mass Meeting in Hattiesburg, Mississippi, January 21, 1964. Reprinted as an appendix to Catherine M. Orr,

"'The Struggle is Eternal': A Rhetorical Biography of Ella Baker" (M.A. thesis, University of North Carolina at Chapel Hill, 1991). See p. 78. Emphasis in original.

20. She made this comment in an interview in New York City on December 27, 1966, with Emily Stoper. See Stoper, "The Student Non-violent Coordinating Committee: The Growth of Radicalism in a Civil Rights Organization," in *Women in the Civil Rights Movement: Trailblazers and Torchbearers, 1941–1945,* edited by Vicki L. Crawford, Jacqueline Anne Rouse, and Barbara Woods (Brooklyn: Carlson Publishing, 1990), 268.

21. Patricia Holt, "Grass-Roots Heroes of Civil Rights," review of Charles Payne's *I've Got the Light of Freedom, San Francisco Chronicle,* "Sunday Review," July 2, 1995, 1.

22. John Britton, Interview with Miss Ella Baker, June 19, 1968, Civil Rights Documentation Project, Moorland-Spingarn Oral History Project, Howard University, Washington, D.C., 79.

23. From the Hattiesburg Address, reprinted in Orr, "'The Struggle Is Eternal,'" 79.

24. Orr, "'The Struggle Is Eternal,'" 79.

25. Orr, "'The Struggle Is Eternal,'" 79.

26. Payne, *I've Got the Light of Freedom,* 101.

27. This remark by Charles Payne is cited in Holt, "Grass-Roots Heroes of Civil Rights."

28. See, e.g., Benjamin Barber, *Strong Democracy: Participatory Politics for a New Age* (Berkeley: University of California Press, 1984); or Harry C. Boyte, *The Backyard Revolution: Understanding the New Citizen Movement* (Philadelphia: Temple University Press, 1980).

29. Paul Gilroy, *The Black Atlantic: Modernity and Double Consciousness* (Cambridge, Mass.: Harvard University Press, 1993), 79.

30. Joseph Road, *Cities of the Dead: Circum-Atlantic Performance* (New York: Columbia University Press, 1996), xi.

31. Cantarow and O'Malley, "Ella Baker," 52.

32. Hogan, "Interview with Ella J. Baker," 34.

33. Hogan, "Interview with Ella J. Baker," 57.

34. Mary King's memory of Baker's questions can be found in her *Freedom Song* (New York: William Morrow, 1987), 60. Cited by Charles Payne, "Ella Baker and Models of Social Change: A Tribute," *Signs* (Summer 1989): 894.

35. James Clifford, "Traveling Cultures," in *Cultural Studies,* edited by Lawrence Grossberg, Cary Nelson, and Paula A. Treichler, with Linda Baughman and assistance from John Macgregor Wise (New York: Routledge, 1992), 96–116.

36. Edward S. Casey, *The Fate of Place: A Philosophical History* (Berkeley: University of California Press, 1997), 303.

37. Casey, *The Fate of Place,* 303.

38. Jerry Frug, "Decentering Decentralization," *University of Chicago Law Review* 60, no. 2 (Spring 1993): 257 n. 12.

39. Frug, "Decentering Decentralization," 272, 273, 310–12.

40. Hogan, "Interview with Ella J. Baker," 22.

41. For an interesting discussion about alternatives to either blood or territory as fundamental "ties that bind," see Daniel Boyarin and Jonathan Boyarin, "Diaspora: Generation and the Ground of Jewish Identity," *Critical Inquiry* 19 (Summer 1993): 693–725.

42. Benedict Anderson, *Imagined Communities* (Cambridge: Oxford University Press, 1983), 26.

43. Anderson's *Imagined Communities* remains a core text in the scholarly discussion of nationalism. Other major works include those of postcolonial critics, e.g., Edward Said, *Orientalism* (New York: Pantheon, 1978) and *Culture and Imperialism* (New York: Alfred Knopf, 1992); of social scientists, e.g., Ernest Gellner, *Encounters with Nationalism* (Cambridge: Oxford University Press, 1994); of theorists influenced by psychoanalytical literature, e.g., Slavoj Zizek, "Enjoy Your Nation as Yourself!" in *Tarrying with the Negative: Kant, Hegel, and the Critique of Ideology* (Durham: Duke University Press, 1993); and of critical legal studies scholars, e.g., Nathaniel Berman, "Modernism, Nationalism, and the Rhetoric of Reconstruction," *Yale Journal of Law*

& the Humanities 4, no. 2 (Summer 1992): 351–80. This is only a sampling of this vast field.

44. Saskia Sassen, *Cities in a World Economy* (Thousand Oaks, Calif.: Pine Forge Press, 1993).

45. Baker's fellow activist Ivanhoe Donaldson, quoted in Jacqueline Trescott's "The Voice of Protest: Ella Baker, Legend of the Rights Movement," *Washington Post,* December 14, 1979, C1.

46. *DoubleTake,* an innovative magazine that combines photography and text, reprints a portion of the poem "The Cure at Troy" on the opening page of every issue as its name comes from it. The poem in its entirety is *The Cure at Troy: A Version of Sophocles Philoctetes* (New York: Farrar, Straus and Giroux, 1991); these lines appear on p. 77.

47. Boyte, *The Backyard Revolution,* 179.

EPILOGUE

1. A great introduction to these ideas can be had by reading the novel *The God of Small Things* by Arundhati Roy (New York: Harper-Perennial, 1998). In the novel, the characters come to grips with the delicate coercions of British culture in postcolonial India. The body of theory to which I refer includes cultural studies and postcolonial theory. For an introduction, there are several good anthologies, including Lawrence Grossberg, Cary Nelson and Paula Treichler, eds., *Cultural Studies* (New York: Routledge, 1992), and Patrick Williams and Laura Chrisman, eds., *Colonial Discourse and Post-Colonial Theory: A Reader* (New York: Columbia University Press, 1994).

2. Angela Harris, cited in Jerry Frug, "Decentering Decentralization," *University of Chicago Law Review* 60, no. 2 (Spring 1993): 311.

3. Jane Tompkins, *Sensational Designs: The Cultural Work of American Fiction, 1790–1860* (N.Y.: Oxford University Press, 1985).

BIBLIOGRAPHIC ESSAY

One could go into a library and not emerge for several lifetimes if one wanted to read everything about landscape as a setting for moral and political instruction in the United States. The literature extends from the history of ideas to art history to the history of science; from children's stories to philosophy; from literary critics' examinations of the pastoral tradition to the behavioral science discipline of environmental psychology. The literature is so vast that there is an almost equally formidable stack of works that purport to summarize and provide an overview of Americans' relationships to nature. Despite the enormous amount of reading material that exists, there are many books still wanting to be written. The one for which I constantly longed was a survey of the subject inspired by the shifts in scholarship since the 1960s. Part of the reason, of course, that I longed for such a new synthesis is that it would have helped me to direct my reading into all the most interesting areas of new scholarship that touch on the question of Americans' complex relationships to landscape.

The first issue that my dream text would have helped me with is how to address race, class and gender. The greatest histories about ideas of nature fascinated me, from Arthur Lovejoy's 1936 classic on *The Great Chain of Being* (New York: Harper & Row, [1936] 1960) to Raymond Williams's *The Country and the City* (New York: Oxford University Press, 1973). Especially Williams I read with a great thirst, as his book so eloquently captured problems I had myself mulled over. But even as I learned a great deal from such texts, I knew that some fundamental absence distorted them. Most studies of landscape myths remain rooted in a scholarly perspective that at best adds women and minorities as an interesting sidebar to the main story. How then to reconceptualize the field?

I got my answers to these questions of how race, class and gender might fundamentally reorient the histories of nature as much from fellow graduate students' emerging work as anywhere else. The West as a symbol and myth was the topic on which my ideas were honed, and it is in western women's scholarship that I found samples of what a reconceptualized perspective might look like. For an example of the shift, I would pair Krista Comer's *Landscapes of the New West: Gender and Geography in Contemporary Women's Writing* (Chapel Hill: University of North Carolina Press, 1999) with Richard Slotkin's standard-bearing texts such as *Gunfighter Nation: The Myth of the Frontier in 20th-Century America* (New York: Atheneum, 1992). Comer writes about authors such as Wanda Coleman, a poet of working-class, African-American Los Angeles, and about the theme of conflict on L. A.'s white beaches. Comer's perspective builds on the work of a long list of scholars who opened the scholarly West to the presence of women and people of color, including especially the crop of 1987: Vera Norwood and Janice Monk, eds., *The Desert Is No Lady: Southwestern Landscapes in Women's Writing and Art* (New Haven: Yale University Press, 1987); and Susan Armitage and Elizabeth Jameson, eds., *The Women's West* (Norman: University of Oklahoma Press, 1987). The year 1987 also produced the landmark reconceptualization of western history by Patricia Nelson Limerick, *The Legacy of Conquest: The Unbroken Past of the American West* (New York: Norton, 1987). For theoretical frameworks, I relied most especially on the works of Peggy Pascoe, Joan Scott and Hazel Carby.

A new synthesis of American attitudes toward nature would not only form itself through a sophisticated use of race, class and gender, but it would also resist the pull toward rural favoritism. In a broader sense, a core insight shared by the scholarship that influenced me the most is that nature myths can be found in a mall as well as in Thoreauvian landscapes. Jennifer Price's wonderfully written *Flight Maps: Adventures with Nature in Modern America* (New York: Basic Books, 1999) refuses to locate the environment solely in the woods, pastures and streams. For many people, it has been hard work to substitute a more fluid definition of nature for the one conceived often by disconsolate urban men in their modern jobs, longing for a freedom they see in wilderness. My own reorientation came mostly through the effect of studying books like Mike Davis's *City of Quartz: Excavating the Future in Los Angeles* (New York: Vintage Books, 1992) as well as a host of postmodern theorists, including Trevor J. Barnes and James S. Duncan, eds., *Writing Worlds: Discourse, Text, Metaphor in the Representation of Landscape* (New York: Routledge, 1992); Jane Bennett and William Chaloupka, eds., *In the Nature of Things: Language, Politics and the Environment* (Minneapolis: University of Minnesota Press, 1993); Dana Phillips, "Is Nature Necessary," *Raritan* 13, no. 3 (Winter 1994): 78–100; and Edward W. Soja, *Postmodern Geographics: The Reassertion of Space in Critical Social Theory* (London: Verso, 1989). My dream text would translate the message of these postmodernists for newcomers into more accessible journalistic prose. In addition, my thinking was shaped in reaction to Neil Evernden's *The Social Creation of Nature* (Baltimore: Johns Hopkins University Press, 1992) and William Cronon's "The Trouble with Wilderness; or Getting Back to the Wrong Nature" as well as other selections in *Uncommon Ground: Rethinking the Human Place in Nature,* edited by William Cronon

(New York: Norton, 1996). To complement and complicate these works, I would single out David Harvey's "Class Relations, Social Justice and the Politics of Difference," in *Place and the Politics of Identity*, edited by Michael Keith and Steve Pile (New York: Routledge, 1993), 41–66.

The change in historical perspective that has loosened "nature" from equivalence to rural or wilderness landscapes is part of a wider turn. Unlike Lovejoy or even Williams, the author of my dream synthesis would recognize how much the definitions of nature or any kind of place depend on contingent, historical and cultural factors. I had been stumbling toward my own profound regrounding when I came upon an article that singularly summarized the trouble with common assumptions about place and identity: Akhil Gupta and James Ferguson, "Beyond 'Culture': Space Identity, and the Politics of Difference," *Cultural Anthropology* 7, no. 1 (February 1992): 6–23. Building on the field of cultural history that I was first introduced to with Warren Susman's *Culture as History: The Transformation of American Society in the Twentieth Century* (New York: Pantheon Books, 1984), together with writings by postcolonial and cultural studies scholars including Edward Said, Stuart Hall and Mary Pratt, the Gupta and Ferguson article confirmed my hunch to define small communities for this book in terms of arising and subsiding allegiances like those of Ella Baker's civil rights activists.

To see landscapes as fluid, not romantically fixed, is a project made much easier by simply becoming aware of other times and cultures. As my notes show, I am much indebted to environmental historians, especially Donald Worster and Richard White but also a variety of others, including Carolyn Merchant, among whose works is a classroom anthology that helped me as much as it did my students: *Major Problems in American Environmental History* (Lexington, Mass.: D. C. Heath, 1993). Also significant to my ideas were Arthur F. McEvoy's "Toward an Interactive Theory of Nature and Culture: Ecology, Production, and Cognition in the California Fishing Industry," in *The*

Ends of the Earth, edited by Donald Worster (Cambridge: Cambridge University Press, 1988), 211–29; and Dan Flores's *Caprock Canyonlands: Journeys in the Heart of the Southern Plains* (Austin: University of Texas Press, 1990). Likewise I was much influenced by cultural geographers, especially D. W. Meinig's *The Interpretation of Ordinary Landscapes* (New York: Oxford University Press, 1979) and *The Shaping of America: A Geographic Perspective on 500 Years of History* (New Haven: Yale University Press, 1986). The lifework of anthropologists Clifford Geertz and James Clifford shaped my thinking, as did a short and excellent article by Narit Bird-David, "Beyond 'The Original Affluent Society': A Culturalist Reformulation," *Current Anthropology* 13, no. 1 (February 1992): 25–47. Another tack is to read landscape ideas as a form of religion, as did Catherine L. Albanese in her *Nature Religion in America: From the Algonkian Indians to the New Age* (Chicago: University of Chicago Press, 1990); John F. Sears in his *Sacred Places: American Tourist Attractions in the 19th Century* (New York: Oxford University Press, 1989); and Jack Fruchtman, Jr., in his *Thomas Paine and the Religion of Nature* (Baltimore: Johns Hopkins University Press, 1993). For the psychology of landscapes, I relied on a journalistic account: Winifred Gallagher, *The Power of Place: How Our Surroundings Shape Our Thoughts, Emotions and Actions* (New York: Poseidon Press, 1993).

The undoing of nature's certainties would be part of the survey text's agenda. More tricky still would be the task of offering a broad, authoritative overview at the same time as living with one's own limits. The role of expert understanding within a deeply philosophical recognition of the local, particular and historical character of knowledge has been a concern of this book. Most of the reading I have done in my life speaks to me on this issue, but I will mention some recent and old favorites, some of which are theoretical and some examples of personalized intellectual inquiries: Stephen Toulmin's *Cosmopolis: The Hidden Agenda of Modernity* (Chicago: University of Chicago Press, 1990); Ludwig Wittgenstein's *Philosophical Investigations,* 3d ed., translated by G. E. M. Anscombe (New York: Macmillan, [1953] 1968); N. Katherine Hayles, "Searching for Common Ground," in *Reinventing Nature? Responses to Postmodern Deconstruction,* edited by Michael E. Soule and Gary Lease (Washington, D.C.: Island Press, 1995), 47–64; Zeese Papanikolas, *Trickster in the Land of Dreams* (Lincoln: University of Nebraska Press, 1995); and James Agee and Walter Evans, *Let Us Now Praise Famous Men* (Boston: Houghton Mifflin, 1939).

In the absence of my dream text, I nevertheless received much guidance from the long tradition of American Studies scholars, historians and literary critics who have tackled similar questions to mine. To mention only the most important to my own study of the topic: Williams, Lovejoy and Slotkin, whom I have cited above; Martin Green, *The Great American Adventure* (Boston: Beacon Press, 1984); Myra Jehlen, *American Incarnation: The Individual, the Nation, and the Continent* (Cambridge, Mass.: Harvard University Press, 1986); Michael Kammen, *Mystic Chords of Memory: The Transformation of Tradition in American Culture* (New York: Vintage Books, 1991); Annette Kolodny, *The Land before Her: Fantasy and Experience of the American Frontiers, 1630–1860* (Chapel Hill: University of North Carolina Press, 1984), and *The Lay of the Land: Metaphor as Experience and History in American Life and Letters* (Chapel Hill: University of North Carolina Press, 1975); Leo Marx, *The Machine in the Garden: Technology and the Pastoral Ideal in America* (New York: Oxford University Press, 1964); Perry Miller, *Errand into the Wilderness* (Cambridge, Mass.: Belknap Press, 1956); Roderick Nash, *Wilderness and the American Mind,* 3d ed. (New Haven: Yale University Press, 1982); and Henry Nash Smith, *Virgin Land: The American West as Symbol and Myth* (Cambridge, Mass.: Harvard University Press, 1950).

Without a perfect guide, I had the advantage of wandering freely among the many novels, autobiographies and oral histories that addressed my gradually formulated focus on social justice and landscape. I will mention only a few clusters. I intend, with this very small selection, to give a glimpse into the types of books I chose in the process of selecting what would become the case studies of this book. One of my hobbyhorses has been to read novels set on family farms, of which there are literally thousands. Among African-American examples, I was struck especially by George Wylie Henderson's *Ollie Miss* (Tuscaloosa: University of Alabama Press, [1935] 1988); Mildred Taylor's young adult fiction about a black family farm, including *Roll of Thunder, Hear My Cry* (New York: Bantam Books, 1978); and Toni Morrison's *Song of Solomon* (New York: Signet Books, 1977). For a regional glimpse, I would select two curious books. One is Robert P. Tristram Coffin's *Lost Paradise: A Boyhood on a Maine Coast Farm* (New York: Macmillan, 1934), a book that would also interest scholars looking for undercurrents of homosexuality. The other is Caroline Gordon's peculiar *The Forest of the South* (New York: Charles Scribner's Sons, 1945), in particular, the title story of this short story collection. I paired my readings in family farm literature with research into utopian and communalist movements. I tarried especially on Charlotte Perkins Gilman's *Herland* (New York: Pantheon, [1915] 1979); Nathaniel Hawthorne's *The Blithedale Romance* (New York: Norton, [1852] 1978); and a journalist's account of recent utopias, Frances Fitzgerald's *Cities on a Hill: A Journey through Contemporary American Cultures* (New York: Touchstone, [1981] 1986). A point of convergence between utopian and rural romances has been the critique of consumerism: I was much affected by Daniel Horowitz's gentle rebuke of moralizers in *The Morality of Spending: Attitudes toward the Consumer Society in America, 1875–1940* (Baltimore: Johns Hopkins University Press, 1985), and also by David Shi's appreciative survey, *The Simple Life: Plain Living and High Thinking in American Culture* (New York: Oxford University Press, 1985). As will anyone who considers the normative aspect of landscape, I engaged in long internal debates with Wendell Berry, who wrote farm-based novels such as *A Place on Earth* (New York: Harcourt, Brace and World, 1966), as well as a landmark nonfiction book, *The Unsettling of America: Culture and Agriculture* (New York: Avon Books, 1977). The critic and novelist John Berger has been a great inspiration, especially his novel *Pig Earth* (New York: Pantheon Books, 1979).

Roaming in the academic and literary fields of utopian and family farm writing laid the intellectual groundwork for my study of Sandoz and Johnson. Woven inside and beside these arenas were the western titles I consumed. Here I pursued what one mentor called a "posthole" strategy, digging deeply into a few individual writers' works in addition to some modest surveying of the whole. The dreams of a good society projected onto the West by Walter Prescott Webb, Wallace Stegner, Larry McMurtry, Sandoz and Johnson were grist for the dissertation out of which this book sprang.

Within the thematic clusters of western, utopian and farm writings, I sought out many titles by non-Anglo writers. However, my selection of Ella Baker's activism as the third case study drew from a different angle of vision. Inspired by postcolonial and multicultural theorists, I realized that the framework provided by my themes foreclosed a deeper understanding of difference. Helped by a reading group at the University of Utah, I became acquainted with some of the major postcolonial thinkers, including Frantz Fanon, Gayatri Chakravorty Spivak, Homi Bhabha and Arjun Appadurai. For an introduction, readers could consult *Colonial Discourse and Post-Colonial Theory: A Reader,* edited by Patrick Williams and Laura Chrisman (New York: Columbia University Press, 1994).

Finally, though many lifetimes would be needed to make a real round of the literature on landscape and social justice, there are enormous pleasures even in a single turn. For the enthusiasm I brought to intellectual inquiry, I am beholden to the many authors I have mentioned here and in the notes but also to a particular person: the late J. David Greenstone, a professor of political science at the University of Chicago, where I was an undergraduate. David Greenstone first introduced me to the great social theorists, including Karl Marx, Émile Durkheim, Max Weber and his own favorite, Wittgenstein. But he also taught when it was time to break for pizza. I am glad to count myself among the students who claim a lifetime debt to his inspiration.

ACKNOWLEDGMENTS
OF PERMISSIONS

Excerpt from "Imagine." Words and music by John Lennon. © 1971 (Renewed 1999) by LENONO MUSIC. All rights controlled and administered by EMI BLACKWOOD MUSIC, INC. All rights reserved. International copyright secured, used by permission.

Excerpts from the works and papers of Josephine Johnson are used with the permission of the Estate of Josephine Johnson Cannon.

The author also consulted the Josephine Johnson Papers, Special Collections, Washington University Libraries.

The excerpt from the last line of the poem "The Summer Day," in *House of Light,* by Mary Oliver, is reprinted by permission of Beacon Press, Boston. Copyright © 1990 by Mary Oliver.

Selected material from the Lenore Bredeson Hogan "Interview with Ella J. Baker" appears here with permission. Copyright © Highlander Research and Education Center, New Market, Tennessee.

Selected material from the Ella Baker Interview, Southern Oral History Program Collection, #4007, G-7, is located in the Southern

Historical Collection, Wilson Library, the University of North Carolina at Chapel Hill, and appears here with permission.

Excerpt from *The Cure at Troy: A Version of Sophocles' "Philoctetes,"* by Seamus Heaney. Copyright © 1990 by Seamus Heaney. Reprinted by permission of Seamus Heaney; Farrar, Straus and Giroux, LLC; and Faber & Faber, Ltd.

INDEX

academia: author's experience of, 83–88, 137, 171; and irony, 45, 197

activists: and intellectuals, 87

act locally, think globally, xvii–xviii, 175, 180; and postnational era, 188

Agee, James, 240

agrarian philosophical tradition, 29; Josephine Johnson's attack upon, 115–127

agriculture, small-scale, 159

Aid to Families with Dependent Children (AFDC), 6

Albanese, Catherine L., 239

Alinsky, Saul, 160

American Studies, 81–82, 85, 240

Anderson, Benedict, 186

anthropology: and Social Darwinism, 218–219n39

antiphony, 173

Appadurai, Arjun, 242

Appeal to Reason (periodical), 71

Armitage, Susan, 236

Austin, Mary: *Cactus Thorn*, 32

Baker, Ella: ancestors of, 162; biography of, 161; and black power, 167; and communism, 167; and democracy, 161, 167; and empowerment, 182; and evolution, 182; and faith versus reason, 168; and freedom, human spirit for, 168, 172, 181; and freedom, psychological, 172; and lack of vision, 168; as localist, 160, 163, 173; and organizing, 166, 169; and politics of courage, 173; and sense of leadership, 163, 165, 174, 181; and sense of the local, xviii, xx, 166, 169, 173; and social justice, xviii, 196; theory of, 174–175; and utopia, 168, 191

Baker v. Carr, 24

Barnes, Trevor J., 237

Barton, Bruce, 113

Text: 11/15 Granjon
Display: Granjon
Composition: BookMatters
Printing and binding: Haddon Craftsmen, Inc.